Ethnic and Religious Identity in Modern Scotland

Culture, politics and football

JOSEPH M BRADLEY

Avebury

Aldershot • Brookfield USA • Hong Kong • Singapore • Sydney

Published by
Avebury
Ashgate Publishing Limited
Gower House
Croft Road
Aldershot
Hants GU11 3HR
England

Ashgate Publishing Company
Old Post Road
Brookfield
Vermont 05036
USA

British Library Cataloguing in Publication Data

Bradley, Joseph
    Ethnic and Religious Identity in Modern
    Scotland: Culture, Politics and Football
    I. Title
    306.609411

    ISBN 1-85972-005-6

Library of Congress Catalog Card Number: 95-79587

Printed and bound by Athenæum Press Ltd.,
Gateshead, Tyne & Wear.

ETHNIC AND RELIGIOUS IDENTITY IN MODERN SCOTLAND

Contents

Tables

Acknowledgements

This book could not have been written without the assistance and participation of many people. Supporters of all the football clubs involved in the survey as well as those individuals who helped me gain access to them have to be thanked. I am grateful to the various members of the Loyal Orange Institution of Scotland and the Irish organisations who assisted me. Church attenders from the Church of Scotland and Catholic denominations were very helpful as were the clergy who prepared the way for the application of my survey. Eddie O Neil assisted with the questionnaire while Dave Marsh of Strathclyde University was an invaluable source of academic assistance. My gratitude to all.

Preface

One of the central arguments of this book is that football in Scotland has acquired characteristics which make it a nationalistic, political and cultural repository. An examination of football allows us to look at characteristics of identity in Scotland otherwise unclear. These identities have their origins in the post-Reformation period in Scotland, Irish immigration into Scotland and Scotland/Britain's historically contentious relationship with Ireland. This book will examine some of the main features of these identities.

It reflects on the development and pervasiveness of Protestantism within society, emphasising its anti-Catholic dimension. Irish immigration to Scotland in the 19th and 20th century is briefly reflected upon within the context of a growing ethno-religious cleavage.

The nature of the cleavage between both Protestant and Catholic cultures is explored. The conclusion establishes that previous studies, although valuable, have omitted to recognise some of the crucial features of religious identity in modern Scotland.

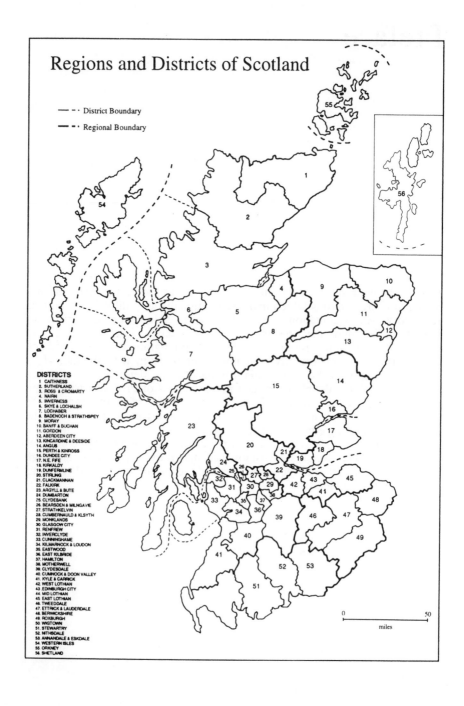

Regions and Districts of Scotland

— - — District Boundary

— ▬ — Regional Boundary

DISTRICTS
1. CAITHNESS
2. SUTHERLAND
3. ROSS & CROMARTY
4. NAIRN
5. INVERNESS
6. SKYE & LOCHALSH
7. LOCHABER
8. BADENOCH & STRATHSPEY
9. MORAY
10. BANFF & BUCHAN
11. GORDON
12. ABERDEEN CITY
13. KINCARDINE & DEESIDE
14. ANGUS
15. PERTH & KINROSS
16. DUNDEE CITY
17. N.E. FIFE
18. KIRKALDY
19. DUNFERMLINE
20. STIRLING
21. CLACKMANNAN
22. FALKIRK
23. ARGYLL & BUTE
24. DUMBARTON
25. CLYDEBANK
26. BEARSDEN & MILNGAVIE
27. STRATHKELVIN
28. CUMBERNAULD & KLSYTH
29. MONKLANDS
30. GLASGOW CITY
31. RENFREW
32. INVERCLYDE
33. CUNNINGHAME
34. KILMARNOCK & LOUDON
35. EASTWOOD
36. EAST KILBRIDE
37. HAMILTON
38. MOTHERWELL
39. CLYDESDALE
40. CUMNOCK & DOON VALLEY
41. KYLE & CARRICK
42. WEST LOTHIAN
43. EDINBURGH CITY
44. MID LOTHIAN
45. EAST LOTHIAN
46. TWEEDDALE
47. ETTRICK & LAUDERDALE
48. BERWICKSHIRE
49. ROXBURGH
50. WIGTOWN
51. STEWARTRY
52. NITHSDALE
53. ANNANDALE & ESKDALE
54. WESTERN ISLES
55. ORKNEY
56. SHETLAND

0   50
miles

IRELAND

Border
County
Boundaries

Donegal
Derry
DERRY
ANTRIM
TYRONE
Belfast
DOWN
LEITRIM
FERMANAGH
MONAGHAN
ARMAGH
SLIGO
CAVAN
LOUTH
MAYO
ROSCOMMON
LONGFORD
MEATH
DUBLIN
WEST MEATH
GALWAY
Galway
OFFALY
Dublin
KILDARE
CLARE
LEIX
WICKLOW
KILKENNY
CARLOW
LIMERICK
TIPPERARY
WEXFORD
KERRY
WATERFORD
CORK
Cork

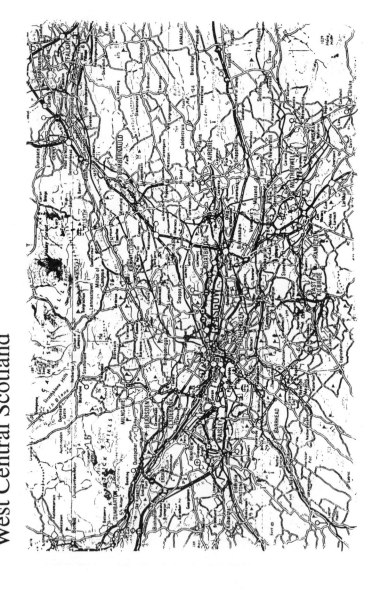

West Central Scotland

Introduction

Despite its historical significance, religious identity (i.e., Protestant and Catholic identity) in Scotland has often been ignored because of its controversial nature.[1] However, its significance has also been recognised by some academics as well as social and political commentators. Unfortunately, previous enquiry, although important, has sometimes been partial.

One of the key problems with much of the literature is that it operates with a narrow understanding of religious identity by using sectarianism as its key concept. As such, many authors ignore the multi-faceted nature of religious identity in Scotland. Although Brown recognises the significance of religious identities he also uses the established terminology, characterising these identities in terms of bigotry and sectarianism. So, Brown argues:

> The silent hope is that by ignoring Protestant-Catholic antagonism, and by denying its political relevance, an unhealthy atavism might disappear. But sectarianism runs deep in Scottish popular culture (Brown, 1987, p. 244).

Although an important work in relation to religious identity in Scotland, Gallagher also adopts this language in his book, Glasgow: The Uneasy Peace:

> If sectarianism is still capable of a last hurrah in Scotland, the evidence presented in these pages suggests that it will not be on the same scale witnessed in Northern Ireland (1987, p. 354).

Murray's popular look at religious cleavage in Scottish society uses a similar terminology:

> Scotland's segregated education system is still the biggest hurdle to overcome in the elimination of sectarianism....(Murray, 1984, p. 275).

1

Media commentators have been most at fault in their treatment of religious identity in Scotland. Religion in Scotland, and the identities arising from it, have long been reduced to spurious and insufficient comments about 'sectarianism'. As defined, sectarianism in turn is treated as an aberrant mentality based on outmoded religious prejudices. In mid 1989, the Sunday Times[2] for example, spoke of aspects of Scottish life which continued to show signs of sectarianism. A short time before this, the London Evening Standard suggested that London football supporters were taking sides with one or other of Scottish football's sectarian rivals.[3] Similarly, Scottish newspapers have over the years consistently referred to 'sectarianism' in reporting on issues from Irish political demonstrations[4] to debates on the controversial subject of Catholic schools in Scotland.[5]

In its Scottish context, sectarianism has been utilised as a concept to explain areas of Scottish life which remain unaddressed or obscured. The term sectarianism has powerful connotations for behaviour and beliefs. These are almost always negative; the emphasis is upon bigotry, religious insularity and hate. However, this usage has been so common in Scottish society as to become the only available terminology to interpret and define religious identity. In terms of our understanding of such matters, the language of sectarianism has helped establish 'tribes of bigotry' on the opposite sides of a wall of ignorance; tribes which simply reflect each other's 'sectarianism' as defined by their religious identity. Such an approach thus involves both an unintentional and, as I will argue later, a culturally dominating distortion of much of the reality of these identities. Not only is it an inadequate concept, but carelessly used, it also denies any connection between prejudiced and ethnocentric individuals and communities, as well as other facets of the larger society.

Of course, the use of the term sectarianism is appropriate in a number of instances, certainly when applied to narrow mindedness, bigotry and intolerance. However, the term has evolved to become a catch-all and evasive phrase to describe many aspects of religious, national, political and cultural identity in Scottish society. Perhaps most importantly, the use of such terminology often implies that it is wrong to have an identity defined in large part by a particular religion or ethnic background. The problem is that most literature alludes only to the surface of these identities and religious cleavage in Scotland. The absence of academic work on religious identity has allowed journalists and other commentators to shape the discussion, at the same time covering up its true nature in part by the use of inadequate labels. Such misreadings in turn mean that an important aspect of cultural identity in Scotland is understudied and misunderstood.

This book aims to move beyond the conceptual confines imposed by the emphasis on sectarianism; rather, I will attempt to identify some of the complexities involved in religious, social, and political identity in Scotland. In addition, I will investigate why and how some of these identities are misrepresented. This concern leads us directly to the question of why football in Scotland says something important about Scottish society.

Of course, some of these commentators are possibly partly motivated by a wish to see a more secular society. Gallagher's sympathy for the Scottish nationalist cause for example, may have affected some of his conclusions, because he wishes to see established a new Scottish identity which will not be cross-cut by religious cleavage or ethno-cultural factors. For Gallagher, the Irish have already taken too long to equip themselves with an identity for living in Scotland (Gallagher, 1991, pp. 19-43). Whether they see such a proposition in a like sense to Gallagher, or they are simply identifying the conditions for their argument, this point is made more explicitly made by Ritchie and Dyer:

> It would be even more helpful to the separatist cause if the Catholic community could also lose its religious and political faith, allowing a reinvented national community [and identity] to transcend historic divisions[6]

It is true certainly that even a cursory glance at contemporary Scottish society suggests that religious cleavage is no longer overtly reflected in certain areas of political and social life. However, an argument here is that although there has been a movement away from overt areas of conflict and cleavage, such conflict has, to a significant extent, been displaced. In an era of general culture, powerful state sectors and apparatuses, globalisation, Americanisation and the increased role of the mass media, there has clearly been an increase in cultural and political conformity. Nevertheless, other popular spheres of culture and different identities still exist, most often associated with institutions which have no overt political significance. These spheres of culture should be recognised by students as important, because they are crucial to 'ordinary' peoples' sense of identity which, in turn, has resonances throughout their relations with society, including political society. Scotland has become a much more complex society during the last two generations and ethno-religious identities have to be re-assessed in that light.

This view finds some support from Brown who suggests that:

> studies of organised sectarianism may underestimate the vibrancy of the popular culture of bigotry. In part prosperity and better education have, in the words of one commentator, taught bigotry 'good manners'.... (1987, p. 244).

Brown implies that the religious cleavage which exists in Scottish society has taken on a new form and character in recent years. A similar conclusion is also reached by Gallagher and Walker (1990, p. 5) in their analysis of the complexity of the Protestant identity. They stress:

> the variety of social, cultural and political phenomena which have a peculiarly Protestant dimension. Protestantism has certainly never been monolithic in Scotland, notwithstanding the daunting rigidity of Calvinist doctrine.

Most of the literature upon the significance of religion in Scotland has sometimes operated with a narrow definition of politics at the expense of other broader definitions. In particular, many studies concentrate upon overt political behaviour and political participation. However, voting should not be viewed as the definitive expression of political attitudes, behaviour or opinion. Indeed, approximately one third of the electorate in Britain does not vote in national elections, while only around 40 per cent of the electorate voted in the 1992 and 1995 local elections in Scotland.

Such figures may represent voter apathy and powerlessness. However, they also indicate that many people regard other political arenas as more important; more relevant to their immediate lifestyles, their attitudes, beliefs and relations with others. In addition, the powerlessness experienced by many people in the political arena, often crucially shaped by the media, may be reflected by holding and expressing social and political attitudes, which not only fail to translate into party political expression, but also become focused on arenas which are outside of higher political processes. Politics for many people can become privatised and translated into spheres of culture and identity. That was the case for example, when the Sunday football team of an Irish pub in Coatbridge turned out in the strips of the Argentinean national side in the midst of the Falklands/Malvinas War in 1982. This was a clear case of a section of the community raising their Irishness, as well as their anti-British attitudes, to the level of a political statement. Political parties and their concerns are often irrelevant to the real concerns of many people. Yet the social and political attitudes of people are important elements of identity and may have a broader political resonance.

Identity: the Scottish dimension

As in the case of other societies, to understand contemporary Scotland, we need to be able to identify its community and cultural 'identities'. Football provides an appropriate access point, because in Scottish society, it provides an important focus of identity. In Scotland, as in Spain, England, Northern Ireland and other societies, football has a larger significance than that of a simple spectator sport; it is a repository of meaning (see Cohen, 1986, introduction) which says a great deal about the society itself. A study of football in Scotland also involves a cultural analysis which links history, national/patriotic identities, politics and social life at a number of junctures. It helps us to explore some of the social and political identities which are intricate parts of Scottish life, whilst it also shows us how and why a particular cleavage came to be expressed in this way.

As will become clear throughout this book, religion in Scotland is much more than theology and liturgy. It involves social and political identities themselves. Religion meets and mixes with society and politics in Scotland in a way in which it does not anywhere else in Britain. On many occasions this century, the Protestant establishment has spoken for Scotland in such a way as to imply that Scotland was solely a Protestant country. In the early 1980s the Catholic Church in Scotland published a book to celebrate Pope John Paul II visit. Not only was it grandly entitled 'Catholic Scotland', but there was no mention of the fact that in all likelihood, there would be little left of the Catholic Church in Scotland but for the influx of the Irish in the 19th and 20th centuries. That contribution was simply omitted. The fact that these things can occur should be of interest to social scientists who aim to draw a more detailed and accurate picture of Scottish society.

4

In fact, religious identity is often the primary basis of substantial football club support in Scotland, while in the rest of Britain a more orthodox loyalty and team success serve the same role (allowing for the fact that it often 'becomes' a medium for other social and political expressions). For this reason, football in Scotland gains a level and an intensity of support which cannot be explained in football terms. It is a communal adhesive that is underpinned by religious, ethnic and political factors.

Football in Scotland throws a particular light upon society. It reflects much of the nature of that society's social networks which are regularly built around religious affiliation and identities. Of course, we also need to establish why football is the popular medium through which this cleavage and certain identities are expressed. In fact, football can be seen as a mechanism through which some of the main cultural codes in Scottish society can be read. It is a means of displaying some of the social and political distinctiveness and separateness involved in Scot's society.

Overall, religious identity provides, for many people in Scottish society, a significant basis of identification (See Brown, 1987, for Church attendance figures in Scotland. Also, BSA, 1990/91. My own survey when applied to the non-Church groups also shows the strength of religious identity despite the fall in overall Church attendance).

Although encompassing the country as a whole, much of the content of this book will focus on the most significantly populated region in Scotland, the Central belt. In addition, the study will concentrate on the historical and cultural relationship between Protestants and Catholics. Much of the comment on Scottish Protestantism focuses on its anti-Catholic dimension, the aspect most relevant to this relationship.

Of course, religion should not be seen as 'the' single tool of social analysis. Scottish society, like most others, does not reflect a single cleavage. This study does not offer a reductionist perspective, but rather one that reflects and explains more thoroughly, social and political life in Scotland, particularly those elements which accrue from religious practice, religious beliefs and religious background, as well as ethnic identity and consequential group interrelations.

It is the task here to make clearer these identities whilst, at the same time, offering some explanation as to how some of them have evolved. In the past there has been little consensus as to the origins and content of these identities. One of the most recent examples of this confusion can be found in the BBC national news reporting of Glasgow Rangers signing of a Roman Catholic footballer, Maurice Johnston, in 1989. The significance of this event was explained by reference to sectarianism in Glasgow. The origins of this sectarianism were located in the First World War period when the Govan shipyards in Glasgow experienced an influx of Protestant, Belfast, shipworkers. This migration was therefore given as the cause of religious tension in Scotland.

Certainly, the explanations of these ethno-religious identities and the consequent cleavage can be firmly rooted in an earlier history. Indeed, an historical perspective is a prerequisite for any contemporary understanding. Thus, in historical terms, Protestantism and Catholicism respectively shaped both the Scottish and Irish characters. In Scotland, 'Presbyterianism was not just a state religion but, for more than three centuries, defined the Scots to

5

one another and to the rest of the world' (Gallagher, in Devine (ed.), 1991, pp. 19-43). O'Farrell offers a similar perspective on the Irish:

> Irish Catholicism has been more than the official pronouncements of the hierarchy: it is a set of values, a culture, a historical tradition, a view on the world, a disposition of mind and heart, a loyalty, an emotional psychology - and a nationalism (O'Farrell, 1972, p. 306).

This emphasis upon ethno-religious cleavage in Scotland differs then from the stress upon class cleavage in Britain as a whole, though the latter has been seen in recent years to be a declining social and political factor.[7]

It will become evident then throughout this book that Protestantism, Catholicism, Orangeism, being Irish, etc., can be decisive in shaping popular consciousness. In Scotland, political attitudes and political activity often reflect an ethno-religious consciousness. Although social life and politics are invariably affected by class, age, gender, residence, etc., this study does not suggest that any of these are unimportant. The aim here is to demonstrate the importance of religious affiliation and identity in certain areas in Scottish life with which it would not normally be associated. This will again reflect Scotland's uniqueness within Britain. However, it will also emphasise its similarity with Northern Ireland where the key cleavage is based on religion through its linkage with cultural and national identities.

Overall, this book argues that some concept of identity is crucial for any understanding of the political attitudes and behaviour of individuals and communities. A concept of identity allows us to begin to explore areas of social and political interest which are largely excluded by inadequate terminology. This book begins from the foundation that everyone has been given identity by virtue of family and community, and that these identities are subsequently layered by environmental, life cognitive and conditioned factors.

It will be the task of this book to explore aspects of these particular religious identities in Scotland as well as their cultural and political expressions. More importantly however, I shall also look at why some of them are not expressed, or at the very least why they are not expressed significantly, in other ways.

Old themes: new approaches

Religion has for almost half a millennium been crucial to Scotland's social and political development. The aim here is to analyse the contemporary situation in Scotland in the light of the cleavage that arose from the mix of indigenous Scots Protestants and the arrival of immigrant Irish Catholics in the 19th and 20th centuries. In particular, much of the focus will examine the historically important anti-Catholic aspect of this emergent cleavage. This book postulates a number of propositions regarding religious identity. It will build on existing material which looks at religious identity in Scotland. In addition however, it both extends and challenges some of this previous work.

6

Overall, the book will offer a less restrictive view of religious identity in Scotland by:

1. Challenging the use of the term 'sectarianism', as such emphasising the variety within the dominant culture, the importance of sub-cultures and of the symbolism relating to such cultures.

2. Analysing football in Scotland in an attempt to widen our understanding of religious identity, thus adding to the developing literature concerning the cultural, social and political features of football which are often ignored in approaches which view it simply as a sport.

3. Establishing the historical, cultural, social and political context of religious cleavage in Scotland. This has been almost totally omitted in most previous related works. This book argues religious identity in contemporary Scotland cannot be understood outwith an appreciation of the historical context of post-Reformation Scotland developing a Protestant identity which incorporated a powerful cultural and political anti-Catholicism. In addition, it can only be understood with reference to the development of Irish Catholic immigration and reactions towards it.

4. Deconstructing popular images of the contemporary Irish identity in Scotland analysing its connections and interactions with the dominant identities and a number of cultural, social and political features of contemporary Britain.

5. Contributing to the growing academic field of identity theory and analysis. It achieves this by adopting some of the paradigms used by contemporary academics who have opened up the question of identity to a more systematic analysis. It also adds to the terms utility by widening its scope using Scotland as the subject matter. The book makes use of the term identity to explore and explain more thoroughly the cultural, social and political resonance that religion has in Scotland. Again, this enables us to appreciate religion as something more than about Church attendance.

In fulfilling these tasks this book has also utilised a wide-ranging innovative survey of aspects of religious identity in Scotland. This survey taps the religious identity of various groups: football fans, members of the Orange Lodge, Irish organisations, etc. While it has limitations, notably given the resources available to me, and the nature of the populations surveyed (the results are partly representative), it is the most innovative survey so far attempted in analysing these questions (see appendix for discussion of the survey).

Book structure

Chapter one offers a short historical insight into the evolution of religious cleavage in Scotland. This chapter therefore stresses the importance of religious identity in Scottish society as well as introducing a less restrictive and inhibiting approach to analysing its contemporary condition. In addition, the concept of football being a transmit and conduit for social and political identities is explored.

Chapters two and three show why and how football is such an important demonstration of identity and cleavage in Scotland. It also highlights the strong relationship in Scotland between football and certain social and political attitudes, practices and activity. It is here that survey material is used to strengthen the analysis.

Identities of course must have content and this is outlined in chapters four, five and six. Orangeism is examined as an ideology, with particular reference to its Scottish application. Its structure and social and political significance are also assessed. Protestantism, in relation to its anti-Catholic aspect and the condition of the Irish Catholic identity in Scotland, are likewise appraised. Finally, the concluding chapter attempts to draw together the findings and analysis in such a way as to construct a framework which sheds new light on the subject.

Notes

1. See M Linklater and R Denniston (eds.) 'Anatomy Of Scotland' Chambers 1992.

2. Sunday Times; 16/12/89.

3. London Evening Standard; 26/8/88.

4. See Sunday Mail for example; 9/6/91.

5. Glasgow Herald; 1/11/90.

6. M Ritchie and M Dyer, in The Herald 25/9/91 and 26/9/91.

7. See M. N Franklin, 1985.

1 Scotland, 1560 and four centuries of transition

This book argues that certain points in history are crucial in showing us the origins of religious cleavage in Scotland, reflecting the salience of the related symbolism, and in establishing a context for current religious identities. The first chapter reviews principal features of Scottish history which provide a key context within which to understand contemporary religious identity. It does not offer an overview of Scottish history in the relevant years. Rather, the aim is to demonstrate that although Scotland was affected by many different social, economic and political forces in the post Reformation period, and despite the ongoing factor of schism within the Protestant Churches, anti-Catholicism was a powerful force which helped to mould Scots society.

The Scottish Reformation took place in 1560. Its main target, 'degenerate Roman Catholicism', was overthrown throughout most of the country. Catholicism had been ailing for many years in Scotland prior to the Reformation and its degeneracy is one of the reasons why Protestantism did not have to struggle too much to establish itself.

In the decades after 1560, the Scots Parliament, itself profoundly affected by the events, backed the new Church of Scotland and the General Assembly. There was therefore, from the beginning of the Protestant history of Scotland a great interlocking of church and state. Secular and religious agencies and bodies thus had a symbiotic relationship in which 'godly discipline' became an all-pervading ethos. The cultural, social and political identity of the Scots people was forthwith intertwined with their Protestant faith.

Inter and intra Protestant dissension and rivalry dominated much of the proceedings of the centuries following the Reformation. The two Protestant systems of presbytery and episcopacy alternated throughout the period until in the end the Presbyterians prevailed and they assumed control of the established Church in Scotland.[1] In addition, the potency of the lingering Protestant-Catholic aspect of politics in Scotland and England reached a climax with the 'Glorious Revolution' of 1688-90.

9

James VII and II acceded the British throne in 1685. He made little secret of his Catholic faith and he pursued a policy of religious toleration towards the various groups in his Kingdom. Opposition to James mounted in both Scotland and England. The King was perceived as a threat to the high status of the Protestant faith (especially to the Kirk in Scotland). In 1686 the Scottish parliament refused to repeal the penal laws against Catholics thus showing their opposition to James. Paradoxically, the Presbyterians derived considerable benefit from James grant of toleration and they were subsequently to grow in strength.

This era also resulted in a more definitive conquest of Ireland by Williamite forces, a time characterised and celebrated in future years by victories in Derry in 1689 and at the Battle of the Boyne in 1690. This revolutionary period not only resulted in manifest political change in Britain and Ireland, but it became the major landmark of much future Protestant ideology in its relation to society, culture and politics in Britain. The 'Glorious Revolution' resulted in the confirmation by the new King William III of the formal establishment of Presbyterian dominance in Scotland. The Episcopalian system dominated in England. In Britain, as well as other long standing disabilities, Catholics were excluded from the monarchy and all offices of state. As a whole, Scottish Episcopalians did not accept William's dynasty and this led to the subsequent Jacobite attacks of the 18th century. This factor is also relevant to the way in which Presbyterianism became equated with allegiance to William and the emerging British state.

Protestantism was the ethos which pervaded all facets of Scottish life. The independence (with reference to the Act of Union in 1707) of the legal, educational and Church systems meant that they remained as formidable institutions in terms of Scottish identity. The Church of Scotland continued to be a significant institutional tier in Scottish national consciousness. In 1968 a committee of General Assembly stated their belief that; 'The Church of Scotland has constantly upheld Scotland's historic nationhood and identity'.[2]

The anti-Catholic dimension

Though varying in degrees of intensity and fervour, one of the greatest features of Scottish Protestantism persisted throughout the centuries; anti-Catholicism. In 1788 the London and colonial Dublin Parliaments passed Catholic Relief Bills. Both statutes were modest, for example the English Act left priests subject to 'perpetual imprisonment' for saying mass, but it abolished the one hundred pounds reward for informing against them for such a deed. When Henry Dundas, the Lord Advocate of Scotland, promised during the debate on the English Bill that a Scottish measure would follow, the Scottish cry of 'no popery' was aroused; this despite the fact that the actual numbers of Catholics in Scotland were few and they constituted no threat (Donovan, 1979, pp. 62-76).

The evangelical party of the Kirk attacked Parliament's intentions for Scotland and immediately launched appeals, sermons and pamphlets to rouse the country against the proposals. Ministers were influential people and many laymen, Presbyterian seceeders and Episcopalians joined them. Secular bodies joined in the agitation and a successful campaign was begun by Scottish town councils and the city corporations. Tolerating the Catholic faith was perceived as being:

> highly prejudicial to the interest of the Protestant religion in Scotland, dangerous to our constitution, civil and religious, a direct violation of the treaty of the union, inconsistent with the King's honour, and destructive to the peace and security of his best subjects (Devine and Mitchison, 1988, p. 154).

Cooney argues that: 'as a result of the denunciations 12,000 Glaswegians vowed to suppress idolatry and to block the relief bill, even though only twenty Catholics mostly Highlanders, were living in that city' (1982, p. 13). Anti-Catholic rioting took place in Glasgow and Edinburgh, while the press also became involved in the struggle against the spectre of revibrant Catholicism. In February 1779 the government decided reluctantly to abandon Catholic relief for Scotland. Ironically, the Scottish success and continued denunciations on the subject led their English allies to restart their anti-Catholic agitation. Demonstrating the extent of anti-Catholicism in Glasgow alone, one commentator relays that in the 1790s, there were only thirty-nine Catholics in the city; this in a community that had at the same time, forty-three anti-Catholic 'societies' (Murray, 1984, p. 93. Devine, 1988, p. 154, notes the latter figure to be 60 in 1791).

In 1823 Daniel O'Connell formed the Catholic Association in Ireland to press for emancipation. Within a few years the agitation in Ireland, and to a lesser extent Britain, caused such an uproar that the eventual granting of such a concession led to the downfall of Wellington's government. In Scotland, although many individuals and some groups favoured this concession (Catholics would now be able to sit in parliament), the protest and antagonism towards the passing of the measure was deep (there occurred a widespread protest in England, but in Scotland it was of a much more virulent and encompassing kind). Stirling Council addressed petitions to the Lords, the Commons and the King. The general Session of Glasgow (ministers and elders of all the Church of Scotland charges within the city) petitioned against concessions. Within a fortnight of the Emancipation proposal; 'with varied words but unanimity of sentiment twelve of the fourteen incorporated trades had sent in their petitions' against it (Muirhead, 1973, pp. 26-42).

Individual parishes outside of the Church of Scotland also joined the chorus. The Presbyteries of Glasgow, Hamilton, Lanark and Dumfries, of Linlithgow, Perth and Stirling; parishes in Aberdeen, the Synod of Ross, as well as the parishes of the far north, all petitioned London against the reform (Edinburgh though was to remain lethargic amidst the uproar). Handley notes that 'ten years after the measure was passed, synods of the Church of Scotland were still drawing up petitions for its repeal' (1964, p. 137). The students and graduates of Glasgow University also sent petitions to parliament protesting against the proposals.

In addition to traditional anti-Catholicism, some of the protest may have been a reaction to the increasing numbers of Irish immigrant labourers present in the country, who would have been viewed as an economic challenge. They were often seen as being ignorant and destitute and lowering social conditions in areas where they settled.

The Rev Dr Muir encouraged the General Kirk Session of Glasgow to petition London in 1829. Five years later, some of the rationale behind that protest manifested itself when he expressed the feeling that it:

> would be advantageous with such immigration stopped, because it would prevent the growth of popery in the west of Scotland, which is the fruitful mother of all evils that at present afflict Ireland; in as much as the word of God asserts that idolatry brings a curse with it (Muirhead, 1973, pp. 26-42).

Anti-Catholic violence also manifested itself at the Trongate in Glasgow and at meetings in Perth. Mob-violence erupted in Inverness and Thurso. Nonetheless, there were some voices of toleration and moderation amongst the Scottish people. The evangelical preacher, Thomas Chalmers, backed Catholic Emancipation, made provisions for the Catholic poor in his social work activities in Glasgow, and preached sermons for religious tolerance in Ulster as well as Scotland'.[3] Paradoxically, he continued to talk of infiltrating Roman Catholicism and of destroying it from within. In Edinburgh, a pro-Emancipation meeting attracted 2,000 people paying one shilling per head whilst 'there was a galaxy of talent, mainly legal'. The Scotsman newspaper frequently refuted the extravagant anti-Catholic claims. It highlighted virtues amongst the immigrant community, such as the chastity practised by the female sex 'even in the most reduced circumstances or the low illegitimacy rate when compared with the native Scottish figure' (Muirhead, 1973, pp. 103-120).

Overall however, it would be accurate to conclude that the vast majority of those who made clear their opinions over the impending bill were against its enactment. Such dissent was geographically widespread and the Scottish collective was viewed as being under threat by Catholic Emancipation. The idea of a religious collective and consequently a collective identity was important to Scottish Protestantism, and transgressions imposed on this community only invited the judgement of God upon them (Muirhead, 1973, pp. 103-120). Apart from overt religious arguments, Emancipation was also seen as a subversion of the Revolutionary Settlement, the Treaty of the Union and the Protestant establishment.

Britain, Ireland and other factors

By the late 18th and early 19th centuries many questions relating to Catholicism were considered with reference to Irish-British relations. The Scottish people had national, cultural, religious and kinship ties with the colonist population of the north of Ireland. It was from Scotland that the majority of Protestant settlers 'planted' in Irelands northern province of Ulster in the 17th century originally came. Ireland was a valuable asset in Britain's Empire and this depended to a large extent upon maintained links with the descendants of the settlers. Native Irish insurgency had almost always had Catholic connotations, generally viewed as the faith of pre-plantation Ireland. If Britain was to remain in control of Ireland then the Protestant ascendancy would have to be maintained. Therefore, any laws relating to the Catholic's position in Britain were carried forward with reference to Ireland.

Muirhead (1973, pp. 103-120) opines that; 'in Scotland anti-Romanism had become a religion and a way of life'. Significantly, the debate against Emancipation was not an isolated event or a reaction to an impending threat perceived from Catholicism; centuries of anti-Popery had left its mark on the national psyche.

Until the arrival of the Irish the membership of the Scottish Catholic Church made up less than one per cent of the Scottish population. As Irish Catholic immigration mushroomed in the 19th century the debate would expand as anti-Catholic activity developed in new ways. The Catholic Church in Scotland between 1603 and 1879 was relegated by Rome to missionary status. The presence of the Irish in the 19th century however transformed that condition. The first substantive display of the changing status of the Catholic Church in Scotland was the building of St Andrews Cathedral in Glasgow. When, in 1805, the then priest Andrew Scott arrived in Glasgow from the north of Scotland to minister to the growing Catholic flock, the city's only priest had under him 450 parishioners (McLelland, 1967. p3). With Irish immigration to the city developing into a trend, by 1822 there were 15,000 Catholics in Glasgow.[4] The cathedral was opened in 1816 but its creation was the subject of anti-Catholic mob violence, press disapproval and Protestant pulpit protest.

The Irish huddled together in the worst parts of the towns and, cities and coming from a rough but simple peasant society, they often found it difficult to adapt themselves. Linguistical differences did not lend to an easier acclimatisation. Many of the stereotyped attitudes that developed towards the Irish did so in this context. The feelings of the native community towards the increasing Irish influx emerged within various facets of Scottish life. Victorian times were characterised for example by 'No Irish Need Apply' notices, a common warning in the employment columns of the contemporary press and the walls and entrances of employment concerns. Pamphlets, lectures and tracts against Ireland, the Irish and Catholics, as well as their rudimentary schools, were common during these decades (Gallagher, 1987, c. 32). A cultural and ideological polemic was waged by many sections of Scottish society against Irish Catholic immigrants.[5]

Whilst some immigrants were immediately sent back to Ireland, the numbers of Irish applying for poor relief rose dramatically. The infirmaries of Glasgow were filled with Irish people in the throes of fever. The incidence of cholera deaths rose at an incredible rate in and around Glasgow. The appearance of cholera and typhus in the industrial towns of Scotland during the years of 1847 and 1848 added impetus to prevalent anti-Irish feeling. Although outbreaks of fever were common in industrial Scotland before the Famine, the Irish in their state of wretchedness, provided the fodder which gave fever, cholera and typhus, epidemic status wherever people abided in large numbers (Handley, 1964. c180).

However, it would be the incomers Catholic religion which would become the greatest focus for attention. Throughout the 19th century, continual waves of Irish immigrants came to Scotland in a bid to escape from the hardships experienced at home. Thousands arrived at different times throughout the 20th century, each new wave almost inevitably mixing and inter-marrying with the previous generations. The Catholicism of the immigrants became the main layer of identity of Irish immigrant life in Scotland.

> The sheer isolation [occasionally of a self imposed nature, though almost inevitably so in the context of religious and national group security in an alien environment] and weakness of the Irish in Scottish society meant that they were despised rather than actively feared by those sections of the population who felt their presence to be uncomfortable (Gallagher, 1987, p42).

Despite this assessment, at an anti-Catholic riot in Kelso in the Scottish border region in 1856, the Catholic church was burnt down. Anti-Irish and Catholic troubles are recorded in Greenock, Port Glasgow, and Dumbarton in the 1850s, whilst a notorious outbreak of 'Orange and Green' troubles broke out in Partick, Glasgow, on the occasion of the O'Connell centenary celebrations of the local Catholic community in August 1875. Catholic chapels, houses and individuals, were the main targets.

As early as 1857 (Handley, 1964, c. 256) trouble in Coatbridge was recorded around the occasion of the 12th of July Orange Parades, and this appears to have been a regular occurrence. During the summer months of 1883, many serious outbreaks of related fighting are chronicled. The weeks prior to the 12th July celebrations, as well as events around the annual 'Home Rule for Ireland' procession in mid-August, resulted in skirmishes, police charges and violence. Such things persist; some outbreaks were also witnessed in Coatbridge during the 1980s and 1990s.[6]

The Scotsman newspaper stood out for its tolerance of the incomers (at a time when there existed a number of anti-Irish periodicals and newspapers). It believed it nonsensical that when 'Protestantism has almost all the rich and influential in the community', and thus had all the odds stacked in its favour, that so many should be so virulently anti-Catholic (Handley, 1964, pp. 249-260).

A number of Protestant ministers became prominent in the anti-Catholic activity of the mid to late 19th century. John Hope and Jacob Primmer of the Church of Scotland were two of the most active of this group. The 20th century meanwhile witnessed both the social and political impact of anti-Catholicism with Alexander Ratcliffe's Scottish Protestant League and John Cormack and the Protestant Action Society (See Gallagher, 1987).

Although national politics was never fully divided along straight ethnic-religious lines, related questions have had an effect on the nature of Scottish political activity. For example, despite their social make-up, the working class wards near the Glasgow shipyards, during much of the early part of the 20th century were dominated by the Conservative and Unionist Party. This was an area affected by an influx of Belfast Protestant/loyalists who came to work in the local shipbuilding trade in the early 1900s.[7] Religious identity's political resonance was also found in other areas of early 20th century life in

14

Scotland. In 1923, Hugh Ferguson was returned to Parliament for the Lanarkshire seat of Motherwell, Ferguson was the candidate of the Orange and Protestant Party, allies of the Tory Party. His beliefs became manifest when he called 'in parliament for another Cromwell to get to work in Ireland.'[8] Sir John Gilmour, as Secretary of State for Scotland from 1924 to 1929, was an honorary deputy grand master of the Orange Order, while Colonel A.D. McInnes Shaw, a Renfrewshire MP, later became Scottish Grand Master of the Order:

> In 1926, McInnes Shaw, along with Sir A Sprot, MP for Lanark, tried unsuccessfully to remove Scotland from the jurisdiction of the Roman Catholic Relief Act which lifted the ban on open-air Catholic processions (Gallagher, 1987. p. 144-145).

In the past therefore, prominent Conservatives clearly had strong links with Orangeism.

The demographic, cultural and religious constitution of Scottish society experienced a gradual change over the course of the 19th and 20th centuries. By 1992-93, from a population of approximately five million in Scotland, 744,600 were Roman Catholic; around fifteen per cent.[9]

Table 1.1
Catholics in the Scottish population (1878-1977)

1878	332,000	9.2 %,	% of Scottish
1901	446,000	10.0%	population.
1931	662,000	13.7%	
1951	750,000	14.7%	
1971	882,000	15.7%	
1977	823,000	15.9%	(Darragh, 1979)

The arrival of the Irish, introduced a new cleavage into Scottish society, one which in particular reinforced already entrenched anti-Catholicism. Anti-Catholicism, with a new powerful ethnic element, subsequently became a framework for determining many features of everyday life from employment and education, to sport and politics.

Identities and ethnicity

Identity is a crucial concept in social science. Identities can be based upon a variety of factors, notably class, ethnicity, race and religion. Such factors or 'classifications' stimulate or promote individual and collective emotions, ideas and practices. This work is based on the contention that society and politics are derived from individual and community patterns of orientation, belief systems and 'identities'. An aim of this book is to utilise a concept of identities to facilitate an understanding of Scottish society. A concept of identity assists the interpretive framework for a social, cultural and political picture of the Irish identity in modern Scotland and its relationship to the wider society.

A task here also is to look at the ethno-religious cleavage which is reflected in Scottish football support. Therefore, I need to explain why an analysis of soccer offers an important contribution to any discussion of ethno-religious identity in Scottish society. This will demonstrate that soccer in some countries can be viewed as a symptomatic expression of various social and political factors not normally associated with the sport. A brief analysis of three societies, Spain, England, and Northern Ireland, should be adequate to show the importance of soccer as a particularly important element in an analysis of socio-political cleavage and identity.

The concept of identities has been used by social and political scientists like John Turner, Sten Rokkan, Derek Urwin and Henry Tajfel. Much of the work of these people concentrates upon both self and group identity, with an emphasis on identities shaped by national, racial, territorial or religious factors. Rokkan and Urwin write:

> On the issue of 'who, what, and where am I', the individual tends to look no further than his own accumulation of attitudes and prejudices which themselves are determined by his own cultural environment. These patterns of orientation provide the individual with an identity and offer him a standard by which he may interpret the world and to which he may adjust his reactions. Collectively, they impose upon a society a set of cultural contours that are enduring configurations. It is in this sense that we can talk of the cultural myth that the ritual practice that ensures the survival of the myth for at least one further generation. (1983, p67):

This, of course, has implications for all kinds of social and political belief, behaviour and activity. The same writers (1983, p. 67) also note that:

> roots are important because they help you know who you are and whom you can trust; they are the lifeblood of cultural identity. But options are equally important, though a surplus of options or misguided options they believe, may lead to 'a heightened depersonalised anonymity'.

John Turner (chap 1, Tajfel, 1981) uses this social identification model, arguing:

> a common social identification is shared and there is more often than not self-perception in being a member, or simply a number, in a particular social category. This definition stresses that members of these social categories seem often to share 'a sort of collective perception' of their own social unity 'and of their difference' - often hostility - from those who are not of the same kind.

Similarly, Tajfel sees 'social identity', as:

part of the individual's self-concept which derives from their knowledge of their membership of a social group (or groups) together with the value and emotional significance attached to that membership....however rich and complex may be the individual's view of themselves in relation to the surrounding world, social and physical, some aspects of that view are contributed by the membership of certain social groups or categories. Some of these memberships are more salient than others; and some may vary in salience in time and as a function of a variety of social situations

This book shares Tajfel's emphasis:

our explicit preoccupation is with the effects of the nature and subjective importance of these memberships on those aspects of an individual's behaviour which are pertinent to intergroup relations - without in the least denying that this does not enable us to make any statements about the 'self' in general, or about social behaviour in other contexts.

Here, I am using the concept of identity in a limited way emphasising its relationship to: 'certain limited aspects of social behaviour:' (Tajfel, 1981, p. 255) and also to certain limited aspects of political behaviour.

Group psychology, social identity, political identity and behaviour all frequently interlace with ideas of ethnicity, ethnic beliefs, behaviour, ideas and traits. A sense of ethnicity is also important for this present study. As Harold Issacs says, words such as tribe, clan, nation, nationality, race, ethnic group or ethnicity, are used by writers to describe social groupings, though each term will be employed to suit the particular taste, bent, or discipline of the writer concerned. What is without doubt is that man has an 'overwhelming urge to belong, to identify himself with tribe or nation and above all with his system of beliefs'. This would indicate that it is common for people to find themselves as part of a group or at least to passively or actively seek out a group of which the are, or they can be, seen to be part. As indicated earlier, we are concerned with 'the general perception of common categories the psychological group membership; the common social identification,' (Issacs, 1974, pp. 15-41) that relates to geography, culture, religion and nationality; a psychological and practical bonding which leads to a perception of some sort of collective identity; both by the group and by attitudes relating to it.

The term identity should not be seen as a rigid one; one that absolutely categorises people into one group or the other. It is simply used to identify common attributes or beliefs which mark out a group of people as having something quite significant in common with one another and, equally, as being different from others. McCall and Simmons (1966, p. 24), note however that, 'cultures are, not all that simple or homogeneous....the best conceptual models of cultures can only state correctly the central tendencies of ranges of variation'. Partial cultures, which are dependent upon the larger one in a different way, and even subcultures, can often be significant aspects of the larger one. Nevertheless, internal differentiation and sub-cultural divergences do not take away from the fact that a centrality of common identities exist. The idea of subcultures is something to which we shall return later.

Some sort of conception of ethnicity then is often useful when ideas of identities are being discussed. Indeed, it is vital to an understanding of this particular project. Referring to United States society, Gordon (1974, p. 167) defines ethnicity in terms of any 'group which is defined or set-off by race, religion, or national origin, or some combination of these categories,' and which results in a 'common social psychological referent'. Similarly, Schermerhorn (1970, p. 12), defines an ethnic group as:

> a collectivity within a larger society having real or putative common ancestry: memories of a shared historical past, and a cultural focus on one or more symbolic elements defined as the epitome of their peoplehood. Examples of such symbolic elements are: kinship patterns, physical contiguity (as in localism or sectionalism), religious affiliation, language or dialect forms, tribal affiliation, nationality, phenotypical features, or any combination of these.

Greely and McCready (1976, pp. 91-106), argue that an ethnic group is a 'collective based on presumed common origin', and with a conspicuous trait that marks them out or even puts them at odds with the indigenous population in the country of settlement. All of these related definitions of ethnicity are important for this analysis. However, 'identity' is the overarching concept throughout this book.

For Rokkan and Urwin (1983, p. 67):

> Identity can be broken down into at least four component parts: myth, symbol, history, and institutional....the mythical aspects of identity may be defined as a set of beliefs [feeling, emotions, aspirations and actions] that creates an instrumental pattern for behaviour in the sense that these beliefs provide aims for their followers....the most significant myth historically has been religion, whilst since the nineteenth century, nationalism as a myth can be regarded almost as a civil religion....the symbolic element represents the enduring expressive aspect of culture, transmitting its values from individual to individual, and from generation to generation.

History is an almost natural occurrence alongside these, juxtaposing itself as part of a collective experience and psyche, whilst the institutional aspect of this breakdown can be seen as the concrete enactment of the so-called myth and the symbol.

Tajfel (1978, p. 283), views the social identities which derive as a result of interactions between these characteristics, as essentially dynamic ones:

> It is not an attempt to view social identity for 'what it is' but rather to see it as an intervening causal mechanism in social situations. The complex dialectical relationship between social

identity and social settings is stressed, in the sense that the salience of a particular social identity for an individual may vary from situation to situation and indeed from time to time within the same situation. Social identity, then, is a blanket term concealing the complexity of the relationship between the clarity of the awareness that one is a member of a group and the strength and nature of the emotional investments that derive from this identity.

It will also be seen here that religious identities and labels, as part of the complexity of the social identity, have an importance in Scottish society that goes far beyond the realms of simple religious practice.

Soccer as a symptom of cleavage: Spain

After twenty-five years of peace, behind the applause could be heard an authentic support for the Spirit of July 18th. In this quarter of a century there has never been displayed a greater popular enthusiasm for the state born out of the victory over Communism and its fellow-travellers....Spain is a nation every day more orderly, mature and unified, and which is steadfastly marching down the path of economic, social and institutional development. It is a national adventure.

Duncan Shaw (1985, pp. 38-42) uses this paragraph from the 'sports pages' of the conservative ABC newspaper in Spain (in the wake of the Spanish national teams European Nations Cup final win over the Soviet Union in 1964), to illustrate how soccer had been politicised in that country, as well as to introduce his reader to the fact that for many people in Spain, football today and in the recent past, has been used as a means of popular protest. Shaw informs us how the success of the famous Real Madrid team of the late 1950s and the early 1960s, as well as victory of the Spanish national team, were used by Spain's 'dictator', General Franco, in the cause of creating a centralised Spain, with its focus in Madrid, and, regaining European acceptance. Because of the undemocratic nature of Spanish society, the effects of Civil War, and the Dictatorship of General Franco; 'Spain was the pariah of post-1945 Europe' (Browne, 1983, p. 79). It is not General Franco's 'successes' which are our concern. However, in a highly diversified country, Franco's actions are pertinent in that his attempts at centralism, in cultural and often linguistic terms, were resented most resolutely by the Catalan and Basque regions of the country, and this rancour was to find an expression in soccer.

Medhurst (1987) argues about these areas:

The Basque and Catalan regions stand apart from the rest of Spain. Their distinctive political characters are derived largely from keen awareness of historic languages and cultures coupled with widely supported local nationalist movements. During Franco's dictatorship, both regions long endured severe political and cultural repression, alienating them yet further from the central government in Madrid, fuelling their demands for regional autonomy, and fomenting opposition groups.

Shaw adds (1985, p. 38-42): 'Rancour towards Madrid emanated most powerfully from Catalonia and the Basque country, and manifested itself through frenetic support for the CF Barcelona and Athletico Bilbao clubs'. More generally, Shaw also notes that under certain conditions (Shaw considers here a political dictatorship), open opposition is silenced and dissent very often finds expression through safer channels. In all probability, many kinds of popular protest, dissent or expression can become manifest through just such channels.

Many regional characteristics were banned by the Franco regime, as its brand of Spanishness was imposed upon society. The native languages and cultures came under attack and it became an offence to fly a regional flag. Such widespread repression meant that a number of otherwise neutral avenues were to develop a para-political and extra-cultural dimension. A football ground, often with vast crowds, invariably became a safer environment for otherwise repressed expressions, and indeed this is what happened to the Catalan Barcelona, and the Basque Athletico Bilbao. As Shaw argues:

> As well as being a focus for Basque emotions at home, the Athletico Bilbao club became a pole of resistance to Francoism right across the country. Hundreds of local supporters clubs were established by workers who had never visited the Basque Country, but who saw in Athletico both a successful working class club, and a powerful symbol of opposition'(1985, pp. 38-42).[10]

It was only from the 1950s, when Real Madrid began to gain their noted successes, that the regime began to associate itself so closely with the club. The obsessive centralism of Franco found its focus in the Madrid team. However, Real Madrid also drew a similar attention from other more independently minded regions which were attracted purely by the success of a big club, but were ignorant of the subliminal message Franco was pursuing. Franco and his like-minded politicians and military men were glad to be seen regularly at such a successful bastion of the new country, the de-regionalised Spain. Real Madrid became simultaneously an internal and an external focus for Spanish nationalism, as defined by the Civil War victors.

In Catalonia, although nationhood is often perceived in linguistic and cultural forms (see Payne, 1971), it can also be reflected in demands for political autonomy. In the Basque region a great stress is placed on shared ethnic identity. The alienation from the rest of Spain shared by the Basques in many ways transcends class divisions. Within the more confident culture of Catalonia, class often appears to take precedent in terms of political struggle (Medhurst, 1987, p7).

By the 1960s, the existence of E.T.A (Euzadi ta Azkatasuna), the Basque nationalist political and militant organisation, had succeeded in reactivating what had until then appeared to be a diminishing force. The re-emerged

Basque nationalism became one of Franco's major problems:

> The steady deterioration of the situation in the Basque provinces proved that the military philosophy of the regime, its doctrinaire centralism, provided no permanent solution for the old problem of Spanish regionalism (Carr & Fusi, 1979, 1981, p. 160).

Even as Franco lay in his death bed in late 1975 the Basque region would continue to cause him major headaches.

Around this period Franco personally insisted on the execution of five Basque E.T.A militants. The following Sunday the Bilbao and Real Sociedad de San Sebastion players ran out wearing black armbands. The police intervened against this blatant anti-Madrid gesture, and the matter was eventually smoothed over by the clubs each claiming that the armbands were to commemorate the death of some extremely obscure figure in their histories. The international indignation at Franco's final major action was reflected in the decision by the Lazio club of Rome to withdraw from playing Barcelona in the UEFA Cup, ironically unaware that the Catalan club had, in fact, been a powerful pole of opposition to the dictator throughout his thirty-six years of ascendancy (Shaw, 1985, pp. 38-42).

After the death of Franco there was a general relaxation of cultural and language repression. Nevertheless, in the Basque region especially, alienation from the Spanish state continued unabated. In Catalonia, outright opposition seemed to diminish, though there existed the possibility of a significant residue of support for the regional cause. Although Basques are divided themselves on their ideas for the future of the region, and a large percentage of the inhabitants of the provinces are economic migrants from other parts of Spain, there is an ever present sense of separateness evident. Spain's democratic evolution after the death of Franco and the election of July 1977, has meant an unprecedented and uninterrupted period of constitutional rule. The regional problems have been tackled in a different way from that of the dictators, but the Catalan and Basque identities remain strong nonetheless (Medhurst, 1987).

This has also meant that the ethnic, cultural and nationalist dimension of Spanish football did not disappear with the demise of Francoism. The regionalist movements have now come out and openly identified with the Barcelona and Bilbao clubs and vice versa:

> Regional leaders like Taradellas and Garaicoechea have realised the importance of the football match as a gathering of regional sentiment, and so have made themselves noticeable there. The fans too, have come out into the open with their flags, and now there is as much red and yellow as red and blue at Barcelona, and similarly at Bilbao (Shaw, 1985, pp. 38-42) .

Although possibly still seen as the quintessential Spanish team, Real Madrid have edged themselves away from the old Franco images with which they were so often equated.

Lincoln Allison, experienced the political and cultural dimension to Spanish football when in the city of Barcelona in 1985, at a time when the club had just won the Spanish League for the first time in over a decade. Allison wrote, that at the subsequent celebrations, Jordi Pujol, President of Catalonia (who was imprisoned under Franco), made a speech which extolled Barca [Barcelona], called for greater autonomy for Catalonia and noted, in passing, that agreement had been reached that day for Spain to join the EEC. Allison recounts how a woman told him:

> I detest football, but Barca is more than football. In the bad days, when we had nothing else, Barca meant Catalonia. People used to go to the stadium just to speak Catalan.

The following weeks match against Gijon was incidental he adds, Catalonian songs were sung with a joy and fervour which can scarcely have been equalled. 'Autonomy and the championship; it was like a nation whose dreams had come true'. For Allison, and in reference to George Orwell's idea's about Spain and socialism, etc., Catalan nationalism and football's symbolism mattered much more than orthodox class struggle (Allison, 1986, pp. 2-3).

Although there are other important conduits of regional and ethnic identity in Spain, football remains symptomatic of the major diversities that exist within Spanish society. More than ever before, despite the onset of democracy, and at least as far as the above clubs are concerned, they are the symbols and the focus, as well as the open vehicles for the expression of ethnic, cultural and nationalistic identities and differences within Spanish society.

England

Immigration to Britain from its former colonies initially took off in the post-War period. Much of the impetus for this immigration began when British industry looked abroad for fresh sources of labour due to the post-war worker shortage. The 1948 Nationality Act made it easier for citizens of British colonies and former colonies to gain UK citizenship. By the mid to late 1950s the number of people from the Caribbean and South Asia in the UK was estimated to be 200,000 or 0.5 per cent of the population. This had increased tenfold by 1988, when about 5 per cent, or 2.6 million people, were of New Commonwealth origin or decent. Over half of this minority were born in the UK (Cashmore, 1989, pp. 80-82). At the same time, between 1944 and 1950, 175,000 European immigrants, mainly Polish, German and Ukrainian, came to Britain to work. In addition, millions of Irish immigrants came to Britain in the 19th and 20th centuries.

Between 1948 and the mid 1950s, Liverpool, Nottingham and the London districts of Notting Hill, were marked by racial riots or attacks upon their non-white populations. Often they 'were encouraged by fascist organisations that were active in the period' (Cashmore, 1989, p. 84). This growing conflict can be seen against a background of increasing economic competition between newcomers and the indigenous population. Even earlier, the black/brown presence had led to other social and political frictions. Many individual MP's were making their voices heard, calling for a restriction of the right of entry of 'coloured colonial immigrants' (Cashmore, 1989, p. 87). In 1948, the Conservative Party's Central Council passed a resolution in favour of immigration control. By the late 1960's, the Conservative Shadow Cabinet MP, Enoch Powell, was making his famous anti 'coloured' immigration speeches. Powell was to attract a remarkable degree of working class support during this time. On the 23rd April 1968, 1500 London dockers marched to Westminster in support of Powell. Three days later, the Smithfield meat porters joined them, whilst during April and May, pro-Powell marches took place in a number of provincial centres.

Several academics have subsequently focused upon the cleavage and low level conflict that has been instigated in England as a result of this immigration and the reactions towards it (see Rex, 1973; Daniel, 1968; and Miles and Phizachlea, 1979). Cashmore and Troyna have helped rationalise it, arguing that, although the British Empire itself might have dissolved:

> the consciousness associated with that Empire has been transmitted through generations and remains largely intact. The idea that being white denotes superiority is not some natural fact, but a remnant of the colonial mentality. The enormous flux of immigrants which the UK received after World War 11 was possible precisely because of the old system of empire; the territories from which the migrants came were parts of the old regime and the new arrivals in the post-war years were, in a real sense, reminders of the empire. The reactions they elicited from both politicians and people in the street can be seen as a legacy of the colonial era which maintained the white man's innate superiority over both black and brown men (Cashmore, 1989, p44).

Rex and Tomlinson (1979, p. 13) opine that; the colonist and imperialist attitudes which characterised the colonial exploiters and their own native population continues, but within a different context and with new manifestations. English football provides us with a reference point for some of that societies ethnic or colour differences.

Talking of England's racial riots of the 1980s, one writer says, 'the racial intolerance which prompted these revolts was nowhere more loudly expressed than at England's football grounds'. He believes black footballers in England in the 1970s and 1980s, 'were sitting targets for concentrated doses of the kind of malice which most had probably been familiar with all their lives' (Hill, 1989, pp. 13-14). With reference to the supposed nationalism, racism and general ethnocentricity of the English working class football hooligan, Hargreaves asserts that:

> Englishness, manliness and belonging to one's local community are all of a piece, and when the chips are down the essence of these qualities is the willingness and the ability to fight for them. Asians are despised...Blacks are seen as taking over the country, including 'our game', black players are vilified with racist abuse, especially when (final insult) they are selected to play for England. (1986, p. 108)

For Hargreaves, this has enabled the National Front and the British Movement to gain support from amongst football supporters (see also, Platt and Slater, 1984). Dave Hill, in his biography of the black footballer John Barnes, adds, in a racial context:

> the football culture perpetuates an idea of Englishness which militates against all the valuable things that football is supposed to represent.

He believes that being white is comprehended as the supreme ethic: 'football has become a microcosm for the country at large' (Hill, 1989, pp. 182-196).

Although Hill states his belief that anti-black feelings pervade English football, he concentrates his research on the city of Liverpool in the north-west of the country, and where two of the country's most successful and most powerful teams originate, the city rivals of Everton and Liverpool Football Clubs. His exploration centres around the Liverpool signing of the Jamaican born, black, footballer, John Barnes, in the mid 1980s. Apart from two players in the 70s who made a handful of appearances each with both clubs, this was seen as a landmark in the area's football. This was despite a strong black population having existed in the area for a number of generations, as well as their active and successful involvement as footballers in the city's amateur leagues. Added to this, was the fact that blacks had become routine features of league teams of all standards in all other parts of the country since the early 1970s.

The lack of black players with both clubs was recognised by the city's blacks and reflected in their thin representation on two of the most populated football terraces in England. 'White Liverpool celebrated at football on a Saturday afternoon'. It is a definition of whiteness which isolates black Liverpool from identifying with two of the foremost and greatest institutions in Northern England. When the black John Barnes made his cup derby debut for Liverpool against the Everton club in October 1987, both he and his club were met with chants of 'Niggerpool, Niggerpool' and 'Everton are White', whilst Barnes himself became the recipient of 'volumes of bananas' (Hill pp. 137-141).

Also significant was that despite this high profile game and the racist chants coming across loud and clear on television and radio, the media hardly mentioned it at all. A league match a few days later witnessed the same display, from fans and media alike. For Hill:

> the BBC's presentation of the match was an object lesson in the way television's production values effectively sanitise football and largely exclude reflection on the social issues connected with it.

The result in the above instance: 'was that an entire, central element of a major football occasion - the violently racist behaviour of the Everton fans - went utterly unremarked'. Some football officials put this down to the actions of a few hundred supporters; as Hill says, 'the lunatic fringe theory'. The focus was always upon how it all affected the skills of the black footballer Barnes; not on the 'broad issue of racism' (Hill, pp. 141-142).

This 'racism' that the Liverpool fans often displayed had seemingly disappeared on the signing of Barnes; 'it was as if the bigots of Anfield [Liverpool's home ground] had been smitten with contrition and the forces of reason had prevailed' (Hill, p. 11). However, anti-black singing and symbols were long a feature of the fans connection and affiliation with the club. Indeed, racism can be viewed as part of the identity they shared with each other, as well as being reflected in the contempt they felt for those who were excluded from this identity.

The signing of Barnes seemed for one newspaper reporter to be a signal that Liverpool were at long last embarking on 'a clean up campaign', attacking racism on the terraces and on the walls of the stadium (where often displayed were the graffiti and slogans 'NF', 'White Power', and 'No Wogs Allowed').[11] However, he had possibly misread the signing, not being able to recognise the true nature or the extent of anti-black feeling in England.

Hill believes that if one was to accept that racism had been struck from the Liverpool repertoire, this would only ignore its real extent and significance. In a match against Watford, John Barnes was substituted and the Liverpool fans sang humorously 'Liverpool are White! Liverpool are White'. In that moment he says, a self awareness became all too manifest. It also indicated the kind of respect that may be judged to be only temporarily and insincerely given to an extremely gifted black player in a white institution. It is significant also that when Barnes was absent through injury the Liverpool fans greeted an opposition's sole black player with cries of derision (1989, pp. 161-164).

This anti-black feeling may be viewed as a symptom of a general attitude within the society itself. Hill again adds, that racism is:

> an inherent part, a logical product of a theory of Englishness acted out behind the goal, which is just the crudest manifestation of the Bulldog [an English symbol] mentality routinely invoked in the name of national pride (p. 194).

Talking of the skinhead element of the fascist groupings (considered by him to be such groups as the National Front and The British Movement) which utilised football stadia in the 1970s (as well as the 1980s and 1990s) for recruiting purposes, Hebdige (1981, pp. 39-41), says that their violence and aggression stood for:

> a way of life, a set of values and attitudes which, according to some social historians, did not emerge until the late 19th century when the British Empire was at its most powerful when imperialism, nationalism and Toryism were beginning to feature prominently in the language of the pubs and the music halls.

Cashmore and Troyna, quoting Martin Baker (1983, p. 63), go so far as to tie this line of inquiry into the nationalism of the Thatcher era, which was particularly manifest during the Falklands/Malvinas War period. This new political rhetoric and action Baker says, derived from the same mind-set as that of Enoch Powell, who's own rhetoric was simply an undisguised expression of many of the feelings which lay at the heart of English/British society. The control and preserve nature of the legal tradition concerning immigration since the early 1960s, was epitomised in 1981 he says, with the passing of 'The British Nationality Act', which meant citizenship was no longer automatically gained by birth and residence in the UK. The Act was specifically aimed at non-white immigration, despite the fact that since the initial inflow of the 1950s, the majority of immigrants into Britain had been white (a parent had to have been born in Britain and to have lawfully settled there for an offspring to qualify for residency). EEC immigration was of course excluded from the Act. Henceforth, there was to be no such category as 'Commonwealth immigrant', but simply 'migrant workers'; thus, such 'migrants' status was now less secure (See Hudson and Williams, 1989).

Baker's assertions are backed up by other commentators. Various writers have made similar claims (often supported by empirical evidence) that English international supporters (who have gained world wide notoriety since the mid 1970s, due to their aggressive behaviour and violence against 'foreigners' and their property) exhibit a form of English/British racism and nationalism. Williams (1986), says that, despite the setbacks and the humiliations of the post-war years, the English continue to feel superior to other nations. He notes a complacent sense of superiority as one British newspaper put it, rooted in the idea that, whatever our failings, we are, somehow, more civilised than they, more secure in our democratic values.

Williams believes that racist abuse has been aimed - unchallenged - at black players in England for years, but that it is either ignored or casually dismissed by the game's administrators. When pressed on such issues, he says that the clubs generally produce statements saying they have none and they wish no political links of any kind. He believes it to be strangely ironic, that only days before the tragedy of the Haysel Stadium riot in Brussels (May 1985), the British government was, once again, ordered before the European Court of Human Rights because of its perceived racist immigration policies (1986, pp. 17-18).

John Hargreaves opines that the motivation that drove Liverpool's fans to such destruction in that year were not simply the actions of a tiny criminal element, but were in fact a constituent element in that culture; at least in so far as the working class was concerned:

> Feelings of national superiority and a suspicion of foreigners and things foreign have rarely been far from the surface of British working-class culture, and the consequent chauvinism and transient xenophobia receive expression in sports (1986, p. 107).

The Norman Chester Centre for Football Research at the University of Leicester, has been operating during most of the period since the 1970s when hooliganism has been a feature of English football. The Centre's main researchers also believe that there is a strong connection between English/British nationalism, anti-black feeling, and the image presented by many football fans at both the local and national level in contemporary England.

In the early 1980s black players began to make their mark in the England national team set-up. Almost immediately they became the focus for booing by sections of the England fans. The Centre's main writers (Williams,

26

Dunning and Murphy) state that:

> until the late 1970s such incidents tended to be individualised, unorganised and sporadic. Then, when black players began to make significant breakthroughs into the English professional game, organised groups from the far right became prominent on the terraces as they stepped up their endeavours to recruit disaffected young working-class males to their racist cause (1984, p. 150).

Again, the same writers also make a connection to English/British culture, nationalism and the Falklands War period. The hooliganism of English football fans in foreign contexts is, in part, an expression of nationalistic feelings and thus not totally dissimilar to the state-legitimised nationalism expressed and officially encouraged in conjunction with the Falklands war.

This relates to the jingoistic coverage of the war which propagated a new national self-image, emitting from such popular newspapers as The Daily Star, The Daily Express and The Sun. The Sun, with daily sales of approximately four million, both captured and helped create the mood of patriotism and nationalism that existed in England (the mood was not so apparent in Scotland) during the time of the conflict.

This heightened nationalistic fervour was reflected in an interview with the then England team manager, Ron Greenwood, who connected his team's forthcoming 'mission' in the Spanish World Cup tournament (1982) with that of the 'Task Force' engaged in the South Atlantic battle.[12] Again, the Task Force image was clear in Spain amongst the England fans, and the song 'Rule Britannia' (with its obvious connotations of a strong and invincible British fleet), became a dominant theme in the repertoire of football songs. The Sunday Observer, was to report that English football fans at the 1990 World Cup could be heard singing, to the tune of 'Camptown Races', 'Two World Wars and one World Cup', while they also rendered a version of The Dam Busters Theme, a tune with images of a powerful British military force from the Second World War.[13] For Williams (p. 16) however:

> the focus that the present English national side provides for the expression of macho-nationalist and racist sentiments is not just a reflection of a post Falklands urge to nail the 'Great' back into Britain. The 'Rule Britannia' brigade also speak more deeply of our national culture and the place of football in it.

Hill sees English football, at both club and international level, as being used as a platform to project this racism (which he implies can be detected at all levels of English society), whilst he also views it as a particular kind of nationalism, where xenophobia and misogamy mix together to define the ultimate in Englishness (1989, pp. 182-196).

The implication here is that deep in the English mind set lies the roots of such ethnocentric, xenophobic and ultra-nationalistic expressions displayed by large numbers of English club and national football supporters. Lorimer (1978, p. 82) notes that in the mid to late 19th century stories in cheap popular fiction which centred on African and Caribbean tales, 'preached the

27

virtues of empire along with an exaggerated racial conceit, that tended to reinforce rather than initiate the growth of racial arrogance'. Although it cannot be stated that English people have a systematic attitude to black and brown former colonial immigrants, a certain cleavage within English society, based upon a reaction towards those people not perceived as being 'of us', can be detected as well as reflected in that section of the society which has an interest in the sport of soccer.[14]

Therefore, football in England displays a number of sometimes well defined but often overlapping features. Racist attitudes, English and British nationalisms, and cultural dominance shown towards diverse individuals and groups, are often manifest in English soccer. The importance of these identities for this book, is the way they can be projected via the football environment. Football in England has become an important setting for the expression of social, ethnic and political attitudes which underlie large elements of English society. In this way therefore, a study of English football reflects how various social and political characteristics can collect and become more demonstrative and conspicuous in such a setting. Football in England can be seen as symptomatic of a number of identities important in social, cultural and political life.

Northern Ireland

Another society where sport, and in a particular way football, has taken on dimensions relating more to the lives of the wider community is Northern Ireland. As with Spanish and English society, Northern Ireland (and Ireland more generally) contains a national or ethnic problem, and one with strong religious undertones. The Catholic population who approximate to the native Irish, and the Protestant population who approximate to the British colonists, have been continually engaged in varying degrees of conflict (with the involvement of both the British Government and Army), resulting in a deep political, social and religious cleavage. Sugden and Bairner emphasise the link between football and politics: 'the development and character of Northern Irish football in general cannot be understood without reference to its political context' (1986, (B), pp. 146-157). Although soccer is played by both communities in Northern Ireland, it is self-evident that it has become an extension of the deeper social, religious and political conflict that is present within that society.

The history of footballs Belfast Celtic exemplifies this conflict. Originating from a Catholic-Irish setting, their fans were often involved in crowd disturbances, especially when they played against the two most Protestant-Unionist-British oriented clubs in the state, Linfield and Glentoran. Although Belfast Celtic had an open recruitment policy and had never claimed the symbolic clothes of Irish nationalism, their fans were overwhelmingly Catholic and nationalist in outlook, seeing the club as a focus for such an identity. For example, in 1920 the club's supporters who waved banners and sang songs in favour of an independent and united Ireland, were met with shots fired by the security forces. Increasingly, Belfast Celtic were viewed as the sporting representatives of the nationalist population in Northern Ireland, whilst:

> the success of Celtic on the field of play and the club's challenge
> to the supremacy of predominantly Protestant teams inevitably
> engendered unionist resentment (1986, pp. 146-157).

This resentment reached a zenith in 1948 when after a Linfield-Celtic clash, Linfield supporters invaded the pitch to attack the Celtic players, one having his leg broken in the melee (one of Belfast Celtic's Protestant players). For Sugden and Bairner (1986, pp. 146-157), this was the 'culmination of long standing inter-community tensions expressed through football'. In the following year, Belfast Celtic decided to disband as they felt they could no longer function in such an environment.

Another club, Derry City, again with a large Catholic and nationalist following, were forced to withdraw from the Irish League (i.e., N.Ireland) for security reasons (this in the early 1970s). In the mid 1980s however, Derry City again emerged, this time as part of the Irish Republic's League of Ireland set up. Although in political terms this revealed few problems for the club and its supporters, in Northern Ireland it meant that a club from the British jurisdiction was playing in another state's league. This decision was not one of free choice however, as Derry had been refused re-admission by the Northern Irish football authorities.

Another club have in recent years replaced Belfast Celtic as the vehicle for 'safe' nationalist expression. Cliftonville, although coming from north Belfast (a traditionally mixed area of the city), have their ground situated close to a predominantly Catholic and nationalist area. They have thus - despite their apparent non-religious character - 'been appropriated by the locals as a symbolically Catholic team' (Sugden and Bairner, 1986, (A), p. 112). Almost inevitably, their support have sometimes become involved in full scale riots with Protestant-loyalist teams supporters as well as the RUC (Royal Ulster Constabulary).

As far as the British Governemnt was concerned football in Northern Ireland took on yet another dimension in the early 1980s. In 1981, as the Irish Republican Army and Bobby Sands, the hunger striking elected Member of Parliament, appeared to be effectively mobilising world sympathy for their cause, the English and Welsh national football teams withdrew from the annual British championship matches in May, which were due to take place in Belfast itself. The Championship as a result collapsed. The cancellation says Hargreaves (1986, p. 201):

> signalled to the world that Northern Ireland was not only an
> abnormal political entity, but that the IRA was winning. The
> government, recognising the ideological importance of sporting
> events in this context, put political pressure on the Amateur
> Athletic Association not to cancel its championships, which
> were due to take place in the province the following month. It
> was decided to launch a counter-propaganda campaign around
> them to convey the message that Northern Ireland was stabilised.

Therefore, in Northern Ireland, clubs similar to Linfield and Glentoran are characterised as reflecting a particular side of the cleavage; that is they are perceived as being loyalist and Protestant, and as symbols of British hegemony. Like Liverpool and Everton, they are often seen as providing the required focal point for expressions of such sympathies. Linfield, largely through supporter and even paramilitary pressure have (until recently) been exempted from attempting to play Catholic players. Although Glentoran have players from a Catholic background, they too have been the object of Loyalist paramilitary threats to desist from this practice (Sugden and Bairner, 1986, (B) pp. 146-157). Linfield supporters will stress at every opportunity:

> their sectarian purity as supporters of a club with an exclusively Protestant playing and administrative staff. For their part the Glentoran supporters, even though most are in all other respects Loyalist and Protestant, are prepared to invert this image and goad their rivals during football confrontations by mimicking Catholic rituals and wearing the green and white of Celtic. This sort of behaviour by Loyalists can be understood only in terms of the special relationship between Linfield and Glentoran (Sugden and Bairner, 1986, (A) pp. 112-113).

Again, the Northern Ireland international team reflects this cleavage. All home matches are played at the home of Linfield football club, which has by far the best facilities available, but which invariably leads to the exclusion of many nationalists who might consider supporting the team. Many other nationalists (almost certainly the vast majority) do not support the team seeing it as a symbol of a divided Ireland, and possibly even as a step towards recognising the legitimacy of the northern state and the union with Britain itself. They, in turn, will often look to the national team south of the border - the Republic of Ireland - to give expression to their national identity, at least in football terms.

Former Glasgow based Celtic and Northern Ireland player Anton Rogan, who is a Catholic, sees himself as a 'victim' of Northern Ireland supporters 'patriotism'; experiencing a level of abuse from the largely loyalist fans in a similar fashion to that of John Barnes in England.[15]

During the 1980s, when Northern Ireland was achieving in football terms a large degree of success (qualifying for two World Cup finals in succession):

> Unionist politicians were pointing to the dogged success of the region's footballers as an example of Protestant Ulster's determination to resist any movement towards a united Ireland (Sugden and Bairner, 1986, (B), pp. 146-157).

The divide over soccer in Northern Ireland manifested itself in February 1990, when the semi-professional side from nationalist west-Belfast, Donegal Celtic, were drawn at home in a Northern Ireland cup tie against Linfield. The game's administrators forced the match to be moved to Linfield's ground, Windsor Park, insisting it was a security threat if they played in the west of the city. This was seen in the Celtic's eyes as being a biased decision favouring their opponents. At the match itself:

30

several thousand Celtic supporters waving Irish tricolours were confined to the Spion Kop end of the ground having been escorted to the stadium by the RUC....Linfield fans sporting their teams red, white and blue colours and waving Union Jacks and Ulster flags, were funnelled into the covered north and south stands.

Significant amongst all the paraphernalia that was displayed and the songs that were being sung, was the large degree of support being expressed for the two big Glasgow clubs, Rangers and Celtic. Amid the nationalist (from both sides) rhetoric and sectarian chants, violence flared, fans clashed, and the RUC fought running battles with the Donegal Celtic fans; plastic bullets were fired at the Celtic fans, and scores of supporters and RUC men were injured.[16]

In response to the game, the editorial of the Irish News, exposed the nature of the sport in Northern Ireland:[17]

> when will the Irish Football Association start to dismantle the bigot-laden edifice which surrounds the core of the game in Northern Ireland? It is time for the European and World soccer authorities to carry out a close examination of all clubs, particularly those at senior level, affiliated to the IFA. Not until then will we be able to say that soccer in Northern Ireland is a sport where all can use the best facilities and where all can enjoy the world's biggest spectator sport. In the meantime, we have to reconcile ourselves to the fact that in Northern Ireland terms, soccer will continue to stagnate in the foetid waters of sectarianism.

Whilst it is true that Protestants and Catholics alike in Northern Ireland, turn out on Saturday afternoons to play soccer, by and large the affiliation of players and community interest tends to break down along lines similar to those outlined for the professional game:

> Schools, churches, Orange lodges, youth movements, old boys associations, housing estates, commercial and industrial organisations serve to structure league and cup competitions according to locally respected sectarian divisions. Thus, while we can fairly say that amateur football is generally not exclusive, on a closer look it is clearly responsive to the socio-political divisions of the province. Even when Catholics and Protestants play for the same club, this says little except that occasionally, within the relatively neutral context of the game itself, divisions can be temporarily suspended (Sugden and Bairner, 1986, (B), pp. 146-157).[18]

Clearly, football in Northern Ireland reflects the cleavage that exists within society there. The identities with which that societies people have and maintain throughout their general lives, permeate aspects of the community's activities which at first sight, to the impartial and untutored observer, may appear to be what is considered normal. In Northern Ireland, sporting activity is simply another level of social interaction where these identities can become manifest, and where national, religious and cultural affiliations are often a determining factor.

Therefore, as a social and political indicator, for some societies football's significance can be seen as being very important. Examples taken from Basque, Catalan, English, Irish/British societies, all point to the idea of a psychological bonding amongst a significant number of people, a bonding that centres around a common identity and which stimulates, or even simply reflects, a religious, cultural and political mind-set that has popular, or at the very least, common images to it. These societies can also be seen as having similarities with Scotland.

Notes

1. In 1929 the vast bulk of previous Presbyterian dissenters rejoined what was to be henceforth called the National Church of Scotland. Since then the Church of Scotland has accounted for more than 90% of 'affiliated' Scottish Protestants.

2. Reports to the General Assembly of the Church of Scotland, 1968, p112.

3. J. F McCaffrey, Scottish Catholic Observer, 29/10/82.

4. Gallagher, 1987, p11, from Johnston, 'Developments in the Roman Catholic Church' p136.

5. However, the rejection of the Irish was not uniform, and again some less antagonistic sources can be found. In a similar fashion to that of the Scotsman newspaper of the Emancipation period, the late 1830s Tait's Edinburgh Magazine spoke admiringly of Irish seasonal labour, whilst the Irishman's patience in the face of "sneers and gibes upon his drawl, his brogue, his idioms, his very dress, airs and manners, as well as upon his religion" (Gallagher, 1987, c116), was to be welcomed.

6. See Airdrie and Coatbridge Advertiser for examples, 1/8/86 & 19/9/86.

7. See Montgomery, 1989.

8. Motherwell Times, 14/12/23.

9. Information from Glasgow Archdiocese.

10. Barcelona were a more insular club, as well as coming from a more powerful economic region. Therefore, they never quite gained the same degree of extra-regional support as the Basque team.

11. Brian Thompson of the Daily Post, 2/7/87.

12. From 'World Cup Review', BBC Television, 11/6/82.

13. Sunday Observer, July 8th, 1990.

14. A recent E.C attitudinal survey reported that Britain was the most racist nation in Europe. Reported in the Glasgow Herald, 11/12/89.

15. See 'The Celtic View' 1988-89, for a number of articles and letters regarding these events.

16. Sunday Life (Ireland) 18/2/90.

17. Irish News, 19th February, 1990.

18. This may be witnessed in the few geographical areas that are less completely divided by religious affiliation, or within college and university football for example.

Other Sources

The Celtic View, 1988-89. Irish News, 19/2/90. Sunday Observer, (including supplementary magazines) 8/12/90, 8/7/90, 11/7/93. Ulster Television, 1989, Documentary history of Belfast Celtic F.C. 'Black Britain': BBC Documentary (four part) series on black perceptions of post 1945 life in Britain. January 1991. Hebdige: Skinheads and the search for the white working class identity; in New Socialist, Sep/Oct.1981, pp39-41. World in Action, 'The Nightmare Returns', ITV, 29/3/95.

2 Soccer and society in Scotland

The introduction and the historical chapter have argued that an examination of the ethno-religious milieu is necessary for a fuller understanding of contemporary social and political life in Scotland. Scottish football provides a link between historical developments, and more contemporary religious and political phenomena in Scottish society. In particular the role of two great Scottish institutions, Glasgow Rangers and Celtic football clubs,[1] can be seen as central to this understanding. Indeed, as will become evident, these two clubs in particular have their own intrinsic political character.

As in a number of other countries, there exists in Scotland symbolic connections between sport, wider social phenomenon and politics. In Scotland, at the end of November 1988, the country's newspapers (quality and tabloids) were dominated by the news that Glasgow Rangers Football Club had been bought by Mr David Murray, an enterprising Scottish businessman. In media terms, that event was overtaken in June 1989 with the news that Glasgow Rangers (who for over a century had essentially practised a Protestant only policy) had signed a Catholic player in Maurice Johnston. Not only did that take up many pages of the Scottish newspapers, but the signing also made national and international news. Quality Sunday newspapers all over Britain, as well as Ireland and elsewhere, included a number of articles discussing the transfer and its more significant and wider applications. This was a rare example of the wider national and international community discovering a feature of Scottish life, long recognised by people in Scotland.

Celtic, Glasgow Rangers and the Scottish game

Football, whether playing or spectating, has been the most popular sport in Scotland for some 100 years.[2] It is also the case that the Scottish game is dominated by both Glasgow Rangers and Celtic. Moreover, approximately 4/5ths of the country's inhabitants live within two hours road travelling time

34

of these clubs home grounds, making them easily accessible to much of the population. Generally, both clubs contain the best and most expensive players, have the largest number of employees, and have the biggest stadia and the corresponding crowds to fill them. In terms of the winning of trophies, they have monopolised the Scottish game since the late 19th century.[3]

Although other countries also have a few clubs which have dominated their respective games (sometimes only periodically), this is generally due to their success which generates a huge support from the normally large population centre where they are located. In contrast, it is the specific origins, subsequent developments, and the very nature of the two big Scottish clubs (and of the Scottish game more generally), which make Glasgow Rangers and Celtic important in terms of cultural, ethno-religious, social and political interpretation.

By the end of the 1880's, football was a popular game throughout Britain. In Glasgow, Brother Walfrid, a member of the Catholic Marist Order, and some of his Irish-Catholic immigrant compatriots saw in the development of the game an opportunity to raise money and feed the poor (largely immigrant Irish) of the east end of the city. Brother Walfrid's intention was to keep Catholics within the reaches of the faith (and therefore out of the reaches of proselytism), while also raising the confidence and moral of that community. Volunteers from this community also helped build a ground for matches (for an account of this period, see Murray, 1984 and McNee, 1978).

At the time of Celtic's founding the vast majority of Catholics in Scotland originated from Ireland and the words Catholic and Irish were interchangeable in the West of Scotland. All the club's founders were expatriate Irishmen or of Irish stock and the new club's support was drawn largely from the swelling Irish community in Glasgow. The donations to charity frequently included some to exclusively Irish causes such as the Evicted Tenant's Fund, then an important aspect of Irish nationalist politics.

> If, as Catholics, the members were concerned about the plight of local charities, as Irishmen they were obsessed with that perennial question of Irish politics, Home Rule. (Campbell and Woods, 1986, p. 18)

For example, John Glass President and Director of the club in its foremost years, was an outstanding figure in nationalist circles; he was prominent in the Catholic Union and was a founder of the O'Connell branch of the Irish National Foresters, as well too as being the treasurer of the Home Government Branch of the United Irish League. Another member, William McKillop, became M.P for North Sligo in Ireland (holding this constituency for eight years before winning in South Armagh in 1908), whilst Michael Davitt (a former revolutionary/Fenian and founder of the Irish Land League), the celebrated Irish patriot, was one of the clubs original patrons. Club officials, players and supporters alike, were often involved in politics; supporting Irish Home Rule, campaigning for the release of Irish political prisoners, opposing what they viewed as British imperialism in the Boar War and South Africa and supporting the contentious Catholic endeavour to have their schools brought within the state-funded system.

Apart from the Sligo born Brother Walfrid, the club's first important Catholic patron was Archbishop Charles Eyre of Glasgow. Many cartoons of the time, in both the Catholic and the secular press, 'included sympathetic caricatures of priests among the crowds at Celtic games', whilst Woods states that the Glasgow Observer, a Catholic newspaper catering to the Irish Catholic community, took a keen interest in Celtic's progress. Other Irish club's also existed at the same time, in Coatbridge, Glasgow and Edinburgh, whom with the same national and religious make-up as Celtic, made efforts to establish themselves. However, it was the remarkable competitive successes of the Celtic club, as well as good organisation and an apt location, which enabled it to prosper (Campbell and Woods 1987, pp. 11-26, also Handley, 1960).

Celtic's charitable contributions helped link the Catholic community with their sporting representatives. Many of the original supporters club's were (as some still are) affiliated to, or had some connection with, the local Catholic parish, while today they have often been seen to maintain the charitable foundations of the club by continuing to donate to charity. In fact in many cases, the tradition has actually been seen to be kept going more by the supporters than by the club itself.[4] Celtic then were founded by and for Irish Catholics, though never exclusively so (for example, they have always included non-Catholics/Protestants in their team). The clubs ethno-religious make-up, along with their early successes on the football field, attracted crowds to football that had never previously been experienced in Scotland (Murray, 1988, p. 19). The club came into existence as the focus for much Catholic and Irish community activity, a setting for that community's broad social and political aspirations.

In contrast, Glasgow Rangers origins were more typical; they began as a purely sporting and athletic institution. Formed in 1872-73, most of the impetus for the origins of the club stemmed from the McNeil family of Gareloch and other budding football enthusiasts from the same place; 'young crusaders who had come to the big city to earn their livelihood, the spirit of adventure was strong within them' (Allison, 1966, p. 186). The team name was proposed by one Moses McNeil, and unanimously adopted by the young men trying to begin their own club. The colours of royal blue and white were assumed, and four grounds were occupied by the new club until the end of 1899 when they finally settled at Ibrox on the south side of Glasgow (Allan, 1923). Unlike the beginnings of their great rivals Celtic, around fifteen years later, none of these Rangers' historians refer to any political, religious or ethnic stimulus. Indeed, the club was a fairly ordinary side in its earliest years, a period when the game itself was amateur, and when another Glasgow club, Queens Park, often dominated.

On the other hand, Celtic's early years were marked by success; the Scottish Cup, the Glasgow Cup, the Scottish League Championship and the Charity Cup were all won by 1893. Glasgow Rangers mounted a successful challenge to 'the Irishmen' in the 1893-94 season winning the Scottish and Glasgow Cups, while Celtic won the League and the Charity Cup. The domination of Scottish football by the two clubs was underway. With large crowds following both teams, and professionalism being adopted within the game before the end of the century, a competitive and financially lucrative environment emerged between the clubs. By 1895, crowds of 25,000 were

36

watching fixtures involving them (Murray, 1984, p. 31).

In 1896 Celtic and Hibernian [an Edinburgh side which had emerged from the Irish community there] were top of the Scottish league, prompting a newspaper, Scottish Sport, to note the dominance in Scotland of two Irish teams and to where the Scottish team was that could challenge them (Murray, 1984, p. 31).

On the field of play the competition between both clubs was already vibrant. At the same time, Celtic were also becoming convinced that they were the victims of some unfavourable decision making by referees and the Scottish football authorities (Campbell and Woods, 1987, chapter 8). Within a similar context, in the 1950's Celtic were ordered by the Scottish Football authorities to take down the flag of the Republic of Ireland which they flew above their ground, with particular acknowledgement to the foundations of the club. After a heated period of disquiet, Celtic eventually retained the 'right' to fly the flag (see McNee, 1975, pp. 63-71; Wilson, 1988, pp. 94-101). Campbell and Woods note (1987, p65):

The Celtic support revelled in the triumphs of the team, compensating as they did for the daily troubles in a harsh life amid uncongenial surroundings; the neutral Scottish enthusiast [distinctive of the already established Glasgow Rangers supporter] understandably resented the nationalist undertones of Celtic's achievements and looked around for a more representative team to cheer for against the Irishmen.

Celtic already had their support. As Rangers became more successful and were viewed as the main challengers to Celtic, the developing transport system enabled football supporters of other teams, like Queens Park and Third Lanark, to change their allegiance and support the most able challenge to 'the immigrants'.

Rangers were a Protestant team in the way in which all senior clubs in Scotland, other than Celtic and Hibernian, were Protestant. However, a combination of factors enabled Rangers to encapsulate, or become the main focus of, a particular Protestant identity which had a strong political, cultural and social character and which was infused with a number of anti-Catholic features. Clearly, Celtic's early successes were resented by society at large. Rangers, through their ability to halt this Irish dominance of Scottish football, assumed a pre-eminent role in defending native prestige. They attracted the strongest attention in the sporting battle with Celtic. Football enthusiasts naturally liked success and this attracted many people to support Rangers. Invariably, the nationalist or ethnic dimension of this particular rivalry proved potent to many Rangers' fans. The very existence of the Celtic club in Scotland therefore spawned a reaction from the rest of Scottish football.

The most significant reaction was witnessed in the growing success and fortitude of Rangers and a strong Protestant political and cultural identity was thus forged within the club. This identity would not have been possible without the presence of Celtic. Being a response to Celtic, it should be considered to be a Protestant identity which was imbued with some of the strongest anti-Catholic and anti-Irish elements in Scottish society. Because of the overriding anti or negative element in the club and its support, and as a reflection of much of the larger society's attitude towards the Catholic Irish in general, forthwith, Rangers Football Club were perceived by many people as being one of the most overt anti-Catholic institutions in society.

The rivalry was threefold; on the field the players fought it out for supremacy; in the boardrooms the directors squabbled for profits; and on the terracings separated under the banners of religion and nationalism. Both clubs could rely on revenue from loyal supporters; Celtic's from a captive audience within the Irish community and Rangers from a populace eager to fix on a side capable of beating the upstarts from Glasgow's east end. No other clubs in Scotland could attract such followings, and it was support that grew with success and the tension of the rivalry (Campbell and Woods pp. 64-65).[5]

Without a doubt the nature of the rivalry added significantly to the potential attractiveness of the game as a football fixture, thus engendering a substantial degree of income for the clubs. Murray also argues:

> Rangers at the turn of the century were a Protestant team, but only in the sense that all teams in Scotland were Protestant. As the one team which could be called upon to keep the Catholics in their place it attracted the more anti-Catholic elements in the Scottish population (Murray, 1988, p. 27).

Thus the mantle of responsibility for defending the indigenous population against these foreign incursions and successes, gradually seemed to focus upon Glasgow Rangers who had the finance, the stadia, the team and the growing support to defend not only the sporting prowess of Scotland but also, in a more sub-cultural way, its national pride and Protestant heritage, at least on the field of sport. They seemed the most able at the time and although other clubs had similar ideas, Rangers became the greatest manifestation of this course. In contrast, Irish Catholics, in a general sense, looked to Celtic as their community's foremost representatives on the field of play, and also as a vehicle for many of their cultural and political aspirations.

Although never embarking on a Catholic only policy it was almost inevitable that young Catholics viewed Celtic as their team to play for, and, historically in competition with many of the forces they believed to be against them. Protestants have always played for Celtic. Indeed their most successful manager Jock Stein was a Protestant, who helped gain for the club its greatest successes, including the winning of the top European club competition. However, a widespread desire to play for the club among Catholics has always meant that it has been easier to choose the best from the community that they represent.[6] It has usually been the case that a Catholic Celtic players upbringing will include supporting that team as a boy. Nevertheless, many of the clubs greatest players have been Protestants, John Thompson (late 1920's and early 1930's) for example, and more recently (in the 1970's and 1980's) Kenny Dalglish and Danny McGrain.

Rangers on the other hand have always had an unofficial Protestant only-no Catholic policy in terms of players, management and staff. This may have been inevitable when one considers that most young Catholics wished to play for Celtic, but it is almost certainly the case that this 'policy' simply reflected similar practices of other institutions and workplaces in Scotland throughout the clubs history. It has become known through recent Celtic history books as well as by way of the players own autobiography, that Danny McGrain was observed as a youth by a Rangers scout. The scout rejected any moves towards the player believing wrongly that because of his Irish name he was therefore a Catholic. Other Rangers players whose relations were found to be Catholic, or who like Alex Ferguson, Bobby Russell, Graham Fyfe and Gordon Dalziel in the 1960s, 1970's and 1980's married Catholic girls, were subsequently to find themselves operating under a cloud or experiencing difficulty gaining a place in the first team. This policy also meant that the Rangers director David Hope (who married a Catholic) was unable to accede to the position of Chairman in the 1970s (see Finn 1994, pp. 91-112).

Rangers Football Club have defended themselves against accusations of sectarianism by arguing that these players were not able to command a regular first team spot. Although a handful of players are reported to have slipped this religious net (see Murray, 1988, pp. 123-124), it took until mid-1989 before this policy was changed by the signing of ex-Celtic player Maurice Johnston (from French league club Nantes), a reputedly non-practising Catholic who came from a mixed Protestant-Catholic background. It has been suggested that this move reflected the good business acumen and driving ambition of the new Rangers directors and management.[7] It was widely commented on at the time in newspaper articles, that Spanish and Italian clubs, coming from notably Catholic countries, would not be prepared to accept such an anti-Catholic institution into a possible future European league. It was also stated by the then secretary of the Scottish Football Association a number of months after the signing, that this move by Rangers removed any inhibitions that he or the Association harboured with regard to the Association favouring Ibrox Stadium (Rangers ground) as a possible venue for Scottish international football games (this in the event of Hampden Park, the traditional site, being disqualified for World Cup matches after 1992 because it was not an all-seater stadium).

At all levels of football in many areas of Scotland, whether it be junior, amateur or whatever, many teams even in mixed areas are perceived as being Protestant. One journalist noted that one of Scotland's most famous junior football clubs, Kilwinning Rangers of Ayrshire, has pursued a policy (denied by the club) barring Catholic players from its ranks.[8] The Lanarkshire amateur football club Bonkle have recently shared a similar practice. A smaller number of Catholic or Irish oriented clubs are also evident on the Scottish football scene at these levels. Football in general terms then can be viewed as not only to an extent mirroring the Rangers-Celtic arena, but more importantly, being an expressive image of this feature of Scottish life.

Celtic and Rangers therefore, emerged from a setting which they would almost inevitably reflect, as indeed did other clubs at the time. Scotland was a country which was fiercely proud of its national and religious traditions. But, it was in a state of continual apprehension over real or imagined submergence of its national characteristics within the larger British state, in the form of Anglicisation. In addition, Irish Catholic immigration was perceived as threatening them from another direction. Catholicism and Popery were anathema to Scottish society at large. Along with their political aspirations for an Ireland 'free from British rule', these were the prominent characteristics of Irish immigrants in the eyes of many Scottish Protestants.

It was perhaps inevitable that the early successes of the Irish football club in Glasgow, which enhanced the self-image of that community, added another dimension to, and stimulated further, the antagonism visibly displayed by almost all who did not relate, via religion or national origin, to the Celtic club. The intolerance displayed towards Irish Catholics in Scotland was partly reflected in the development of football. As well as becoming an environment where ethno-religious identities became a pre-dominant feature, a strong sectarian aspect (see conclusion) to these identities was also to manifest itself.

Overall, various religious related identities emerged in the Scottish football environment. A complex mix of sport, culture, tradition, nationalism, religion and politics, were thus closely linked to the establishment and evolution of the Rangers and Celtic football clubs. The nature of this rivalry will become clear through the subsequent analysis of the Irish identity in Scotland, and, the anti-Catholic dimension of the Scottish Protestant identity.

The cleavage manifest: attitudes and perceptions

Rangers and Celtic are a social and cultural phenomenon contributing directly and indirectly to socio-political life in major areas of Scotland. By focusing on Scottish football, we are able to witness the perceptions which indicate a similar attitude and consciousness which marks out football in Spain, England and Northern Ireland. Because various interests and identities cohere around certain football teams in these countries, it is such comparable examples in Scotland (and which attract a similar kind of experience), which become symbolic of ethno-religious identity there.

In 1988, the following football letter appeared in Scotland's most popular Sunday newspaper, The Sunday Mail.[9]

> On holiday in Scotland, I watched football in Aberdeen, Dundee, Edinburgh and Glasgow - and it was first class. Certainly better than anything I've seen down here. The only thing that puzzled me was when Celtic played Dundee at Parkhead the home fans [Celtic's] were all waving the Republic of Ireland flag. How confusing !

If the writer was confused, he would probably have been more confounded had he also picked up the words of many of the football songs being chanted by the followers of the clubs he saw playing. Regardless of the ignorance of the visitor, these confusing audio and visual displays are in fact intrinsic to the game. Such letters and songs convey social and political attitudes and identities for many people who attach themselves to football in Scotland.

In reference to the S.A.S Gibraltar killings of three I.R.A personnel in early 1988, a large section of the Motherwell football Clubs fans have chanted to the followers of the Celtic Football Club, ' S.A.S, 1,2,3....S.A.S, 1,2,3' (or alternatively, ' bang, bang, bang').[10] Celtic football fans, whether at a match or social occasion, will be heard to sing not only supportive chants for their own club, but also a collection of songs and anthems which reflect a desire for an independent and united Ireland (including support for militant nationalism). The chorus of one of the most frequently sung Irish 'rebel' songs reads:

> And the radio said there's another shot dead
> and he died with a gun in his hand,
> But they didn't say why Billy Reid had to die,
> For he died to free Ireland[11]

An observer may also hear derogatory references from many Celtic fans aimed towards the British Royal Family, as well as the Masonic and Orange Institutions in Scotland.[12] In the aftermath of the 1988 Scottish Cup Final in which Celtic played Dundee United, a game which was witnessed by the Prime Minister Margaret Thatcher, a national newspaper reported that; 'Celtic supporters waved tricolour flags and sang choruses of Irish rebel songs, and there were chants of anti-British slogans from sections of the crowd'.[13]

One of the most popular football songs in Scotland is the 'Billy Boys'.

> Hello, hello, we are the Billy Boys.
> Hello, hello, you can tell us by our noise.
> We're up to our knees in Fenian blood, Surrender or you'll die.
> For we are the 'Billy Billy' Boys.[14]

Celtic fans note that this anti-Catholic song is sung by the followers of Hearts, Dundee, Ayr United, Kilmarnock, St Mirren, St Johnstone, Airdrie, Motherwell, Falkirk, Queen of the South and Morton; that is, clubs from all over Scotland.[15] Such taunts are so widespread that they were heard from the fans of then Highland League club Inverness Caledonian in their 4th round Scottish Cup tie against Stirling Albion in early 1990.[16]

These songs are generally seen in Scotland as being most popular with the fans of Glasgow Rangers. As well as the 'Billy Boys' and other songs (which are seen as supporting the union of Great Britain and Northern Ireland and condemning the Pope, the Catholic faith and the I.R.A), songs are sometimes sung which state support for the loyalist paramilitary tradition in Northern Ireland.[17] The anti-Catholic chorus of one of the most popular Ibrox renditions declares:

> No, no Pope of Rome, No chapels to sadden my eyes.
> No nuns and no priests, no rosary beads,
> every day is the twelfth of July[18]

The followers of Edinburgh's most popular side, Heart of Midlothian, share some characteristics with Rangers fans. Former chairman of Hearts, self-made millionaire Wallace Mercer, indicated the nature of the Hearts club, and possibly much of that of Scottish football itself, when he stated:

> The first day I joined the club I was invited to join the Masons. My father was a Mason and I wouldn't say anything to criticise the organisation. But I decided the moment I took over the mantle of responsibility for Hearts it would be a non-religious, non-political club. Since then I've followed my own course, irrespective of my own private views.

The Masons in Scotland are a semi-secret organisation which pervades many corridors of power including the police, banking, the Scottish media and numerous employment concerns. Generally, they are perceived by Catholics to be anti-Catholic as far as Scotland is concerned. In this view one of the Masons key aims is to perpetuate a Protestant influence and hegemony. Mercer's rejection of free masonry can be interpreted as good business acumen from his perspective.[19] To other observers, such actions (as well as those of David Murray's in signing Maurice Johnston) reveal a normally hidden side to the Scottish game. Although Mercer stated that he desired a non-religious and non-political club, the fact that he considered it provident to make this statement, can be interpreted as a subliminal indication of such a feature within Scottish football.

Related incidents reported in the Scottish press reflects this tension in various areas of Scottish football. So, in the aftermath of Rangers' 1990 League title win, television showed the Rangers players celebrations in their own dressing rooms. They sang songs common enough with their support. 'The songs were notably anti-Catholic with obscene references to the Pope'.[20] A few weeks later, in the Scottish Cup Final (which was finally decided by penalty kicks), Pat Bonner, the Celtic goalkeeper was seen by millions of television viewers to make the sign of the cross before each of the penalty kicks taken by the Aberdeen footballers. Again, letters opposed to such incidents poured into the most popular selling newspaper in Scotland, the Scottish Daily Record, whilst Scottish Television and the local Radio Clyde also became a focus for complaint (the actions of Bonner were seen by many of his critics as being 'sectarian', although this is a common among Catholic footballers in other countries).

After some controversial scenes in the Rangers - Celtic 1986 League/Skol Cup Final, when a Celtic player crossed himself and some refereeing decisions were seen by Celtic as favourable to Rangers, the then Celtic manager stated: 'if it were up to me, Celtic would apply for membership of the English league tomorrow'. This reflected the belief of the Celtic support that their club is the victim of anti-Catholic/Irish forces which on the soccer field as reflected in anti-Celtic refereeing decisions (This belief has held widespread currency among Celtic fans throughout their history. Further examples of this perception are evident throughout Celtic history books. See footnote 21).

This general Celtic perception was indicated after the above match when the then chairman of the club, Mr Jack McGinn said; 'Some aspects of the Skol Cup Final left us feeling rather aggrieved....We will not allow the Celtic Football Club to be deflected by any amount of adversary from any source'. The Sunday Observer newspaper commented that McGinn's statement might have been read from the steps of the General Post Office in Dublin (it was here that Padraic Pearse announced the Easter Proclamation which began the 1916 Irish Rebellion), thus making a strong reference to the clubs Irish nationalist tradition.[21]

One writer to the Glasgow Herald,[22] replying to a Celtic supporter's attack on Ranger's supposed sectarian, playing staff policy, wrote:

> I suggest that, when the flag of a foreign and frequently hostile state, whose constitution impudently claims sovereignty over part of the United Kingdom, and whose land and people the present pope has declared to be 'Mary's Dowry', no longer flies from the mast-head of 'Paradise', there may be, I say only may be, less 'bigoting' in the stands of Ibrox.

The foreign state is the Republic of Ireland, Mary is the Virgin Mary and Paradise is the colloquial Celtic language for Celtic Park. In such views, religion, politics and football are compounded.

Much of the larger population belt of Scotland, from Ayrshire, Dumbartonshire, Lanarkshire, Glasgow, Fife and the Lothians, as well as towns and villages in other parts of the country have clear ethnic and religious identities. Towns and villages throughout much of Scotland are sometimes known in the popular mind as Protestant or Catholic. Although such religious/geographical identities do not match the intensity of those in Northern Ireland (see Boal and Douglas, 1982), Coatbridge, Glenboig, Chapelhall, and Carfin, in Lanarkshire, and Clydebank, Calton, Gorbals and Garngad, in and around Glasgow, are popularly known as Catholic areas or 'little Irelands'. Likewise, Larkhall, Ferniegair, Airdrie, Bridgeton and Kinning Park in Lanarkshire and Glasgow; as well as areas of Stirlingshire, Ayrshire, Fife and the Lothians, are characterised by their Protestant and sometimes Orange-Unionist make-up. Coatbridge, for example, has the largest percentage of Catholics per head of population in Britain, whilst Larkhall, with a population of around 20,000 people, contains under 2,000 Catholics and is constantly referred to in the west of Scotland for its strong Rangers and Orange sympathies.[23]

In footballing terms, it can be argued that Celtic and Glasgow Rangers are crucial to the interest in, and perhaps the quality of, Scottish soccer.[24] Regularly, Celtic and Rangers between them attract 60 per cent or more of all the active spectators who watch Saturday afternoon professional football in Scotland (there are forty Scottish league clubs). The visits of Celtic and Rangers, with their substantial travelling supports, enhances the income of the home club to such an extent that it becomes the high point of the season for many of them. Take both clubs out of Scottish football and it could be argued that the sport would be rendered moribund at the professional level.

For many years it has been a complaint of the management of Scottish football clubs and media observers, that vast numbers of football supporters leave their local town and villages to give allegiance to either Rangers or Celtic.[25] In addition, both clubs attract a regular following from England (mainly people from a Scottish or an Irish background). Each has approximately sixty registered supporters clubs there.[26] Ireland too is a prime source of this kind of support. Celtic have approximately twenty supporters clubs from the Republic of Ireland, whilst they have around fifty-five from the North. In Northern Ireland Glasgow Rangers have over one hundred supporters clubs. Table 2.1 reflects the strength of Celtic's support in the various parts of Scotland, whilst other clubs maintain only a handful of supporters from outwith their own localities.

Table 2.1
Scottish geographical support for Celtic FC

Glasgow area and the west (including Paisley, Renfrewshire, Dumbartonshire, Clydebank, Erskine and Greenock)	250 clubs
Lanarkshire	125 clubs
Edinburgh, Lothians and Borders region	60 clubs
Fife, Perth, Stirling and Falkirk areas	40 clubs
Ayrshire and South-West Scotland	30 clubs
Highlands and Islands	15 clubs
Dundee and Aberdeen areas	10 clubs

(clubs can range from approximately 20 to 100 people in size)

Former Celtic director, Tom Grant, believes that contrary to popular comment regarding Celtic as a Glasgow club, proportionately, most of their support comes from the Lanarkshire area of the country,[27] whilst Rangers believe that only 40 per cent of their support comes from Glasgow. Managing director David Murray supports this view by adding; 'we have really become a Scottish team'.[28] Rangers and Celtic are clearly representative of 'widespread sections' of the population of Scotland. The significance of this widespread support is that it indicates that both Rangers and Celtic have a large and geographically well spread appeal.

The clubs attract a more than local support because of the identities that the respective clubs represent. Both clubs have become important Scottish, Irish, Protestant and Catholic, cultural, social and political experiences..

Identities: the national football culture

If national or ethnic identities appear to take on a wider significance in a Scottish football context, the involvement of Rangers, Celtic, Aberdeen, Hearts and other clubs players in the national side, might be taken to indicate that this apparent football cleavage disappears at that level of the game. Nevertheless, here also there are also signs which indicate that football is not an isolated social phenomenon.

After a Scotland versus Poland international match during May of 1990, the following letter appeared in the Daily Record:[29]

I stood on the East Terracing [the traditional Celtic end of the national stadium], puzzled by the sound of silence when Flower of Scotland [the unofficial Scottish national anthem] was played.

44

I didn't realise there were so many Polish immigrants in Scotland for the only spark round me was when Celtic double-act Dziekanowski and Wdowczyk were on the ball.

Another letter stated:

At the traditional Celtic End, my wife was upset by the abuse Mo Johnstone got from some of the fans after scoring his goal. Some fans were even willing Jacki Dziekanowski [one of Celtic's two Polish international players] to score for Poland. Surely this is not what football is all about?[30]

Because of their repetitiveness and thematic consistency, such letters can be viewed as typical of a widespread perception that Celtic fans' have a negative view of the Scottish national team (as well as other things Scottish).[31] In the view of these letter writers, the Celtic fans were not supporting Scotland's national team (this, despite the presence of a Celtic player and a few ex-Celtic players in the side).

Not so apparent among these letters, though referred to in many of the following Sunday newspaper match reports, was the constant booing and antagonism being displayed towards the Celtic player Dziekanowski from major sections of the crowd. Around the same time the Scottish team played a pre-World Cup friendly against the reigning World Champion's Argentina. After the game the following letter appeared in the Daily Record's sister newspaper, the Sunday Mail: 'Wasn't it moving to hear Brian McClair and Roy Aitken [both ex-Celtic players] booed onto the park against Argentina? This must have lifted the team'. [32]

Although it may be true that some newspaper editors choose letters to print which attract readers to a particular column or page, the letters referred to here are typical of the widespread perceptions of football and football fans which exist in Scotland. Indeed, there is a long history of such letters in the Scottish press. They are but another aspect of the wider context of religious identity in contemporary Scotland. They should be viewed together with other letters cited in this book on a variety of religious related topics. Along with the survey itself, interview material, secondary evidence and the primary sources referred to, the letters are another manifestation and context for the expression of ethno-religious identity and cleavage.

In reply to a newspaper article which criticised the selection of a particular Celtic player for the Scottish side, a Celtic fan replied:

Your correspondents article is just another example of the treatment Celtic players have received at the hands of the so called Scottish supporters down through the years. The late Jimmy McGrory, the most prolific scorer in the history of the game in Britain, amassed two caps against England, a handful in all. Jimmy Johnstone was hounded out of the team by the abusive chants of Rangers fans at Hampden. Kenny Dalglish was never a popular choice for Scotland - when he was a Celtic player....Mr Traynor's article implies that Celtic supporters have a 'chip on their shoulder'. These same Celtic supporters have

45

recently seen on television [in a recent documentary] how 20 per cent of the police force are members of a secret organisation, some of who broke the law of the land to protect and help their fellow members. It was also pointed out that membership of this organisation was proportionately higher in Scotland than in England or Wales. I wonder if any of our referees and linesmen know the existence of this organisation.[33]

In conjunction with the other letters referred to, this reflects the attitude towards the Scottish international football team, as well as to some of Scottish football's main representatives, from a majority of Celtic football fans. In response to the survey question which asked the fans which international side they supported or liked, no Celtic fans indicated a preference for Poland (see tables 2.2 and 2.3). However, the Celtic fans didn't identify with Scotland, the team they might be expected to.

Surveying football fans in Scotland: substantiating the perceptions

Although identifying with the Scottish national team is seen by the wider football community (including the media) as being natural, this is not the view of Celtic fans. In fact, a majority of the Celtic fans surveyed indicated an 'ambivalence' towards the national side; 54 per cent of their fans said that they never attended the matches of the Scottish team, 43 per cent went sometimes, whilst only 3 per cent 'always' attended. All other categories of Scottish football fan were significantly more likely to attend Scotland matches than were Celtic fans. Thus, there are faint ties between this significant symbol of the modern Scottish identity (See Moorhouse; 1987, pp. 189-202) and the Irish club which has its home in Scottish football.

The Scottish football supporters who most actively support Scotland are drawn from a number of clubs. At Rangers, 80 per cent of their fans always or sometimes attend the international teams matches. This is much higher than the Celtic figure but lower than the 95 per cent of Hibernian fans who go always or sometimes, closely followed by Kilmarnock, (92 per cent) and Motherwell (88 per cent). In fact, as can be seen from tables 2.2 and 2.3, the fans of all clubs other than Celtic are similar in terms of their attachment to the national team as the ultimate standard bearer in Scottish football.

Table 2.2
Percentages of fans attending Scottish international team games (all
percentages in this and subsequent tables have been rounded to the nearest
whole figure)

Group	Always	Sometimes	Never	Row Total
Rangers Fans	17.0 (15)	63.0 (57)	20.0 (18)	20.0 (90)
Hearts Fans	10.0 (4)	65.0 (26)	25.0 (10)	9.0 (40)
Aberdeen Fans	12.0 (7)	78.0 (46)	10.0 (6)	13.0 (59)
Kilmarnock Fans	14.0 (7)	78.0 (39)	8.0 (4)	11.0 (50)
Celtic Fans	3.0 (3)	43.0 (41)	54.0 (52)	22.0 (96)
Motherwell Fans	15.0 (5)	72.0 (23)	12.0 (4)	7.0 (32)
Hibernian Fans	17.0 (3)	78.0 (14)	6.0 (1)	4.0 (18)
Dundee United Fans	4.0 (1)	82.0 (18)	14.0 (3)	5.0 (22)
St Johnstone Fans	6.0 (2)	79.0 (27)	15.0 (50)	8.0 (34)
Column Total	11.0 (47)	66.0 (291)	24.0 (103)	100.0 (441)

The cleavage within Scottish football, and the distinctiveness of Celtic, is
clear from the answer to the question; do you support or like 'any other'
international football team? (table 2.3). The majority of all the other clubs
supporters questioned indicated no preference for any country other than
Scotland. Where the fans did feel compelled to express a like or a degree of
support for another national side, many chose Brazil and (West) Germany,
two of the top international sides since international competition began
seriously after the Second World War. Holland also received a significant
degree of support; that country playing some of the most attractive football
in world competition during the 1970s and 1980s. Aberdeen fans indicated a
liking for Holland at a time when they have recently had a number of Dutch
players. Similarly, Rangers fans showed a strong preference for England
which in part reflected their employment of English talent from the second
half of the 1980s. We might also conclude that the Orange historical
significance of the collective, Northern Ireland, England and Holland, have a
part to play here, and that some Ranger's fans view this support as being
linked to their Protestantism.

Table 2.3
Fans who support 'other' international teams

Group	Ireland Republic	None	Ireland North	England	Holland	Other	Row Total
Rangers Fans	1.0 (1)	57.0 (48)	6.0 (5)	13.0 (11)	6.0 (5)	17.0 (14)	21.0 (84)
Hearts Fans	3.0 (1)	67.0 (22)	3.0 (1)	6.0 (2)	9.0 (3)	12.0 (4)	8.0 (33)
Aberdeen Fans		55.0 (28)			16.0 (8)	29.0 (15)	13.0 (51)
Kilmarnock Fans		67.0 (32)	2.0 (1)	2.0 (1)	4.0 (2)	24.0 (12)	12.0 (48)
Celtic Fans	52.0 (47)	35.0 (32)			2.0 (2)	11.0 (10)	23.0 (91)
Motherwell Fans		69.0 (20)	4.0 (1)		7.0 (2)	21.0 (6)	7.0 (29)
Hibernian Fans	12.0 (2)	50.0 (8)		6.0 (1)		31.0 (5)	4.0 (16)
Dundee Utd Fans	5.0 (1)	75.0 (15)				20.0 (4)	5.0 (20)
St Johnstone Fans	3.0 (1)	57.0 (17)	3.0 (1)	7.0 (2)	7.0 (2)	23.0 (70	7.0 (30)
Column Total	13.0 (53)	55.0 (222)	2.0 (9)	4.0 (17)	6.0 (24)	19.0 (77)	100.0 (402)

Although almost all clubs fans denoted no preference for any other international team, this was the response of over 50 per cent of Hibernian fans and 75 per cent of Dundee Utd fans, again there was one significant departure from this picture. Only 35 per cent of Celtic fans expressed no preference. Few Celtic supporters chose any European or South American sides and only Dundee Utd fans resembled Celtic fans in their lack of support for England and Northern Ireland. Where the Celtic fans stood out was in their support for the Republic of Ireland; 52 per cent indicating this preference.

Since the late 1980's the Irish soccer team has emerged as a surprising force and has subsequently gained a much higher media profile. This has been especially so in Britain, where all of the Republics players play their football and indeed where many of them were actually born, as second and third generation Irish. Soccer fans within the Republic, although bombarded with English soccer on television, have during this time displayed a strong affection for Celtic. Many of their songs will be sung, whilst their soccer shirts and memorabilia are popular amongst the Republic's support.

This is reciprocated to a degree. In the same period many Celtic supporters have not only displayed the symbols of Ireland, a long time habit of theirs, but also worn the Republic of Ireland's international jersey. It appears that for a majority of Celtic fans that exhibiting this support is an adjunct of the 'Celtic culture' itself. For Celtic fans, there are clear parallels between themselves and Northern Irish Catholics who do not identify with their 'national' side. However, it is also a manifestation and expression of a particular identity which is not clearly reflected in other ways.

Summary

The historical development of football in Scotland parallels the evolution of aspects of relations between indigenous Protestant and immigrant Irish Catholics. The anti-Catholicism often displayed by Scots in the post-Reformation period, was added to with the arrival of large scale Catholic immigration in the 19th and 20th centuries. Ethno-religious tensions thus became a part of the way of life for both Protestants and Catholics in areas of Catholic settlement.

The establishment of Celtic Football Club provided an environment where many of the Irish and their offspring congregated, and where there was a sense of security and expectation that was difficult for them to come by in other areas of life. Scottish attachment to football was of a more diffused kind. Glasgow Rangers however, assumed an extremely strong presence as the institution which was best equipped to deal with the early successes of a club which was in every way perceived as alien to the Scottish people. An ethno-religious cleavage was thus created within the context of Scottish football. It was a cleavage which reproduced, in a much narrower sense, the social reality experienced by many people in Scotland more generally.

Notes

1.   Glasgow Herald 23/4/88 and 5/8/89.

2.   The following crowd figures reflect the popularity of the game in Scotland: European club match record attendance; Scottish Cup Final at Hampden Park, Glasgow, 24th April 1937. Celtic v Aberdeen, 146,433. It was also judged that there remained 30,000 locked out of the stadium. European Cup record attendance. Semi-Final tie between Celtic and Leeds United (England), at Hampden Park, Glasgow, 15th April, 1970. 138,000. European League match record. Glasgow Rangers v Celtic, Ibrox Park, Glasgow, 2nd January, 1939. 118,567. International match record for Europe. At Hampden Park, Glasgow, played only days after the above Celtic v Aberdeen game, 149,547, Scotland v England.

3.   Since the first League Championship in 1890/91 when Dumbarton and Rangers shared it, the following has been the situation up until season 1994-95: Celtic 35 times (22 runners up): Rangers 45 times (23 runners up). As well as contesting a number of finals and semi-finals Celtic and Rangers have also won the premier competitions in Europe; Celtic won the European Cup in 1967 and Rangers won the

European Cup Winners Cup in 1972.

4.   Examples of this charity come from the 'The Celtic View', the club newspaper. 17th Aug, 1988, the paper reported on some of the activities of the David Hay CSC. This club were the prime movers in establishing the Paul Rafferty Appeal Fund, to raise funds for Glasgow's Yorkhill Hospital to buy brain scanning equipment. In a period of a few years the club had raised £350,000. 31st Aug, 1988; Starry Plough CSC Glasgow, announced efforts to raise funds for the Gateside School for Deaf Children in Paisley. Celtic also played a match against the Portuguese club Benfica in the mid 1970's, donating the gate receipts to UNICEF.

5.   Woods notes that rivalry and profit to be derived from it was the cause of the clubs being linked in the ambiguous sobriquet the 'Old Firm', a description half distasteful and half admiring, as many unsympathetic cartoons in the papers showed the clubs treasurers bearing bulging money bags to the bank (1987, pp64-65).

6.   Catholic footballers who have made the grade with other clubs in Scotland often make known their yearning as a boy to play for Celtic (this can be attributed to Rangers players also). Kevin Gallacher, the Scottish internationalist who plays in England, and Michael O'Neil, the Northern Irish internationalist who plays in Scotland, are both contemporary examples of this attitude.

7.   See relevant features in the Sunday Observer 16/7/89 and Sunday Times 16/7/89. Also Daily Express 22/8/88, Observer Scotland Sunday 3/6/90, and Evening Times 11/7/89.

8.   Glasgow Herald: 16/10/89.

9.   Sunday Mail: 1/5/88.

10.   Witnessed, 25/8/90 and 6/11/90.

11.   Ballad of Billy Reid.

12.   Jack Webster of the Glasgow Herald wrote an article in that newspaper (28/8/89) mainly relating to this aspect of the Celtic 'cause', and in response to the debut of Maurice Johnstone in his first 'Old Firm' match (for Rangers). His article invited the wrath of the Celtic support, who wrote to their own club newspaper complaining about his derogatory remarks.

13.   The Sunday Mirror: 15/5/88.

14.   The 'Fenians' was the name of the mid-19th century Irishmen who engaged in military struggle against Britain. Today in west-central Scotland and Northern Ireland it is often derogatorily used to describe

Roman Catholics. The 'Billy Boys' is the name which approximates to anyone of a Protestant religious label identifying themselves as followers or supporters of the 'attitude' which epitomises Northern Irish and Scottish loyalism. This song often includes the words "the Brigton (Bridgeton/Glasgow) Billy Boys", which denotes a gang from that area of Glasgow, and who engaged in fights with rival Catholic gangs, particularly from the Irish-Catholic Gorbals area. The Bridgeton gang were also involved during the 1930s, in pro right-wing street violence.

15. Interview with ex-Celtic director Tom Grant. Also see Glasgow Herald: 23/2/90.

16. Inverness Caledonian have often been referred to as the Rangers of the north.

17. The Ulster Defence Association are the main (legitimate until August 92) Loyalist-Unionist paramilitary organisation in Northern Ireland. They have a monthly publication called Ulster, in which one of the sections is called 'Tartan Talk', and which often pertains to Glasgow Rangers FC. See February and March 1988 for examples.

18. The 12th of July being the celebratory date for the Battle of the Boyne of the 1st July 1690 (old calendar).

19. Profiles of Wallace Mercer in, the Glasgow Herald, 19/9/90 and Observer Scotland section, 3/9/89.

20. Daily Record: 23/4/90. Such singing on the part of Rangers staff was also heard by viewers of 'Faith, Hope and Calamity', a series of documentaries on Scottish football, STV, 22/10/94.

21. Irish Post: 22/8/87. Also, H.F Moorhouse (1984, pp, 285-315), writes; 'A large number of Scots believe that Rangers are favoured by the authorities in matters of ground selection, fines and selection of internationalists. Referees are thought to award them more than their fair share of penalties and to ignore their own rough play. All these charges plus the belief that the Scottish media are favourable to Rangers are a persistent feature of the Celtic club histories. The former Celtic chairman [Sir] Robert Kelly says that his father and the Celtic manager at the start of the century reckoned Rangers got five points a season via refereeing decisions'. Former 1960s player, Alex Ferguson, noted that in his time with the club, some referees would indicate their affinity with Rangers during matches via bias comments and decisions. See footnote 20 for STV reference.

22. Glasgow Herald: 6/5/90.

23. Stewart Lamont in the Glasgow Herald: 9/2/91 makes a key point regarding some of these areas when he suggests that; 'in Scotland

there are still several places where to be identified as a Catholic or a Protestant is to be at once caught in the deepest distrust which exists in a given community'.

24.   Archie MacPherson in the Sunday Mail: 25/11/90 commented that 'Without the Rangers-Celtic game Scottish football would be as world renowned as the Upper Zambezi Ladies' Netball League'.

25.   Jack McLean in his article 'The Beautiful Game' in the Glasgow Herald: 6/9/90 states that: 'The Old Firm have been the Upas trees of Scottish football for most of this century; their fans hail from the Hebrides to Berwick and beyond, to the detriment of local football'.

26.   Information from Celtic FC.

27.   Interview, Tom Grant.

28.   Interview of David Murray by Kevin McCarra, in, 'Skol Cup Final Magazine' 25/10/90. Rangers Football Club refused the author and a professor at Strathclyde University any information regarding the club. Later, one director, Hugh Adams, did phone the writer and an interview was conducted via telephone.

29.   Daily Record: 26/5/90.

30.   Daily Record: 21/5/90.

31.   See Herald 12/10/92 for article by sports journalist James Traynor, in which he argues for a 'united' support for the Scottish team. The appeal is essentially aimed towards Rangers fans Ulster-Loyalist culture and to Celtic fans Irish identity. However, it is also an appeal which exemplifies a lack of understanding of religious and ethnic identity in Scotland. The Irish identity and anti-Catholicism are construed as opposites and therefore both are condemned in the guise of 'neutrality' and 'unity'. Despite its high claim (and one which is a popular one), Traynor fails to recognise cultural and ethnic diversity and seeks to marginalise a large proportion of the Irish community by invalidating their identity (see conclusion). In addition, Rangers fans are entitled to have a British identity above or alongside that of a Scottish one. A similar view was expressed by the same writer in a later column (22/8/94, Sports Section, p9) which argued that Rangers in Europe in 1994 should be supported by everyone in Scotland. Everyone had to set aside their 'trivial little loyalties' while 'only the most bigoted' would not allow themselves to support Rangers.

32. Sunday Mail: 1/4/90. In addition, in 1993 some evidence for this scenario emerged with the release of a Glasgow Rangers audio tape. Part of the tape related a story concerning a referee (who also belonged to the Free Masons) who boasted that during eighteen years of refereeing, he had always officiated over an unbeaten Rangers side. See Irish Post, 24/7/93 for reference. Also footnote 21.

33. Glasgow Herald: 25/10/89.

Other Sources

The Celtic View (weekly during the football season).The Rangers News (weekly during the football season).The Absolute Game: A Scottish Football Fanzine. May/June1993 pp12-13, 'Bigotry and Sectarianism', by Bert Moorhouse, of Glasgow University.

3 National and cultural identities: other indicators

The fans of both Rangers and Celtic (as well as a number of others) habitually sing songs which refer to the conflict in Northern Ireland. Added to this, the vast numbers of supporters and supporters clubs in Northern Ireland reflects the cultural and political attachment that many people there give to both institutions in Scotland.

A street scene from east Belfast which began the 1990 ITV series on the John Stalker affair, showed children playing football whilst wearing the jerseys of Glasgow Rangers Football Club.[1] Glasgow Rangers' jerseys are a common sight at matches involving Linfield Football Club, while they are regularly worn by the street supporters of Orange demonstrations in Northern Ireland. Scottish international football shirts are reciprocally worn by many of the younger Orange travellers from Northern Ireland, as they journey from Northern Ireland for the west of Scotland's annual Orange parades. This reflects the strong national and cultural attachment of Northern Ireland Protestants for Scotland. Scottish symbols like the St Andrews and Lion Rampant flags are common at many of the Orange parades as well as on Unionist-Loyalist wall murals in Northern Ireland. In a BBC television documentary a Loyalist prisoner in Northern Ireland, was interviewed whilst wearing the soccer shirt of Glasgow Rangers.[2] Rangers tattoos, posters and football jerseys also formed an important part of the photographic record of 'The Life Of Brian, a diary of violent [Loyalist] youth in Belfast', in a Sunday Observer magazine special.[3] A newspaper reported in 1991, that:

> A Scottish magazine with links to the Loyalist prisoners Welfare Association [in Northern Ireland] and the Independent Orange Lodge is targeting individuals and families for attack....The Red Hand....sells between 4,000 and 5,000 copies mainly at Glasgow Rangers and matches in the Winter and at loyalist marches in the Summer[4]

The Celtic football jersey can be seen in the nationalist areas of Northern

Ireland, giving it an important religious and cultural significance. This was reflected at the British based 'Time To Go' campaign's (which called for a British withdrawal from Northern Ireland) main march in London in 1989. Beside Labour MP's Ken Livingstone and Jeremy Corbyn at the front of the march, were two women wearing the Celtic soccer jersey.[5]

In west Belfast, teenager Seamus Duffy was shot dead by the R.U.C during rioting. One year later at the inquest it was reported that Duffy, as well as the youth who it was believed was throwing petrol bombs at the time, was wearing a Celtic jersey.[6] An Irish Republican newspaper reported what they viewed as a sectarian attack on a Catholic in the city:

> Jim Burns....was stopped by a gang of loyalists, who demanded to know, 'Are you a taig or a snout'? As they surrounded him, they saw that he was wearing a Celtic t-shirt and immediately began punching and kicking him to the ground.[7]

The newspaper reported the loyalists as wearing Rangers' shirts and scarves. In a loyalist gun attack on a Catholic bar in Belfast, newspapers described how loyalists, who were shooting indiscriminately, seemed to pick out a small boy wearing a Celtic football top and shot him.[8] In a similar vein, another Republican publication reported that:

> One of our best areas for sales is Glasgow, so we were surprised to find 60 copies of our last issue returned unsold. However, our puzzlement turned to sympathy when we read the accompanying note. 'Enclosing some unavoidable returns which would have been sold at Parkhead if Celtic hadn't done so poorly this season'.[9]

Clearly the implication is that lower attendances at Celtic Park due to Celtic's poor season had an affect upon the sales of this pro-Republican magazine.

Indeed Rangers and Celtic jerseys and emblems are frequently worn in areas of Northern Ireland. Rangers have become strongly identified with the cause of Northern Ireland Unionism/Loyalism and Orangeism, whilst Celtic emit a Catholic identity and of a brand of Irish nationalism. In this way, the 'football opposites' also become social, religious and political ones.

Religious and political sensibilities

Glasgow Rangers and Celtic also provide a setting within which the cleavage over the Northern Ireland issue is expressed within Scotland. These political and cultural expressions are clear in the responses of the Scottish Football fans to questions concerning the historical-political situation in Northern Ireland.

In relation to questions on the political and constitutional position of Northern Ireland, almost three-quarters of Rangers fans surveyed believe that Northern Ireland should remain in the United Kingdom (Table 3.1). This figure indicates the 'loyalism' of the Rangers fans. As over 90 per cent of Protestants in Northern Ireland support the continuation of the union with

Britain, it is apparent that Glasgow Rangers fans share an affinity with them in relation to this area of political partisanship. (See BSA, Curtice and Gallagher, 1990/91, pp 183-216).

Most Motherwell, Hearts and Kilmarnock supporters support the 'keep Northern Ireland British' option; a position which is reflected in some of the vocal opinions of their fans in games. A large number of Aberdeen fans were 'don't knows' (39 per cent) with the rest split evenly between supporters of the status quo and of a united Ireland.

Although Table 3.1 shows 61 per cent of Hibernian fans and 64 per cent of Dundee United fans favourable to a united Ireland position, the numbers involved are low. Nevertheless, this may indicate the Irish elements in the background of both clubs. Anti-Irish or Catholic songs, common enough at many other clubs, are not sung by Hibernian fans and rarely heard at Dundee United. However, both clubs are now Scottish in disposition (as well as secualr) and only limited sections of the Hibernian support give any hint of their Irish background. Nevertheless, each of them has a proportion of supporters with an Irish background and who are Catholic (see later tables) and this factor probably explains the relatively high levels of support amongst their fans for a united Ireland.

Significantly, every team apart from Celtic, and to a lesser extent Hibernian and Dundee United, has a much smaller proportion of supporters favouring a united Ireland than are to be found in the wider British population. Curtice and Gallagher assert that: 'British Governments clearly lack widespread public support for Britain's continued association with and involvement in, the province'. Although this evidence does not invalidate the findings of Curtice and Gallagher, their conclusion is not so accurate when the opinions of Scottish football fans are considered.

Given the extent of the support for Rangers, such evidence is an indication of the variation of attitudes towards the Northern Ireland question in Scotland as compared to the rest of Britain. Whereas many people in Britain have become exasperated by the continuing violence associated with the problem (a view forwarded by Curtice and Gallagher) and for this reason wish to end Britain's involvement in this violence, my survey indicates that a significant number of people in Scotland have a partisan view of the problem/solution. The view that: 'all shades of British opinion believe that the best future for Northern Ireland would be for it to be part of a united Ireland' is also be seen as less true in Scotland. (BSA, 1990/91, pp. 183-216).

The most striking figures are for the Celtic fans who identify most closely with a united Ireland. Four out of five Celtic supporters supported a united Ireland, in contrast to the 55 per cent of the general British population (BSA) who take such a view, as well of course as the majority of other Scottish football fans who adopt this perspective. This result also suggests a strong politico-cultural connection between Celtic fans and Ireland; one which is highly distinctive in terms of the broad spectrum of Scottish football fans.

Table 3.1
Fans solution to the Northern Ireland conflict

Group	Remain in UK	Reunify with Ireland	Other Answer	Don't Know	Row Total
Rangers Fans	73.0 (65)	11.0 (10)	6.0 (5)	10.0 (9)	20.0 (89)
Hearts Fans	42.0 (16)	21.0 (8)	18.0 (7)	18.0 (7)	9.0 (38)
Aberdeen Fans	25.0 (14)	29.0 (16)	7.0 (4)	39.0 (22)	13.0 (56)
Kilmarnock Fans	47.0 (24)	22.0 (11)	8.0 (4)	23.0 (12)	12.0 (51)
Celtic Fans	5.0 (5)	79.0 (77)	6.0 (6)	9.0 (9)	22.0 (97)
Motherwell Fans	48.0 (15)	29.0 (9)	10.0 (3)	13.0 (4)	7.0 (31)
Hibernian Fans		61.0 (11)	22.0 (4)	17.0 (3)	4.0 (18)
Dundee United Fans	9.0 (2)	64.0 (14)	14.0 (3)	14.0 (3)	5.0 (22)
St Johnstone Fans	38.0 (13)	41.0 (14)	3.0 (1)	18.0 (6)	7.8 (34)
Column Total	35.0 (154)	39.0 (170)	8.0 (37)	17.0 (75)	100.0 (436)

Table 3.2 also reflects the different views of the Celtic support with regard to Northern Ireland; 85 per cent of Celtic fans supported the withdrawal of British soldiers from Northern Ireland. In contrast, 69 per cent of Rangers fans said they would oppose the withdrawal of troops. Celtic and Rangers fans can be placed at the opposite ends of the opinion scale on these questions. Indeed, they can be construed as each other's polar opposites on such a scale.

Table 3.2
Fans supporting or opposing a withdrawal of British troops from Northern Ireland

Group	Supp Strongly	Supp a little	Oppose a little	Oppose Strongly	Don't Know	Row Total
Rangers Fans	13.0 (12)	8.0 (7)	8.0 (7)	61.0 (55)	10.0 (9)	21.0 (90)
Hearts Fans	31.0 (12)	23.0 (9)	3.0 (1)	31.0 (12)	13.0 (5)	9.0 (39)
Aberdeen Fans	21.0 (12)	16.0 (9)	11.0 (6)	27.0 (15)	25.0 (14)	13.0 (56)
Kilmarnock Fans	23.0 (12)	18.0 (9)	12.0 (6)	23.0 (12)	23.0 (12)	12.0 (51)
Celtic Fans	67.0 (64)	18.0 (17)	2.0 (2)	4.0 (4)	9.0 (9)	22.0 (96)
Motherwell Fans	10.0 (3)	16.0 (5)	10.0 (3)	42.0 (13)	23.0 (7)	7.0 (31)
Hibernian Fans	67.0 (12)	17.0 (3)		17.0 (3)		4.0 (18)
Dundee United Fans	50.0 (11)	18.0 (4)	9.0 (2)	18.0 (1)	18.0 (4)	5.0 (22)
St Johnstone Fans	12.0 (4)	21.0 (7)	12.0 (9)	26.0 (10)	29.0 (4)	8.0 (34)
Column Total	32.0 (142)	16.0 (70)	28.0 (124)	16.0 (70)	7.0 (31)	100.0 (437)

Despite support for the position of Northern Ireland within the UK from a majority of fans who have an opinion, many of the surveyed clubs supporters are more ambiguous on the question of the withdrawal of British troops. Apart from the Celtic, Dundee United and Hibernian fans (who are above the BSA average), the other surveyed spectators were less likely than the general population to support a troop withdrawal from Northern Ireland. Motherwell Football Club fans oppose troop withdrawal and come nearest to Rangers fans on the matter. Rangers fans themselves are less opposed to a troop withdrawal than they are to a united Ireland. St Johnstone fans, from the east of the country, have two in five of their fans opposed to a troop withdrawal.[10]

The Orange, loyalist or unionist consciousness is greater amongst the supporters of Rangers and Motherwell than in the other clubs, and a socio-political Protestant identity takes meaning in these British nationalist expressions. A Protestant identity appears to be strong also in other clubs (considering that the vast majority of supporters denote themselves as of the Protestant faith; Table 3.4), but it does not show itself quite so well with reference to Northern Ireland.

Of course, the responses of both the Rangers and Celtic fans are particularly important because of the strength of club support. In recent years, Rangers have had an average of over 40,000 fans per home game while Celtic have attracted almost 30,000 (for other clubs see Table 3.3). It is also important to recognise that in the case of Rangers and Celtic, the active support does not reflect all the people with strong feelings towards the institutions. Of course, Rangers can be expected to have a greater support than Celtic due to the simple historical fact that there are fewer Catholics in Scotland. Such Rangers' appeal means that their kit replica is the biggest seller in Britain with 165,000 per year.[11] The kit jersey in fact sold 72,000 in its first week of release onto the market in May 1992.[12] Such figures give a more accurate indication of the depth of support existing for Glasgow Rangers.

Table 3.3
Other major supported clubs in Scotland
(average home gates, 1993/94)[13]

Hearts	11,010	St Mirren	2,593
Aberdeen	12,723	Motherwell	7,897
Hibernian	9,718	Dunfermline	4,495
DundeeUtd	8,595	Kilmarnock	9,157
Dundee	5,646	Raith Rovers	4,880
St Johnstone	5,877	Partick Thistle	6,729

If we see Rangers and Celtic at opposite ends of a religious and socio-political continuum the remaining clubs will fall in between; most of them associated to a greater or lesser degree with a number of the attitudes of Rangers supporters. This is reflected in the songs and paraphernalia displayed by many of the followers of football in Scotland as well as in the data collected. Although not quite as partisan as Rangers fans, the supporters of clubs like Hearts, Motherwell and Kilmarnock have views on Northern Ireland which to an extent correlate with Rangers fans.

Of course attitudes to Northern Ireland do not in themselves explain the cleavage that exists between major sets of football supporters in Scotland. Scottish football creates a stage for the assertion of certain political beliefs, and provides a major context in which to analyse the social and cultural identities of the fans. As Moorhouse notes; 'Scottish football, at a number of levels, reveals how sport can represent and enliven all kinds of divisions pertinent in society' (Moorhouse, 1984, pp. 285-315).

Religion

Football fans in Scotland therefore exhibit a variety of political attitudes. How far are these attitudes related to the religious identities of Scottish football fans?

Table 3.4 shows that football clubs in Scotland are overwhelmingly supported by Protestants. Motherwell and Glasgow Rangers are the most exclusive in this respect. Motherwell fans are almost wholly drawn from Church of Scotland identifiers (87 per cent); they have a sparse number drawn from other Protestant faiths, and a small number claiming 'no religion'. There was only one Catholic amongst the Motherwell fans surveyed. Seventy-three per cent of Rangers fans are Church of Scotland identifiers and 15 per cent are from other Protestant denominations. No Catholics were found amongst the Rangers support; 11 per cent expressed themselves as having no religion.

Hibernian, Dundee United and Hearts (i.e., club's from outwith the west-central belt) have a similar percentage of supporters who describe themselves as having 'no religion', as has the British public generally (34 per cent as determined by the BSA survey. The UK Christian handbook 1992/93, estimates that 38 per cent of the Scottish population has no religious affiliation). Despite Hearts popular image as a Protestant and anti-Catholic club, 40 per cent of their fans do not describe themselves as Protestant. However, Protestant identity is important for a majority of Hearts fans. My figures indicate a comparatively high level (though a less than dominant one) of secularism within the Edinburgh area, at least in the context of football (Edinburgh being the place where the vast majority of both clubs fans originate; i.e., 95 per cent in the case of Hearts and 83 per cent for Hibs). Aberdeen and St Johnstone from the east also have a number of fans who claim a 'secular identity', though again the vast majority of both clubs fans claim a Protestant label.

The importance of religion in the west-central population area, is clearly demonstrated by the figures for Celtic, Rangers, Kilmarnock and Motherwell fans. Indeed, all of these club's have fewer non-religious adherents than is the case in Northern Ireland; 'Only 12 per cent of people in Northern Ireland said they did not have a religion' (BSA, p. 184). Of course, all of these percentages are well below the one third in Britain who claim likewise. Overall, despite the clear indication that religion is of less significance in the east of the country than in the other parts, the figures still confirm the greater importance of religious identity in Scotland as compared with England.

In relation to this, with religion so important in the political and social divide in Northern Ireland and a number of Scottish Football fans having strong beliefs on the Northern Ireland problem, Protestant and Catholic identities in Northern Ireland therefore can be seen to have some bearing on the corresponding identities in the Scottish west-central belt.

Table 3.4
Religious denomination of fans

Group	Church of Scotland	Other Prot Church	R.C	Other Religion	None	Row Total
Rangers Fans	73.0 (67)	15.0 (14)		1.0 (1)	11.0 (10)	21.0 (92)
Hearts Fans	57.0 (23)	5.0 (2)	10.0 (4)		27.0 (11)	9.0 (40)
Aberdeen Fans	55.0 (31)	9.0 (5)	16.0 (9)	4.0 (2)	16.0 (9)	13.0 (56)
Kilmarnock Fans	75.0 (39)	4.0 (2)	11.0 (6)		10.0 (5)	12.0 (52)
Celtic Fans	1.0 (1)	3.0 (3)	93.0 (90)		3.0 (3)	22.0 (97)
Motherwell Fans	87.0 (28)	3.0 (1)	3.0 (3)		6.0 (2)	7.0 (32)
Hibernian Fans	6.0 (1)	17.0 (3)	39.0 (7)		39.0 (7)	4.0 (18)
Dundee United Fans	32.0 (7)		32.0 (7)	4.0 (1)	32.0 (7)	5.0 (22)
St Johnstone Fans	71.0 (24)	6.0 (2)	3.0 (1)		21.0 (7)	8.0 (34)
Column Total	49.0 (221)	7.0 (32)	28.0 (125)	1.0 (4)	14.0 (61)	100.0 (443)

One of the focus for attention has also been the fans of Dundee United and Hibernian. These clubs have the largest number of Catholic supporters outside Celtic, though in both cases they have as many secular as Catholic fans. In Dundee United's case, they have the same proportion of Catholic adherents as Protestant and secular ones. Hibernian have fewer Protestants, though they still make up almost one quarter of their fans surveyed. These figures underpin the fact that these two clubs have the least 'tangible' religious identities, in terms of the songs and overt expressions from their fans. Although they have more supporters who are Catholics than other clubs they have no particular affinity.

In religious terms, the secular figures for the supporters of both these clubs match the more general BSA and Scottish Christian survey estimates. Notwithstanding, as both club's have lower levels of support than a number of other club's (especially Celtic and Rangers), their importance should not be overstated. Indeed, Dundee United, though by far the more successful of the two clubs in the city of Dundee, have frequently attracted a smaller support than the less successful Dundee. In this light, it might be significant that it is the Dundee side who are popularly viewed as 'the' Protestant club in Dundee, and the one which therefore has the greatest potential support.

The club which stands out from all the others is Celtic. Only 4 per cent of their followers are Protestants, while 3 per cent have no religion. Ninety-three per cent of Celtic fans are Roman Catholic, thus bearing out the longevity of the religious dimension of the club. The club obviously has a significance for the Catholic population that it does not have for members of other faiths. Celtic fans are seen even more clearly as Catholic if we analyse the answers to the question concerning church attendance.

Table 3.5
Attendance at church

Group	Once or More	Every two weeks	Every month	Some- times	Once a year	Never	Row Total
Rangers Fans	5.0 (5)	2.0 (2)	6.0 (6)	36.0 (33)	13.0 (12)	37.0 (34)	21.0 (92)
Hearts Fans	2.0 (1)		2.0 (1)	27.0 (11)	5.0 (2)	62.0 (25)	9.0 (40)
Aberdeen Fans	20.0 (11)	5.0 (3)	4.0 (2)	23.0 (13)	11.0 (6)	37.0 (21)	13.0 (56)
Kilmarnock Fans	2.0 (1)	2.0 (1)	2.0 (1)	29.0 (15)	19.0 (10)	46.0 (24)	12.0 (52)
Celtic Fans	61.0 (59)	2.0 (2)	1.00 (1)	15.0 (15)	1.0 (1)	20.0 (19)	22.0 (97)
Motherwell Fans	3.0 (1)	12.0 (4)	6.0 (2)	19.0 (6)	9.0 (3)	50.0 (16)	7.0 (32)
Hibernian Fans	6.0 (1)			33.0 (6)		61.0 (11)	4.0 (18)
Dundee United Fans	4.0 (1)	4.0 (1)		14.0 (3)	9.0 (2)	68.0 (15)	5.0 (22)
St Johnstone Fans	9.0 (3)	3.0 (1)	3.0 (1)	29.0 (10)	18.0 (6)	38.0 (13)	8.0 (34)
Column Total	19.0 (83)	3.0 (14)	3.0 (14)	25.0 (112)	9.0 (42)	40.0 (178)	100.0 (443)

A strong majority of the Celtic fans (61 per cent) indicated that they attend church/mass once a week or more (a higher proportion of church attending Catholics than for the Catholic population as a whole), giving further substance to Celtic's popular image as a Catholic club. Despite the high levels of self-religious labelling, very few of the fans of the other clubs surveyed indicated any church attendance at all. This suggests that despite the Protestant make-up of most clubs fans, their faiths' are of a secular nature, at least as regards formal church practice. Moderate proportions of most of the club's spectators do attend church 'sometimes', but the largest proportion of supporters in all clubs, other than Celtic 'never' attend church services. Clearly the Protestantism of many of these fans is not defined by regular Church attendance. This indicates once again that Protestant identity in Scotland has strong cultural overtures and characteristics. It is an argument here that this identity is partly, and in a number of instances strongly if not solely, defined in relation to Catholics.

The Rangers results deserve brief comment. Only 8 per cent are regular Church attenders while 36 per cent of Rangers fans go 'sometimes' to church; the same proportion 'never' go at all and 13 per cent make the trip once per year (Although including 'all' Church attenders, a Scottish Church census of 1984 stated that 17 per cent of the population attended Church either on a daily or a weekly basis). Therefore, regardless of the strong 'religious' content in the make up of Rangers fans, for the vast majority (86 per cent, including the 10 per cent who have no religion), formal religious practice plays no part in their lives (only 5 per cent of their fans attend church once per week and 2 per cent once every two weeks). Again, using the same criteria (and including those of no religion); all other clubs indicate a similar picture to that of the Rangers fans. Aberdeen have the next highest proportion of church attenders after Celtic, with 20 per cent going once per week or more and 5 per cent attending every two weeks. An important point here, is that in a similar sense to the larger society, and despite the presence of 'religion' in Scottish football, there appears to be little difference in the religious practice and identity of football supporters (apart from in the case of the Celtic support) and the wider society.

Overall, apart from Celtic, almost all other teams are followed by fans who are Protestant; a fact often audibly projected from the terracing. However, Rangers Protestantism in particular, is an identity which is fundamentally anti-Catholic and anti-Irish, as well as secular. The principal expressions of the Rangers identity have long been anti-Catholic and anti-Irish. These expressions are manifest in the songs and symbols of the Rangers support and in the long history of the club's policy of refusing to sign Catholic players. As many other clubs fans in Scottish football project similar expressions, the conclusion must be that at least for some sections of the Scottish population, their Protestant identity is also strongly characterised by anti-Catholicism.

Despite secularisation, a cultural standard involving Protestantism as a means of self and group identity, has been constructed by many 'football fans'. Such Protestantism has a high cultural and social content which is rarely reflected in actual religious practice. Its cultural content (as far as the football fans are concerned) appears to include a key characteristic of Scottish Protestant culture since the Reformation; antagonism towards Catholicism. Despite secularisation and low church attendance by many Protestants, this remains strong; at least amongst these sections of the population. In addition, for fans of Rangers and Motherwell (as well as others) the national and religious cleavage and divisions in Northern Ireland have a strong bearing on some of the anti-Catholicism considered here.

The religious aspect of the Celtic support is determined largely by these fans ethnic background. Approximately three in five of that clubs fans perceived themselves as being ethnically Irish, whilst four per cent said they were part Irish. One third of the Celtic support classified themselves as from a Scottish background. The fact that Ireland, along with Poland, has the highest levels of church attendance in Europe,[14] has more than likely some bearing on the high degree of religiosity amongst Catholics in Scotland (though much less than the Irish and Polish figures of around eighty-five per cent), as has the immigrant experience itself. The fact that a majority of Celtic fans denote themselves as having an Irish background (within the past three or four generations) is at variance with other football fans in Scotland. This then is another factor which marks them out as different from the other supporters.

Unsurprisingly, the vast majority of other football fans in Scotland see their background as Scottish (Table 3.6).

Table 3.6
Supporters origins

	Scottish origins	Scottish & 'other' origins
Motherwell	94%	3%
Kilmarnock	90%	2%
St Johnstone	82%	
Dundee Utd	82%	4%
Aberdeen	81%	5%
Rangers	74%	3%
Hearts	73%	12%
Hibernian	72%	6%

Few clubs had a significant number of fans coming from the same background as the Celtic fans; only Hibernian with 11 per cent and Dundee United with 14 per cent had a significant proportion of fans who claimed Irish origin. One other response to this question is worthy of comment; 16 per cent of Rangers fans claimed a British heritage, reflecting to a degree the popular image of 'Britishness' frequently remarked upon by observers of the club.

Ethnic, cultural, and religious differentiation becomes clearer concerning the fans responses to the question of 'ascriptive identity'. A degree of Scottish or Irish consciousness can be detected with the 'identifying' symbols included in the questionnaire, in order to give further evidence of the depth and type of difference which exists between those from a Scottish Protestant and those from an Irish Catholic background. A number of Scottish and Irish symbols were identified.

Scottish		Irish	
The Thistle	symbolic/emblematic	The Harp	symbolic/emblematic
The Bagpipes.	symbolic/emblematic	Shamrock	symbolic/emblematic
Robert the Bruce	political/historical/cultural	Patrick Pearse	political
The Corries	political/cultural	Wolfe Tones	political/cultural
John Knox	religious	St Patrick	religious
Robert Burns	cultural	W B Yeats	cultural

As table 3.7 indicates, respondents were asked with which of these symbols they identified. As far as the Scottish symbols were concerned the Thistle was well favoured by all fans, except the Celtic supporters, of whom only 21 per cent chose it. The highest identifiers with the Thistle were the fans of Motherwell (76 per cent) and Dundee United (74 per cent). The Bagpipes were also chosen as a 'symbol' of Scottish identity. Once again, Celtic fans were significantly different from the fans of all the other clubs; only 15 per cent displaying any kind of attraction for the Bagpipes. In contrast, identification with the Bagpipes was the highest among fans of Kilmarnock (60 per cent), Aberdeen (58 per cent) and Motherwell (48 per cent).

Of the more political symbols, the Corries (a Scottish Folk group whose songs often relate to Scottish independence), received most support among Aberdeen (29 per cent), St Johnstone (32 per cent), Motherwell (25 per cent) and Kilmarnock (24 per cent) fans. Robert the Bruce was approved by Dundee United (63 per cent), Aberdeen (61 per cent), St Johnstone (61 per cent) and Hearts (56 per cent) fans. Celtic fans (17 per cent) were again the lowest in this category of ascriptive identity.

John Knox, a religious symbol of Reformation and Protestant Scotland, was not as popular as might have been expected. However, this lack of affinity with Knox is a reflection of the lack of religious practice (and the related lack of 'religious' knowledge) amongst football fans in Scotland, despite strong religious identity. One third of Motherwell fans did choose him, approximately the same proportion as the Hearts fans. Perhaps more significantly, slightly over half of the Rangers supporters surveyed choose Knox. This support augmented their Protestant self-image.

The contemporary popularity of Robert Burns was reflected in him being chosen in such high numbers by many of the fans. A massive 70 per cent of Kilmarnock fans (partly a reflection of the poet's own origins in this area), 59 per cent of Hearts fans, 57 per cent of Rangers supporters and 54 per cent of St Johnstone fans, bear out the popular image and potent symbolism of the Ayrshire poet. With only 13 per cent of Celtic fans choosing Burns as an important element in their cultural identity, they again reveal their difference from the other fans.

As far as the Irish symbols are concerned, the Harp does not claim many identifiers. The Shamrock also proved of little attraction for most of the fans. No Rangers, Kilmarnock or St Johnstone supporters at all related to this; and only nine fans from the rest of the clubs did so. In contrast, and not surprisingly seeing that it is a specific emblem of the club itself, over half of the Celtic fans positively identified with the shamrock, a most significant Irish symbol.

Padraic Pearse, the leader of the 1916 Irish Uprising, was also relatively popular among Celtic fans, almost one quarter identifying with him. Most Clubs fans did not choose Pearse at all; only five in total from all other Clubs. This possibly reflects his unfamiliarity to non-ethnic Irish people. Similarly, only five fans in total from clubs other than Celtic picked the Irish ballad/folk group, the Wolfe Tones, a band noted, like the Corries, for their nationalist singing. In contrast, a significant 53 per cent of Celtic fans singled out this group. The Celtic fans choice of Pearse and the Wolfe Tones confirmed the links between Celtic fans and Irish nationalism.

The Irish religious figure of St Patrick proved popular with almost a third of the Hibernian fans (31 per cent); almost exactly the percentage of Catholics among them. Yet again however, just five fans of any club other than Hibernian or Celtic expressed any attraction to St Patrick. Once again, Celtic fans were different with half of their fans favouring the Irish saint.

Table 3.7
Symbols identified with (football fans)

Group	Pearse	The Harp	The Thistle	Bruce	Row Total
Rangers Fans		3.0 (3)	55.0 (48)	44.0 (39)	21.0 (87)
Hearts Fans			68.0 (26)	58.0 (22)	9.0 (38)
Aberdeen Fans			67.0 (35)	61.0 (32)	13.0 (52)
Kilmarnock Fans		2.0 (1)	62.0 (29)	49.0 (23)	11.0 (47)
Celtic Fans	23.0 (22)	16.0 (15)	21.0 (20)	17.0 (16)	23.0 (95)
Motherwell Fans			76.0 (22)	55.0 (16)	7.0 (29)
Hibernian Fans	6.0 (1)	12.0 (2)	44.0 (7)	50.0 (8)	5.0 (16)
Dundee United Fans	16.0 (3)	5.0 (1)	74.0 (14)	63.0 (12)	5.0 (19)
St Johnstone Fans	4.0 (1)	7.0 (2)	64.0 (18)	61.0 (17)	7.0 (28)
Column Total	7.0 (27)	6.0 (24)	53.0 (219)	45.0 (185)	100.0 (411)

Table 3.7 (continued)

Group	Yeats	Tones	Corries	Knox	Row Total
Rangers Fans	1.0 (1)		11.0 (10)	51.0 (44)	21.0 (87)
Hearts Fans			13.0 (5)	34.0 (13)	9.0 (38)
Aberdeen Fans	4.0 (2)		29.0 (15)	6.0 (3)	13.0 (52)
Kilmarnock Fans	2.0 (1)	2.0 (1)	25.0 (12)	13.0 (6)	11.0 (47)
Celtic Fans	7.0 (7)	53.0 (50)	9.0 (9)		23.0 (95)
Motherwell Fans		3.0 (1)	24.0 (7)	34.0 (10)	7.0 (29)
Hibernian Fans	6.0 (1)	12.0 (2)	12.0 (2)		4.0 (16)
Dundee Utd Fans		5.0 (1)	10.0 (2)		5.0 (19)
St Johnstone Fans	4.0 (1)		32.0 (9)	11.0 (3)	7.0 (28)
Column Total	3.0 (13)	13.0 (55)	17.0 (71)	19.0 (79)	100.0 (411)

Table 3.7 (continued)

Group	Burns	Patrick	The Bagpipes	The Shamrock	Row Total
Rangers Fans	57.0 (50)		41.0 (36)		21.0 (87)
Hearts Fans	60.0 (23)	5.0 (2)	45.0 (17)	3.0 (1)	9.0 (38)
Aberdeen Fans	48.0 (25)	4.0 (2)	58.0 (30)	2.0 (1)	13.0 (52)
Kilmarnock Fans	70.0 (33)		60.0 (28)		11.0 (47)
Celtic Fans	13.0 (12)	50.0 (48)	15.0 (14)	54.0 (51)	23.0 (95)
Motherwell Fans	59.0 (17)		48.0 (14)		7.0 (29)
Hibernian Fans	31.0 (5)	31.0 (5)	37.0 (6)	31.0 (5)	4.0 (16)
Dundee Utd Fans	47.0 (9)	5.0 (1)	47.0 (9)	10.0 (2)	5.0 (19)
St Johnstone Fans	54.0 (15)		36.0 (10)		7.0 (28)
Column Total	46.0 (189)	14.0 (58)	40.0 (164)	15.0 (60)	100.0 (411)

Few Celtic fans identified themselves with the Scottish symbols. The majority adopted one or other of the Irish ones; St Patrick on the religious side, the Wolfe Tones on the political/cultural front and the Shamrock as an emblem. Almost no other fans chose these. The Scottish symbols of Robert Burns, Robert the Bruce and the Thistle were the principal figures and emblems as far as the other club's fans are concerned.

Clear differences of identity are conspicuous between Celtic fans and other football supporters. This reflects powerful cultural differentials rarely addressed in Scotland. If they are addressed, it is normally within a sectarian context. We can see therefore that the cleavage first noted in the songs being sung at many Scottish football grounds has a much broader resonance. The most striking factor is the vast difference between the cultural symbols of identity which are significant to Celtic as contrasted with the other clubs' fans. This is a clear indicator of the constitution of a contemporary community which derives from Irish immigration.

Identity and Scottish politics

Are these attitudinal differences and perceptions on a diversity of interrelated topics related to political affiliation in Scotland? Are these diversities of opinion, at least between Celtic and the other supporters, particularly fans of Glasgow Rangers, reflected in party political partisanship?

Approximately 20 per cent of the fans surveyed indicated no party preference (see table 3.8), while a handful of Rangers and Hearts fans designated themselves as British National Party supporters.

Table 3.8
Fans political party support

Group	Labour	Conservative	Lib Dems	S.N.P.	Soc Dems	Other	None	Row Total
Rangers Fans	33.0 (29)	32.0 (28)	1.0 (1)	14.0 (12)		7.0 (6)	14.0 (12)	20.0 (88)
Hearts Fans	45.0 (18)	12.0 (5)		20.0 (8)	2.0 (1)	2.0 (1)	17.0 (7)	9.0 (40)
Aberdeen Fans	26.0 (15)	17.0 (10)	9.0 (5)	33.0 (19)			14.0 (8)	13.0 (57)
Kilmarnock Fans	58.0 (30)	10.0 (5)	2.0 (1)	21.0 (11)			10.0 (5)	12.0 (52)
Celtic Fans	85.0 (83)	3.0 (3)	1.0 (1)	4.0 (4)		2.0 (2)	5.2 (5)	22.0 (98)
Motherwell Fans	34.0 (11)	9.0 (3)		37.0 (12)		3.0 (1)	16.0 (5)	7.0 (32)
Hibernian Fans	33.0 (6)	11.0 (2)		17.0 (3)			39.0 (7)	4.0 (18)
Dundee United Fans	32.0 (7)	4.0 (1)		41.0 (9)			23.0 (5)	5.0 (22)
St Johnstone Fans	12.0 (4)	29.0 (10)	3.0 (1)	23.0 (8)			32.0 (11)	8.0 (34)
Column Total	46.0. (20)	15.0 (67)	2.0 (9)	19.0 (83)	0 (1)	2.0 (10)	15.0 (65)	100.0 (441)

The Scottish National Party was the most popular preference amongst the fans of Dundee United (41 per cent), Motherwell (37 per cent) and Aberdeen (33 per cent). A substantial number of Hearts, Kilmarnock and St Johnstone fans indicated a similar partisanship; over one in five supporters on average being SNP adherents. Support for the SNP was lowest among the Celtic supporters (4 per cent). This is not surprising considering Celtic supporters lack of affinity with the symbols of Scotland, including the national football team, as well as the fact that Catholics are generally less likely to be SNP supporters (see Brand 1978 and Miller 1981). Miller asserts that often the irreligious tend to be SNP supporters in Scotland (pp144-146).

Giving some substance to Millers claim, the survey found Dundee United as having one third of their fans with a 'no religion' label. Therefore, the 41 per cent denoting themselves as SNP supporters among the Dundee United fans, correlates with the actual parliamentary vote for the SNP during the 1980s in the two Dundee constituencies. Although small, such figures are important to the overall socio-religious picture of Scotland in that this indicates again the lesser importance of religion in the eastern area of the country.

Motherwell fans, who generally originate from the town area itself, are above their constituency average (13 per cent) in their support for the SNP, although once again the figures are quite small. Hearts, coming from a multi-constituency city, are difficult to relate to the immediate locality and electoral constituency. Nevertheless, the 20 per cent designating themselves SNP is above the general Edinburgh voting average for the Party during the 1980s. Aberdeen fans too, with one third supporting the SNP, are well above the figures for local SNP adherence , though it should be noted that the club have a wider support from the north east of Scotland generally, an area more noted for SNP support (See Parry, 1988. These figures take into consideration the local elections of the same period). Considering these figures overall as well as reflecting on the potential importance of international football teams (and often sport generally) for national identity, it is clearly possible that football raises a particular consciousness, in either social and political terms in Scotland.

The indications from the survey is of a possibility that for a number of club's fans, a Scottish football identity has evolved which often translates into political support for the most obviously Scottish of parties. This of course can result from two factors: those with a particularly strong Scottish identity in political terms may collect around a club they feel projects well this image (possibly when the club plays abroad for example), or/and, the fans themselves may bring a particular identity to the club environment which subsequently develops. In terms of the symbols associated with fans of clubs from the north-east of the country, in the late 1980s and 90s groups of their supporters began to display Scottish flags as opposed to the more common Union Jack flags of other Scottish clubs or the Irish Tricolour adopted by Celtic fans. This perhaps reflects a stronger Scottish identity among fans of these football clubs, as opposed to the Irish Celtic, British Rangers and other 'Protestant' club identities.

However, football supporters generally give allegiance to the national team, and this is very much the case with the fans of all of the teams, except Celtic, who support the national side in large numbers (Table 2.2). Although there are supporters of all political parties involved actively or passively in supporting the national side, it is plausible that the cultural significance of supporting the national team (see H.F Moorhouse, 1987) does, at various junctures, translate into support for the nationalist party (See Brand's hypothesis, 1978). This analysis appears supported by the fact the many fans of Scottish clubs, other than Celtic, are as likely as, or in most cases more likely to support the SNP, than the Scottish or regional averages.

The figures for Conservative Party support are lower among clubs than is generally the case. This is probably due to the more working class nature of football supporters, as well as to the stronger emphasis on support for political nationalism. As far as the football supporters of St Johnstone are concerned however, their support for the SNP, Conservatives, and the Labour Parties, more or less reflects the local electoral support for each of them in the 1980s.[15]

Although Rangers and Celtic supporters originate from a much wider geographical area than any of the other sides, it is here that we find the most striking figures in terms of party political support. Despite Rangers fans having the same social make-up as supporters of other clubs (though middle class employment and student status were slightly more common among

Aberdeen and St Johnstone fans), they appear to maintain a strong Conservative Party connection; the largest of all the clubs surveyed. Since the 1987 General Election in Britain support for the Conservative Party has hovered around the 14-26 per cent mark in Scotland;[16]Rangers therefore are well above the Scottish average in this respect. It is the Rangers' fans Protestantism which is expressed in a national political setting through a significant degree of support for the most Unionist (and British 'nationalist') of the main British political parties (see later for connections with Orangeism and Protestantism generally). Thus the vocal and symbolic British-Protestant identity projected by the Rangers fans, is partly expressed in a high degree of support for the Conservatives.

Even so, it is the Celtic fans who reveal the clearest pattern. In the General Election of 1987, Labour achieved its best ever Scottish General Election result with 42.4 per cent of the poll. However, 85 per cent of the Celtic fans indicate support for the Labour Party. Celtic fans are of course overwhelmingly Catholic and working class and Catholics and the working class tend to support the Labour Party (Miller, 1981, pp 144-146. See also Irish Post survey reported during December/January 1992/3). Nevertheless, the figure of 85 per cent is a massive one. Again, this result suggests that consciousness is raised and/or reinforced within a football setting. The raising of consciousness in this way, whether political, or social or religious, can thus give substance to the proposition that football in Scotland often provides the platform and the context for the expression of supposed 'non-football' sentiments and identities.

As noted in chapter 1, discrimination in employment was the experience of Irish Catholic immigrants and their immediate offspring. Although such discrimination is often difficult to detect, we can still gain some insight into our respondents 'perceptions' of discrimination. Fans were asked whether they believed that Protestants and Catholics in Scotland who applied for the same job had the same chance of getting it.

Table 3.9
Protestants and Catholics: perceived job chances

Group	Same Chance	Different Chance	Doesn't Matter	Don't Know	Row Total
Rangers Fans	60.0 (53)	24.0 (21)	8.0 (7)	9.0 (8)	20.0 (89)
Hearts Fans	64.0 (25)	18.0 (7)	13.0 (5)	5.0 (2)	9.0 (39)
Aberdeen Fans	50.0 (29)	10.0 (6)	26.0 (15)	14.0 (8)	13.0 (58)
Kilmarnock Fans	56.0 (29)	21.0 (11)	11.0 (6)	11.0 (6)	12.0 (52)
Celtic Fans	17.0 (17)	71.0 (70)	4.0 (4)	7.0 (7)	22.0 (4)
Motherwell Fans	44.0 (14)	31.0 (10)	16.0 (5)	9.0 (3)	7.0 (32)
Hibernian Fans	44.0 (8)	22.0 (4)	6.0 (1)	28.0 (5)	4.0 (18)
Dundee United Fans	57.0 (12)	5.0 (1)	33.0 (7)	5.0 (1)	5.0 (1)
St Johnstone Fans	58.0 (19)	3.0 (1)	27.0 (9)	12.0 (4)	7.0 (33)
Column Total	47.0 (206)	30.0 (131)	13.0 (59)	10.0 (44)	100.0 (440)

Table 3.10
Group most likely to get a job

Group	Did not answer	Protestants	Catholics	Don't Know	Row Total
Rangers Fans	12.0 (11)	30.0 (28)	5.0 (5)	53.0 (49)	21.0 (93)
Hearts Fans	10.0 (4)	25.0 (10)	2.0 (1)	62.0 (25)	9.0 (40)
Aberdeen Fans	25.0 (15)	12.0 (7)	2.0 (1)	61.0 (36)	13.0 (59)
Kilmarnock Fans	17.0 (9)	23.0 (12)	4.0 (2)	56.0 (29)	12.0 (52)
Celtic Fans	3.0 (3)	73.0 (72)	3.0 (3)	20.0 (20)	22.0 (98)
Motherwell Fans	25.0 (8)	19.0 (6)	6.0 (2)	50.0 (16)	7.0 (32)
Hibernian Fans	11.0 (2)	22.0 (4)	6.0 (1)	61.0 (11)	4.0 (18)
Dundee United Fans	18.0 (4)	14.0 (3)		68.0 (15)	5.0 (22)
St Johnstone Fans	32.0 (11)	9.0 (3)		59.0 (20)	8.0 (34)
Column Total	15.0 (67)	32.0 (145)	3.0 (15)	49.0 (221)	100.0 (448)

On average over half of the fans who answered the question (table 9) believed the same chance existed for both Protestants and Catholics. A large percentage of them did not know, or did not believe that it mattered which religion a person was when entering the job market. These figures are similar for most of the clubs involved other than Celtic. Almost three quarters of that club's adherents believed that discrimination did exist and was based on one's religious identity.

The fans were also asked which religious group benefited from discrimination (table 10). The most striking answer again emerged from the Celtic fans; three quarters of them believed that Protestants would be most favoured. Approximately one quarter of Rangers, Hearts, Kilmarnock and Hibernian fans agreed with Celtic supporters. These figures are very similar to those of the Northern Ireland Catholic respondents to a similar question in the BSA survey. It would appear plausible therefore that the discrimination and prejudice which often exists in Northern Ireland in employment (see later references), is replicated in some fashion in Scotland.

Conclusion

Overall, these results confirm the main proposition that a religious, cultural, and ethnic cleavage is being played out in many of the stadia of Scottish football, particularly with regards to clubs' interaction with Celtic. The analogies with Northern Ireland, Spain and England are valid in this context.[17]

The outstanding feature of the survey so far is the distinctiveness of the Celtic support on a wide range of issues and attitudes; including attitudes to Northern Ireland, party preference and discrimination. Most Celtic fans also chose Irish symbols over Scottish ones. In addition, they are not on the whole supportive of the Scottish international football team. Indeed, their identity is partly defined by their support for the Republic of Ireland soccer team.

The non-Celtic supporters in the survey do not share social and political attitudes. However, the degree of divergence among them on the questions asked is not so startling or consistent, as the distinction between them and Celtic fans. It is at all times the Celtic, and thus the overwhelmingly Catholic team's support, which is distinct. On a number of questions, including ones relating to Northern Ireland, and in their choice of the father of the Protestant Reformation John Knox as an important symbol of identity for example, Rangers fans adopt polar opposite views to those of Celtic. Nevertheless, many of the Rangers fans do share views with the supporters of other clubs except Celtic.

The comparison between Glasgow Rangers and Motherwell fans is particularly interesting. They share many views, but Motherwell fans, unlike the Rangers ones, ignore the traditional Catholic ties with Labour and give majority support to their own more 'natural' class party. Rangers and Motherwell fans (and to a degree those of Hearts and Kilmarnock), all, except Hearts, from the west and central parts of the country, make a connection between their Protestantism, anti-Catholicism and the Northern Ireland issue. The statistics for Celtic fans reflect their concern with this issue; one that is broadly nationalist in perspective. Dundee United and Hibernian fans show the regional variations which exist within this ethno-religious cleavage commented upon. These are the clubs in which the religious identities so prominent in Scottish football generally, are less clear; their more secular labels are also reflected in the low level of religious commitment of their supporters. They also carry a smaller support than which might be expected from teams from apt locations and who have experienced recent success. Although they have a significant percentage of Catholics among their support, the style and nature of Catholicism here is of a different sort to that of Celtic fans. An Irish background, Irish cultural factors and regular church attendance, are all less important outside of this Celtic environment.

These findings suggest that we need to examine the nature of contemporary Irish immigrant culture - in particular, its vital Catholic component - in Scottish society. This will be the focus of chapter 6. However, the next two chapters analyse the current character of anti-Catholicism and cultural content of Scottish Protestantism in this context.

Notes

1. This related to the then Chief Constable of Manchester's investigation into the shooting dead by the R.U.C of five republican activists, and one civilian in Northern Ireland in the early 1980's; the so called 'shoot to kill' policy.

2. BBC, 'Inside Story Special' 'Enemies Within' 20/11/90.

3. 'The Life Of Brian' 20/5/90.

4. An Phoblact Republican News: 24/10/91.

5. Irish Post: /8/89.

6. Irish News: 13th, 14th, 15th June,1990.

7. An Phoblact Republican News: 9/11/89.

8. Daily Record and Herald: 23/12/91.

9. The Captive Voice, vol. 3, no 2.

10. During the carrying out of the survey, one Kilmarnock fan stated to the interviewer; "there are many people - especially Masons - in Kilmarnock, who were quite prepared to go to Northern Ireland if 'troops out' was threatened, to fight alongside their Protestant/British brethren" .

11. Herald: 29/10/91.

12. Evening Times: 11/5/92. In addition, corresponding to the establishment of 'Rangers Financial Services Limited' in 1993, the club delivered to the homes of 50,000 Rangers supporters (i.e. only those on their mail delivery list) details of this service; itself a reflection of the strength of the clubs support. See Herald, 22/4/93.

13. Figures from the Scottish Football League, 1993/94. Most other 'middle status' clubs (for example Airdrie and Ayr United) average around 2,500 fans for home fixtures, while the lower division of clubs attract an average of 300-600 fans.

14. Quoted by the Catholic Bishop Joseph Devine, in the Scottish Catholic Observer: 28/5/85.

15. Nicholas Fairbairn was Conservative MP for the Perth (and Kinross) area since 1983, until he died in early 1995. The SNP usually generate around one quarter of the vote cast, while Labour are normally the fourth place party

16.   The Glasgow Herald regularly carries out surveys which bear out these figures.

17.   Writing about the first Celtic versus Rangers match of season 1989/90, which was significant for the first appearance of former Celtic star Maurice Johnston; Glasgow Herald writer James Traynor commented (28/8/89); "Johnston's about turn, which delivered him into the embrace of the enemy in return for their coin, had fuelled the primitive prejudice which divides the people of Scotland".

Other Sources:

The Scotsman, for a Celtic profile, 11/7/88; William McIlvanney, 'The Sport of Politics,' in the Glasgow Herald, 10/9/88; and Jack McLean on Rangers and Celtic, in the 'Blue and Green', Glasgow Herald, 23/4/88. 'Not The View'; A Celtic Fanzine. Tiocfaidh ar la: A Celtic Fanzine. 'Follow, Follow'; A Glasgow Rangers Fanzine. 'The Absolute Game'; A Scottish Football Fanzine. Various Scottish Football Club Fanzines.

4 Orangeism in Scotland

Scottish Orangeism is another facet of religious identity in Scotland. Originating in the north of Ireland in the late 18th century (Senior, 1966, p. 153), as a response to nationalist political and agrarian disturbances, it was built upon an anti-Catholic and pro-colonist ideology, which gave a strong backing to all things Protestant within Ireland and Britain. It was first brought to Scotland by soldiers returning to south Ayrshire, who had completed their period as part of the British army in Ireland (Sibbet, 1939).

The Orange tradition has its origins in the colonial campaign in Ireland of 1689-90, when the forces of the Protestant British King William of Orange (though Catholic troops also fought for William) defeated the aspiring Catholic King James's troops and secured British and Protestant supremacy in Ireland; as well as confirming the Protestant ascendancy in Britain itself (the conflict generally having as much to do with political and cultural power as it had to do with religious hegemony). Many of the dates and symbols which for three hundred years have helped sustain the Orange tradition originate in this period.

From its earliest days Orangeism had a belligerent nature, pursuing what they perceived as defensive actions against the growing militancy among the Irish peasantry and opposing any sort of relaxation of the Penal Laws, which basically viewed Catholics as non-persons. Orangeism centred around a growing semi-secret organisation and rapidly spread throughout the colonial settlement of Ireland, having by far its greatest impact in the most heavily settled area, the province of Ulster. From its birth, Orangeism contained; 'a fairly elaborate ritual and system of secret signs and passwords, based loosely on the Freemason tradition and the models of earlier Protestant defensive associations' (McFarland, p. 58).

It is almost certain that many of the men (early Orangeism was for men only) who joined the lodges when they emerged in the south-west and the west of Scotland were Protestant migrants from Ulster. It was probably true that these Protestants, at a time of developing Irish Catholic immigration, desired not only to join together in a sort of Protestant Friendly society, but to set themselves apart from this 'other' immigration, whilst making welcome their Scots co-religionists. As Senior (p. 152) asserts in a similar context:

> in this manner they might hope to protect themselves against the hostility of Catholic Irish immigrants and, at the same time, win the approval of the English who normally regarded Irish immigrants with contempt.

Scotland had its own powerful, and longer, tradition of anti-Catholicism. Its 'equivalent' of the early institution in Ireland was the 'Protestant Association'; an 'ill-defined amalgam of extra-religious and extra-parliamentary forces, 'whose sole intention was to block any progress to Catholic relief. (Black, 1963, pp. 183-211).

This movement was successful and its support widespread. The main point here, is that:

> such early developments are very significant. Above all they emphasise the need for sensitivity towards Scotland's unique cultural and ideological identity in particular underlining the strength of militant Protestant sentiments here, which despite similar themes and rhetoric were articulated quite independently of Orangeism (McFarland, p. 86).

The Protestant Association preceded the Orange Institution in Scotland by over twenty years. It was spread over most of Scotland. McFarland also points out that it had a sizeable bourgeois membership, particularly in Glasgow. 'The Orange Lodges however were concentrated in the West and were strongly proletarian in character' (McFarland, p. 86). A Protestant 'nationalism' and no popery culture provided the Orange Institution with the conditions it needed to make an impact in Scotland.

By 1807 there were Orange lodges in Maybole, Tarbolton, Wigtown, Girvan, Stranraer and Argyle, and by 1813 one in Glasgow. In 1821 the first ceremonial parade took place in Glasgow. The following year the police and the military had to intervene as Irish Catholics confronted the marchers. The year 1824 witnessed the first 12th July demonstration take place in Lanarkshire in the town of Airdrie. Due to the violence engendered at Orange marches, it was the 1840's before such parades began again. This lack of opportunity to publicise their cause probably affected the ability of the Lodge to attract new members and the Institution barely expanded. Nevertheless, it is argued by one of the Institution's historians that Glasgow was a fertile ground for Orange development:

> a city which loyally supported William of Orange in 1689, raising the bulk of the Cameronian regiment from amongst its own citizens greeted the arrival of Bonnie Prince Charlie and his rebel highlanders with scorn; celebrated the centenary of the Glorious Revolution with zeal; in that same year saw 12,000 of its citizens vow to suppress idolatry and block a Catholic Relief Bill; and within a year or two had no less than forty three anti-Catholic societies, more than the number of its Catholic

inhabitants (McCracken, 1990).

The organisation in Scotland was largely made up of the proletariat, which at that time were denied any political muscle. Throughout much of the 19th century, it was an organisation of the 'industrial working class, with possibly also a petty bourgeois component' (McFarland, pp. 131-143). From the very beginning therefore, it differed from its Ulster relation in the complexion of its membership; in Ulster it was intertwined with the powerful elite of colonial society. Local gentry, magistrates, and later industrial magnates all tended towards the Institution in Ireland, seeing it for what it was, a Protestant anti-Catholic organisation. In addition, it was a popular vehicle for maintaining contact with the motherland and for jobs and social advancement at the expense of the native Irish. Political Unionists and Conservatives of consequence thus identified with the Lodge or, at least, with the principles and attitudes it promulgated. Such conditions were not replicated in Scotland as that country's recent political, social and historical past was of a different sort to its neighbour.

Church, class, geography and ideological references

Another distinction in Scottish Orangeism was that it began independently of Scottish Church influence. This remained the case for most of the 19th century until the 1870s, when there was a growing involvement of some ministers with the movement. Orangeism in Ireland was strongly influenced by Episcopalians who had a Hanovarian and Constitutionalist background. However, in Scotland, the Episcopalians were different by way of their history, worship and class. For much of the 19th century in Scotland there were also few Episcopalians. The ritual practices of Scottish Episcopalians was also a factor in distancing them from the incoming Ulster Protestants; this to such an extent that Grand Lodge feared Orangemen from this background becoming unchurched altogether (McFarland, pp. 207-235).

Orangeism gradually became a major form of mass mobilisation in Scotland, especially among the working class, though it has always had middle class members. Although the Order made slow progress in the first half of the 19th century, by the 1850s and 1860s, single Orange demonstrations in Airdrie, Paisley, or Glasgow were attended by five hundred per march. However, as McFarland says (pp. 108-110):

By the early 1860s Orangeism in Scotland had gained a high public profile, but largely in terms of a 'party' or fighting society and certainly not as a credible organisational mechanism for propagating militant Protestantism. For, despite apparently favourable developments in the socio-economic structures and ideological climate of Scotland, the Institution did not attract significant bourgeois or gentry support or even mobilise effectively the anti-Irish sentiments of the Scottish working class. Behind this lay a further failure to anchor itself in the specifically Scottish tradition of anti-Catholicism and appear anything other than a misgrowth and 'unwelcome import'.

79

Despite not being integral to recent Scottish developments, and failing to have any significant impact upon the Highlands, Edinburgh and the east, late in the century it was common to have thirty-thousand at the larger demonstrations. The 1880s and 90s saw Irish Home Rule agitation grow in Ireland and Britain and, as a consequence, Orange numbers and activity further developed. As the Institution entered the new century, official membership stood at around twenty-five thousand with eight thousand of these in Glasgow. Even though official institutional relations with the main Protestant churches in Scotland was weak, a Church of Scotland Report of 1923 was moved to comment, that there was no; 'complaint of the presence of an Orange population in Scotland, they are of the same race as ourselves and are readily assimilated to the Scottish population' (although this was more in reference to the Ulster Scots Protestants than the L.O.I itself).[1]

However, this statement also indicates an attitude towards the Institution which has characterised many Protestants in Scotland. Since the early days, Orange marches had become strongly associated with petty violence and drunkenness. Given this, and its predictability and repetitiveness, marches were poorly reported.[2] The Order suffered because it was perceived as an institution bound up with Irish issues and quarrels. Many Protestants thus greeted the Order with suspicion and hostility because they regarded Protestant respectability as an all important ethos. Although the 1923 Church of Scotland Report empathised with the Institution, there always remained scope for it to distance itself from the more 'degenerative undertones' of Lodge activity. Today there are few if any links between the Church of Scotland and the Orange Institution (although most Orangemen claim to be informal members of the Church) .

At a political level, Scottish Protestant working class adherence to the Conservative Party was influenced by:

> a series of politico-ecclesiastical issues which arose from the 1860s, dramatically convincing Orangemen that their 'Protestant faith' and the 'Protestant nature of the British constitution' were seriously in danger. Crucially, these factors further convinced the LOI that the Liberal Party had profound 'popish' sympathies and the Order should be politicised by offering their active support to the Tories as 'the Protestant Party' - this of course, marking a seachange from the Glorious Revolution when Toryism had Catholic and Jacobite undertones (McFarland, p. 365).[3]

However, the Institution wanted to be regarded primarily as a religious institution; 'too close' links with any party endangered this position. The link then with the Conservatives had to remain a conditional one and it depended upon that party's ability and reputation for forwarding Protestant interests, fighting church disestablishment and combating Irish nationalism. At all times, Protestantism, in the context of a typecast Scots/British nationalism, was the policy of the Grand Lodge in Scotland. As C.I Paton, in his inaugural address as Grand Master in 1875, said:

It is no political participation which is the bound of our union. The principles which animate us belong to a higher and nobler sphere. Political parties are always fluctuating and changing, their watchwords and battle cries are soon forgotten but our principles are not changeable and our course of action must be the same till victory crowns our efforts and till the cry arises 'Babylon is fallen, fallen....'[4]

Church and ideology today

As Roberts argues, despite the Orange Order consistently claiming to be:

> primarily a religious oriented institution in both purpose and practice....the Order has never claimed that its political purposes and activities are unimportant and the function of Orangeism as a creator and preserver of a complex political and social identity need not be regarded as purely a latent one. The motivation for many a member and leader has been political, not religious, and the political endeavours and successes of Orangeism may well be more apparent to non-members and enemies than any religious aspect (1971, pp. 269-282).

It is nevertheless undeniable that religion is intrinsic to the Institutions ideology. The 'Basis of the Institution' in the 'Laws and Ordinances' of Orangeism, states:

> The Institution is composed of Protestants, united and resolved to the utmost of their power to support and defend their rightful sovereign, the Protestant religion, the Laws of thye Realm, the Legislative Union, and the succession to the Throne in the House of Brunswick.

The religious content of Orangeism is clear to aspiring members. A love for, and a steadfastness in, Jesus Christ, 'the only Mediator between God and man', is important as a condition for entry, whilst the new member should:

> love, uphold and defend the Protestant religion, and sincerely desire and endeavour to propagate its doctrines and precepts; he should strenuously oppose the fatal errors of the Church of Rome.[5]

Implicit religious beliefs and practices do lie among the tenets of Orangeism's character, identity and ethos. The consensus of all published Orange opinion shows the clear desire of the leaders that the Orange Order be regarded predominantly as a religious institution.

Despite this, a review of the Orange Torch, the official monthly organ of the Institution in Scotland, reveals that little more than one quarter its contents could be considered religious. Indeed, the largest proportion of this highlighting the 'degeneracy' of Roman Catholicism. Whether historical or contemporary (an appropriate interpretation of history is of vital importance to Orangemen in general), the rest of the content of the monthly is made up of Orange social news and outright political testimonials and articles. For Orangemen, religion, society and politics, cannot be separated while threats from Catholicism and Irish nationalism are persistent and immutable. The Reformation was not simply a religious affair but a social and political revolution. Orangeism sees Catholicism as being alien, disloyal and militantly against the Reformed Order, whilst it also condemns what it views as the lack of civil and religious liberty associated with Roman Catholicism and exemplified in countries with Roman Catholic political influence and 'domination'.[6]

A fusion between the Orange Scottish Protestant faith, British/Scottish patriotism, anti-Catholicism and idea of 'No Surrender', is thus recognisable in Orange thinking:

> In celebrating the Battle of the Boyne and taking the name 'Orange' we recognise with thanksgiving to Almighty God, the services rendered to this nation's people by the Prince of Orange in answering this country's call in a time of great need....The people being predominantly Protestant, secured a Constitutional Monarchy which would recognise the right of its subjects, and the authority of Parliament ensured that the throne, by law, would never again be occupied by a Roman Catholic. It is this first principle of our Constitution that Orangemen and women wholeheartedly support....Our twin pillars are the Protestant faith and loyalty to our Queen and country....[and members] must be both Christian and Patriotic.[7]

In recent years both the Church of Scotland and the Catholic Church have attempted to come closer in ways that might assist in healing centuries old wounds (see Gallagher, 1987, p. 19, p. 263). Although historically the Protestant identity in Scotland has been at odds with the Roman Catholic faith, in 1986 the General Assembly of the Church of Scotland decided that articles containing derogatory references to the Catholic mass, idolaters and the Pope as the anti-Christ, should be removed from the Church's 'Westminster Confession of Faith'. This reflected the ecumenical mood of the 1980's.[8] Regardless of how significant these proceedings have been (joint church services, combined social statements, etc.), the Orange Order in Scotland (as in Northern Ireland) is set against any moves towards ecumenicism, seeing it as a diminution of Protestant identity and inevitably involving subordination to Rome; with all the religious, social and political implications that would entail for Protestant ideology and culture. Orange rhetoric allows a number of Protestants to draw ideological and symbolic boundaries between themselves and their adversaries. In such a process, Orangeism gains a significance for the identities and sub-cultures which prevail in the west-central belt in Scotland.

Regardless of how the prime ecumenical players perceive their own enterprise, the Orange Order in Scotland is clear on its abhorrence of any symptom of Christian (i.e., Protestant and Catholic) togetherness. It condemns the idea that the Roman Catholic and Protestant Churches are simply different branches of the same church; each leading, although by different routes, to the same goal:

> In fact they stand for totally, fundamentally irreconcilably different religions which lead to goals as far separated as hell is from heaven. No Bible-believing Christian can intelligently be, or become, a Roman Catholic[9]

The Orange Institution denies that it is anti-ecumenical, stressing that its followers are members of, or have links with, every Protestant denomination (Table 4.1). In a fundamental religious sense, Orangeism is a part of the Reformed Faith and it welcomes members from any of its various branches. In a more secular vein, it is also claims to be a cultural umbrella covering all the branches. However, they reject any accommodation with the Church of Rome. In doctrinal, social and political matters, the Orange Order in Scotland is absolutely opposed to, and at odds with, the Catholic Church.

Table 4:1
Religious denominations of Orangemen

Church of Scotland	73%
Other Protestant Churches	26%
Other	1%

Organisation and numbers

In the early 18th century the Lodge had only a few hundred members. By the turn of the century they claimed approximately twenty-five thousand members and was one of the strongest and most coherent of groupings within society. Today, the Loyal Orange Institution of Scotland is made up of four County areas; Ayrshire, Glasgow, Central Scotland and the East of Scotland. These Counties are, in turn, made up of sixty-two Districts; the vast majority of which are in Glasgow, Lanarkshire, and Ayrshire. A District is a collection of Lodges in a specific geographical area. The size of a district and the size of the Lodges can vary.

Within a district there exist men's, women's and juvenile lodges, with each lodge having a chaplain, who more often than not will be a layman. There are approximately one thousand lodges throughout the country and their members comprise the Loyal Orange Institution of Scotland. In addition to the 'official' Orangemen, other Protestants participate in the traditional 'bands' which contribute the colour and sound to Orange demonstrations. Only half of the young men and women who march are members of lodges; the rest identify themselves with the movement via this involvement.[10]

In the popular mind, the banner of Orangeism also covers membership of the Imperial Black Chapter of the British Commonwealth or the Royal Black Perceptory. This part of the movement is more secret than the main, or more popular, body, and it concerns itself more with ceremony and ritual. Its members tend to look at themselves as a more respectable arm of the organisation. The status of Orangemen and members of the Royal Black

Perceptory (forthwith also referred to as Orangemen) is marked in relation to a system of degrees. Colour is the most notable symbol of a persons standing within the Order and essentially a higher colour is achieved via a ritual involving knowledge and elaborate interpretation of the scriptures.

There is also the Independent Orange Order, which is a breakaway, more militant, arm of Orangeism. By the early 1990s it was developing a structure and organisation in Scotland based upon its parent body in Northern Ireland. The most prominent member of this organisation in Northern Ireland is Euro MP, Reverend Ian Paisley.

My main concern here is to look at the social significance of the institution and its role as a focal point of identity. To the population at large, the most outstanding feature of Orangeism are the frequent parades and demonstrations. For example, there are approximately fifteen hundred parades in Strathclyde every year. Around half of all police escorted parades in Strathclyde are Orange.[11] West Lothian and Central region experience around half such marches. Various estimates of the size of these demonstrations are disseminated by the Institution, as well as by the media and police. Actual numbers are difficult to judge due to the nature of the 'Walks' themselves. On the most significant day, the Saturday prior to the 12th July each year, many people will engage in varying degrees of involvement in the celebrations.

Many Orange demonstrators will begin their day at around 7.00am by marching around their own locality. Orange members will often march from a central meeting place to their local lodge hall or a bus pick-up point. Full regalia will be worn by the marchers and, frequently, a lodge will be headed by an Orange band who have been hired for the day's events. These bands include both sexes and all age groups, but are typically composed of young men in the sixteen to thirty age group (the Institution itself includes both sexes, and all age groups). The names of many of these bands reflect their intended loyalty to Protestantism, the Crown and the British state.

Demonstrators will march or be driven to a meeting point, where the Institution begins to congregate for the major 'Walk' of the day to a hired ground or park. Here, the Orange hierarchy will make political speeches, say prayers (often with a political content) and propose resolutions. It is quite normal for a sitting Unionist Member of Parliament from Northern Ireland, who himself will more than likely be a member of the Northern Irish side of the Order, to be invited to Scotland to make the appropriate speeches. John Taylor, Rev Robert McCrea and Rev Martin Smyth were all frequent visitors in the 1980s and 1990s.

In 1990 in Scotland, the main Boyne demonstrations took place on the 7th July, and apart from the inclement weather (which inevitably depressed crowd numbers), it was a typical 'Big Walk' occasion. Approximately 8,000-10,000 demonstrators walked in Glasgow on the day, with the same amount of followers and active onlookers. The numbers marching in Glasgow approached twenty thousand.[12] The County Grand Lodge of Central Scotland held its demonstration on the same day in the village of Shotts in Lanarkshire. At the same time, around five-thousand marchers and five-thousand supporters were on parade in Renfrew, Ayrshire.

These figures (probably a few thousand fewer than usual due to the poor weather) suggest that around forty-five thousand people in the west and central Scotland areas were actively celebrating the annual Boyne commemorations in 1990. However, this does not accurately reflect the number of participants who share in the Orange 'identity'. Many bands and lodges will depart from, and return to, well wishers and celebrants whose involvement in the big day is limited to contributing numerically to these and other stages of the occasion. Often a village, a housing development or a part of a town, will have its own symbolic focal point where people will congregate to enjoy a short period of the spectacle and where a degree of solidarity is expressed with the main marchers.[13] Many of these people will join the marchers on their return in the social atmosphere of an Orange social club. For these reasons the figure of forty-five thousand Orange Lodge members and ardent followers, can reasonably be doubled if we count those who make a minimal, though significant, contribution to the day's events. All this suggests that the frequently self-quoted formal Orange Lodge membership figures of eighty-thousand,[14] includes all active sympathisers. Even if this figure intentionally inflates the formal membership, such sympathisers clearly share important elements of an Orange identity.

Nevertheless, the July march is the major demonstration of the year, every year in Scotland. As a comparison, 1989/90 witnessed the most notable anti-Poll Tax demonstrations in Scotland, demonstrations about a highly contentious political issue which affected millions of families and individuals and from all classes of people. Various demonstrations attracted thousands of marchers. However the largest demonstration in mid 1990 attracted thirty-thousand. Similarly, as few as three to six thousand congregated on the streets of Glasgow to march for peace on the eve of the threatened war in the Gulf.[15] Although Orangeism is very much steeped in a 'Walk' culture and this probably contributes to the popularity of its annual occasion, in Scotland Orangeism remains the greatest popular manifestation of overt cultural, religious and political activity (each of these will vary in nature, emphasis and content depending on the individuals concerned). It attracts the largest numbers and it does so on a consistent basis.

The Institution's greatest strength is its capacity as a strong social organisation to provide a key focus of identity. In addition, it provides a social centre in much of the West-Central belt. A number of lodges collectively own social clubs which provide an Orange environment for drinking and other activities.[16] There are around thirty of these clubs in which not only Orange members, but people who have a sympathy for or feel comfortable in such surroundings, spend free time. An obvious empathy, solidarity and identity is expressed by a social life which either revolves around, or frequently experiences, such a setting. The Bellshill club in Lanarkshire, for example, has a membership of six-hundred people, while it is regularly visited by many others who do not feel the need to become formal members, but who are sufficiently associated with the attitudes that the Institution embraces to be drawn towards its social network and culture.

Orangeism's position as a focus of social activity is clearly one of the reasons why it remains potent in today's society. For the Lodge, the development of a social club presents a pragmatic manoeuvre in a society with countless counter attractions.

The extent, if not the vitality, of Lodge membership (and associated membership), is the most overt indication of organised Scottish anti-Catholicism. It is an anti-Catholicism which is often identified with the 'Troubles' in Northern Ireland.[17] With the upsurge in the troubles in the late 1960s and early 1970s, the Institution apparently experienced a consequential rise in membership applications, though Grand Lodge is reluctant to quantify this rise.

My survey of Lodge members recorded their attitudes to Northern Ireland and their role in relation to Orange solidarity. More broadly, the survey results provide an indicator of the various social and political attitudes shared by an organised and formal body of strident and uncompromising Protestant identity.

It is not surprising given that the Orange Institution has throughout its Scottish history continually referred to its Irish concerns, that Scottish Orangemen are nearly unanimous on the issue; firmly believing that Northern Ireland should remain within the UK (Table 4.2). Comparatively speaking, and in reference to the football findings, they stand at the opposite end of the continuum from Celtic fans. In addition, they are similar to, but more homogeneous than, Rangers fans.

Table 4.2
Orange solution to Northern Ireland conflict

Remain in the UK	98%
Reunify with the rest of Ireland	0%
Other answer	1%
Don't know	1%

With regards to the issue of a British troop withdrawal; 87 per cent oppose such a 'solution' (Table 4.3). Although large numbers of Church of Scotland attenders and football fans also prefer this option, again Lodge members are more united on this issue. Similarly, most (79 per cent) believe that a united Ireland in twenty years time is very unlikely (see Table 4.4).

Table 4.3
Orange views on withdrawal of British troops from Northern Ireland

Support strongly	7%
Support a little	3%
Oppose strongly	84%
Oppose a little	4%
Don't know	3%

Table 4.4
Orange prediction on united Ireland

Very likely	2%
Quite likely	2%
Quite unlikely	15%
Very unlikely	79%
Don't know	2%

The results confirm that a strong correlation of attitudes and beliefs concerning the national and political condition of Northern Ireland is a central aspect of a certain kind of Protestant identity in Scotland. Any move which is perceived as threatening the integrity of the Northern Ireland state, and as a consequence the hegemony of the Protestant-unionist population, is firmly rejected by Scottish Orangemen.

The 'New Ireland Forum' was set up within Ireland in the early 1980s to discuss a possible solution to the Northern Ireland conflict. It consisted of most shades of political opinion in Ireland, except that of Sinn Fein who were excluded and the Unionist parties (although invited) who refused to participate. In 1984 its proposals were rejected out of hand by the Grand Lodge in Scotland, as they also were by British premier Margaret Thatcher:[18]

> Joint authority between the United Kingdom and a foreign state, the Republic of Ireland, would be abhorrent to the majority in the United Kingdom and unworkable without the co-operation of the Ulster Unionist people.

As a protest against the signing of the Anglo-Irish Agreement, Orangemen in Scotland attempted to organise politically in some constituencies for the 1987 General Election. However, the relative insignificance of Northern Ireland as an election issue in Britain and the positive light in which the Anglo-Irish Agreement was presented, proved an insurmountable barrier for this grouping. Their lack of political leadership, a perfunctory pre-election performance, an underlying if intermittent fear of violence in Northern Ireland spreading to Scotland, its lack of credibility with the press and the fact that Orangeism is also significant in areas where Labour is traditionally the main Party meant that, despite Orangeism's popular appeal, this initiative had no impact. (It has also been suggested by one political observer that in Ayrshire, where the new party was threatening to stand candidates, local Conservatives acknowledged the potential negative impact upon their own constituency and informally requested that the new Party refrain from challenging them [19]).

Nevertheless, in protest at the Agreement, Orange leaders in Scotland did advise Orange Conservative voters to turn away from Conservatism in the election.[20] In 1987, although the Conservative Party won in its third consecutive term in office, its vote and number of seats in Scotland fell dramatically. Of course, Mrs Thatcher was popularly seen in Scotland as being unconcerned with the economic condition of people in Scotland during much of her premiership (indeed, she was popularly perceived as having added to it) and this was clearly a major factor affecting the fall in her party's Scottish support. Nevertheless, haemorrhaging of the working-class 'Orange vote' (see table 4.6), may also have been a factor. Four years later Mrs Thatcher conceded that she believed; 'The Anglo-Irish Agreement had alienated some pro-Ulster supporters in crucial constituencies'.[21] In all probability, this information derived from the grass roots of the party and was detected during pre-election campaigning. Many, if not most, of these pro-Ulster supporters would have been members and supporters of the Orange Institution in Scotland; they after all are the very people who feel so strongly about the political situation there.

The Orange Institution of Scotland are vehemently and vigorously opposed to all aspects of Irish nationalism. Orange opinion in Scotland simply reflects Orange opinion in Northern Ireland on such matters. Political communication between Britain and the Irish Republic on extradition matters, border security, etc, have all been frequent concerns of Lodge members in Scotland. They are also involved in confrontations with anyone in Scotland and Ireland who support closer relations with the Irish Republic. Such attitudes have clearly reflected in the statements from Grand Lodge itself:

> Ban Sinn Fein! It is utterly incredible that the organisation everyone knows is a mere political front for the IRA has not been proscribed long ago. Introduce selective internment now! Today we are told that the IRA godfathers are 'known'. If the legal system is not adequate for the situation - let's get the terror leaders locked away now![22]

Political identity

Orange Order affinity for the Conservatives may seem contrary to the largely working class make-up of Orange membership and identifiers (Table 4.5). Almost three-quarters of Orangemen in my survey identify themselves in skilled, semi or unskilled manual employment, while slightly more indicate their father as having a similar kind of job for most of his life.

Table 4.5
Social status: Orange employment

Skilled manual	42%
Semi or unskilled manual	43%
Professional or technical	5%
Management or administration	6%
Clerical	1%
Sales	2%
Never had a job	1%

There are many more Orange Lodge members supporters of the Conservative Party than amongst any of the other groups surveyed. In addition, these statistics are substantially above both the Scottish and British ones for Conservative support. This is evidence of an accent on cultural, religious and political matters important to Orangemen. It clearly reveals the legacy of the noted 19th century attachment to the Tories. It also gives some substance to Orange claims that they have a degree of political coherence (though in all likelihood much smaller than they argue) and have the capacity to affect electoral results in a few parts of Scotland.

Table 4.6
Orange political party support

Labour	17%	Conservatives	52%
Liberal democrats	1%	S.N.P	15%
Other	3%	None	13%

This affinity with Conservatism is succinctly summarised by two leading Orangemen in Scotland:

> We haven't deserted the Tories, it is they who have deserted us....Thousands of ordinary working-class Orangemen have loyally supported the Tory Party because they were regarded as the Party of the Union and the Constitution. It is unbelievable to us that the so called Conservative and Unionist Party could flagrantly breach the Union by agreeing to Dublin interference in a sovereign part of the United Kingdom....So be it. If the Union is no longer safe in Mrs Thatcher's hands, we will just have to rid ourselves of Margaret Thatcher (Scottish Grand Master, Magnus Bain).

> One of the many things the Tories fail to appreciate is that thousands of Scottish Orangemen and women vote Conservative, not because of any political or economic policy, but because they see that as representing the sovereignty of the Queen and the unity of the United Kingdom. (Grand Secretary of the Grand Lodge of Scotland).[23]

Table 4.6 also indicates that Labour Party support among Orangemen is dramatically lower than that among any other grouping surveyed (apart from the much smaller grouping of St Johnstone football fans at 12 per cent). This reflects the organisations often strong antipathy towards the Labour Party. However, it is more difficult to determine the wider Orange communities ties to the Conservative Party and alienation from Labour, though the above can be considered to be a partial indicator of this. Antagonism for Labour Party beliefs and actions exists at both national and local levels. For example, the Labour Committee on Ireland, and Labour MPs noted for their 'unorthodox' political views on Northern Ireland, are constantly condemned.[24]

However, despite some degree of Orange support for Labour (and indeed some Orangemen's membership of and involvement with the Party) there are many examples of Orange vitriol being directed towards that Party, especially in Scotland. It is also within an ethno-religious frame of reference that this criticism and derision becomes particularly conspicuous. Although non-Orangemen may see it as some form of Orange paranoia, the following piece from the Orange Torch (ironically, a similar quote is reproduced in chapter 5, this time originating from a Scottish Church source), is quoted at length to give an indication of some of the thinking behind such criticism:

> For years it has been evident to discerning people that like the Eirish in New York, Glasgow's Roman Catholics, at least 98% of post-1870 Eirish stock, are out to capture civic power in Glasgow by the infiltration of the Labour Party. As part of a wider ambition to rule Britain, including Scotland, through their grip on the media, the trade unions, and the 'Labour' Party. Study the [Irish-Catholic] names of some of the 'Labour' candidates elected....What do Glasgow's Protestant clergymen think of this situation? What do the genuine patriots, in the SNP's rank-and-file, think about it? There are thousands of men and women of distinction in Glasgow, in medicine, financial expertise, commerce, industrial management, technology, etc., etc., not forgetting the teaching staffs at the universities, and how do they relish the thought of their city - the birthplace too of so many famous Scots - being run by a bunch of Roman Catholics of immigrant Eirish stock (that's 'nationalism' not 'racialism') hardly outstanding for their talents, culture, or general education? Some Glasgow Roman Catholics may claim to be 'lapsed' Roman Catholics (who never criticise their Church), but they are never 'lapsed' Eirishmen! There isn't a Scoto-Eirishman in Scotland, a Lally, a Murphy, or a Gaffney, who is not Eirish under his skin. Scratch them and their Eirish bit comes out. That is why their priests are so committed to segregated schooling. To teach them 'history' with a Roman Catholic and Eirish slant. To pump into them whatever politics suits at the time and place. The children leave the Roman Catholic schools in this country semi-prepared or conditioned to vote Labour. Just as something new, Cromwell's 'Model Army', had to be brought into being to beat Charles 1 army, something new - a new instrument, a new method or technique, must be created to overcome Catholic action in Scotland, and the place to start is in Glasgow, and in the municipal struggle in Glasgow[25]

Irish immigration to Scotland, Irish Catholic and Scottish Protestant identities and nationalisms, 17th century religious wars in Britain and the issue of Catholic schooling, are clearly all crucial issues for the Orange Institution. The framework of identity which derives from an emphasis upon these historical and contemporary foci, help construct both a core of contempt and a background against which to make anti-Catholicism an everyday live issue. An absolute line is drawn between the identity of the native Scot and that of the immigrant Irish or 'Eirish'. The political intention is clearly to portray the Labour Party as dominated by Catholics.[26] As such, this view sees Protestants wasting their vote on the Labour Party, at the expense of fellow Protestants in the Conservatives. The Orange view is that it is a Protestant's patriotic duty to vote for the party which best guarantees the national identity. Such a wasted vote also allows the immigrants to make their way in Scottish society.

Despite Orange polemics, between 1920 and 1974, 'only 16 per cent of [Glasgow's] councillors were Catholics, with no tendency for the number to increase towards the end of the period' (Keating, Levy, Geekie, Brand, 1989). However, by the late 1980's half of Glasgow's councillors described their religion as Catholic; this is twenty per cent above the proportion of Catholics in the city's population and therefore calculated to draw strong criticism from Orangemen. As far as Orangemen were concerned this was compounded by the fact that until early 1995 the previous seven of Glasgow's Lord Provosts elected by the council were also Catholics.

Antipathy towards political representatives who are also Catholic seems to be based on tribalistic considerations.[27] There is no evidence indicating any biased treatment for the city's Catholics as against its Protestant population. Indeed, the council hosted a civic reception for the Institution to commemorate their Tercentenary celebrations of the Boyne victory (as did other councils - Motherwell and Monklands for example). This seems to suggest that many councillors were apprehensive or politically cautious about being identified as Catholic.[28]

Disdain for Labour, as well as disillusion with the Conservatives, may have contributed to the recent rise in the number of young militant right-wingers. The growth, numbers and prominence of those associated with militant 'far right' politics in Scotland is of increasing social and political significance. The organisers of these parties and bodies acknowledge as likely sources of new members both Orange Institution and Glasgow Rangers supporters.[29] In England, race has become an important cleavage; in Scotland many tensions have revolved around religion. 'Extremist' right-wing parties recognise this and build on 'sectarianism' which resonates with, and relates to, much of the nationalist ideology which exists within the Orange and Rangers sub-cultures. Where talk in far right circles in England may be about a Jewish conspiracy, in Scotland, as can be seen from this evidence, the talk is of a Papish conspiracy. In addition, British National Party and the National Party activity has been strongly in evidence outside the football grounds of a number of Scottish clubs, including Rangers, Motherwell, Hearts and Dundee.[30]

Identity and hegemony

In a similar way to that which evokes the Northern Ireland Protestants' siege mentality,[31] Scottish Orangemen are particularly conscious of Catholic social advancement within Scotland. They are firmly of the belief that this Catholic 'advancement' is to the detriment and at the expense of the indigenous population.

The field of employment reflects a pre-occupation with possible Catholic or immigrant advancement. This is an area which is important to Orangemen in that it is viewed as reflecting Protestant dominance in cultural, social and political matters. Unlike any of the other 'Protestant' groupings surveyed, a large number of Orangemen believe there exists the possibility of job discrimination in favour of Roman Catholics (tables 4.7 and 4.8). This opinion, strongly contrasts with those of Catholic Celtic supporters, and Catholics generally (chapter 6), who believe that Protestants are more likely to find favour in the job market. Nonetheless, given Orange-Protestant ideology, it seems plausible that Orangemen would actively discriminate against Catholics in employment or other fields.

Such an attitude was partly reflected in a speech by Independent-Orange-Unionist MP, Mr Ian Paisley, in 1959. Speaking to fellow Protestants in east Belfast about housing for Protestants and Catholics, he said:

> You people of the Shankill Road, what's wrong with you? Number 425 Shankill Road - do you know who lives there? Forte's ice-cream shop, Italian Papists on the Shankill Road! How about 56 Aden Street? For 97 years a Protestant lived in that house and now there's a papisher in it. Crimea Street, number 38! Twenty-five years that house has been up, 24 years a Protestant lived there but there's a Papisher there now.[32]

Table 4.7
Protestants and Catholics: perceived job chances

	Orange Lodge	Church of Scotland
Same chance	52%	66%
Different chance	41%	16%
Doesn't matter	5%	10%
Don't know	2%	8%

Table 4.8
Group most likely to get a job

	Orange Lodge	Church of Scotland
Protestant	14%	9%
Catholic	31%	5%
Don't know	44%	64%

Ian Paisley's argument has a resonance for the contemporary Orange Institution in Scotland, and this is reflected in an article in the movement's Scottish paper:

> Two top positions for officials in Strathclyde Region are expected to come up soon and even before the advertising starts Roman Catholics are being tipped for the posts....In the field of education there is a vacant post created by the retirement of Dan

Burns from the position of Senior Depute Director of Education but even before the post was advertised, four names were being mentioned, three of them Roman Catholics. Interesting in a region where overall RC's are probably less than 25% of the population.[33]

One other result from tables 4.7 and 4.8 is worth noting. The 'us and them' mindset, which invokes an image of watchfulness against Catholic and Irish transgressions and progress, is shown to be of much less overall concern to the Protestants of the Church of Scotland generally. The idea of an ongoing conflict with Catholic and Irish forces officially holds little appeal for the Church; this represents a gradual change from the era prior to the Second World War when the opposite was the case (See S.J. Brown, 1991, pp. 19-45).

Football, ethnicity and other questions

Maintaining the theme of football as a social and political mechanism through which to enter the larger society, we find that the majority of Lodge members surveyed, and who answered the football question, supported Glasgow Rangers. Other teams supported were Hearts, Motherwell, Queens Park, St Mirren, Partick Thistle and Airdrie, as well as a number of junior and amateur teams. Although Bryce states, 'all Orangemen are not Rangers supporters, and all Rangers supporters are not Orangemen,' it is unsurprising to find a strong correlation between the two. This connection is also reflected in the fact that Orangemen conduct their annual religious service each summer in Ibrox stadium. This occasion attracts an estimated fifteen thousand.[34]

Although its probable that the vast majority of the Orange community regard Glasgow Rangers as their sporting representatives, the fact that they are also to be found at other clubs indicates the widespread infusion of Orange-linked attitudes outwith a Rangers-only environment.

Like many other football fans (apart from those of Celtic), and indeed like many of the other people surveyed, most Orangemen (see Table 4.9) favoured no other international football team than Scotland (63 per cent). Nevertheless, 27 per cent mentioned one of Northern Ireland, England and Holland. Again, these three are the countries which play an historically symbolic role as part of the psychological framework that contributes to British-Ulster loyalism.

Table 4.9
Orangemen supporting other international teams

None	63%
Northern Ireland	12%
England	8%
Holland	6%
British countries	1%
Other	9%

The question of ethnic origin presents a number of problems for Orangemen. In the early part of the last century for example, many Orangemen came to Scotland from Ulster to look for work and a large number of these were crucial to the Institutions' development here. Of course, these people were part of a settler community in Ireland which itself originated mainly from Scotland. What we have therefore is an interesting question as to how Orangemen articulate their own 'ethnicity', bearing in mind their indeterminate genealogical past.

Reflecting the history of the Institution in Scotland, a number of Orangemen denote themselves as Irish (clearly invoking Northern Ireland or Ulster), with 6 per cent claiming Irish ancestry and 13 per cent claiming both an Irish and a Scottish background. Presumably, a number of those who identified themselves as British (14 per cent) also fall into this category, though of course the wholly British identity is also important to Orangemen. Again, this wholeness (i.e., a sort of amalgam of the nations of Britain) of the British identity is reflected by the 6 per cent who ticked a number of boxes; Scottish, British, English, Irish, etc. The dominant identity nonetheless was Scottish, with half of the Orange respondents giving this as their ethnic identity. Nonetheless, this is the lowest percentage of respondents stating a solely Scottish identity among all the groups of Protestants studied.

Ulster Protestants also identify themselves in a multitude of ways (British, Ulster, Northern Irish), and their report of their ethnic identity is often affected by the context and situation in which they find themselves. There is no unanimity (see Bell, 1976). This variety of identities reflects the number of heritages which are interrelated. This is one of the reasons why Ulster Protestants can identify with Scotland. So one commentator declared in a TV documentary that young male Derry Protestants found their identity in Scotland with Glasgow Rangers. These Derry Protestants were almost certainly also members of the Orange Institution in Northern Ireland.[35] The overriding and most important aspect of these identities is the Protestant one.

The idea of Protestant identity assuming the proportions of a national one is logical when one considers the importance placed by Orangemen on an interaction of religious, historical, national, cultural and political matters. It would appear to be the case that many Orangemen in Scotland are more interested in their Protestant identity than a Scottish one, and this is reflected in the spread of nationalist ties, though all within a British context. The comparatively lesser emphasis on a Scottish identity is also affected by strong Orange affiliation with various British symbols (the Monarchy, the Union flag, etc.) and this invariably affects the perception of having a singular Scottish identity. Orangemen are still Scottish, but their sense of Scottishness is very much influenced by their powerful sense of also being British.

The vast majority (73 per cent) of Lodge members cite themselves as members of the Church of Scotland (Table 4.1). However, there are also a strong number (26 per cent) of the brethren attached to other Protestant churches (among them, the Baptists, Pentecostals, Memorials, etc.). According to one member of the Institutions hierarchy in Scotland, Danny Houston, there is in fact an increase in the number of members who are becoming attached to other Protestant churches as opposed to the Church of Scotland. It is argued that much of this is related to the national church increasingly 'detaching itself from the Reformed tradition', and many people of an Orange leaning turning instead to these other churches. Elsewhere, it has been claimed that the Church of Scotland is losing somewhere in the region of twenty-thousand of its members per year whilst such evangelical churches (churches which on the whole are fundamentalist and more strictly based within the Reformed tradition) have been expanding.[36]

According to the survey, and contrary to popular belief (particularly that of Catholics and Church of Scotland church attenders), most Lodge members are regular church attenders (table 4.10). This is unlikely to be the case in the larger Orange community, who generally see their Protestantism in a more secular light. In this survey, half of the Institutions membership claim to attend church weekly, and almost one quarter go either once or twice per month. Accepting the possibility of deception, for the Brethren have an obligation to attend church regularly, it is clear that such figures are high, and do display a strong formal religious attachment. The homogeneity of this religious attachment is confirmed by the answers to the question concerning the faith of the respondent's marital partner (table 4.11). All married Orangemen (the term also includes Orange 'women') married someone of the Protestant faith; the proportion was significantly higher than among the other Protestant groups surveyed.

Table 4.10
Orange attendance at church

Once or more per week	46%
Every two weeks	12%
Every month	11%
Sometimes	28%
Once a year	1%
Never	2%

Table 4.11
Orange marital partner

Church of Scotland	73%
Other Protestant	27%

Another significant element in Orange identity is their strong affinity with the 'defenders of the faith'; the Queen, and the Royal Family. For Orangemen, the Royal Family symbolises the Protestantism that was instituted with the rule of King William during the 'Glorious Revolution'. It is contemporary evidence of the victory over Popery and an everlasting representation of Protestant hegemony in Britain itself.

Not surprisingly therefore, we find an almost complete feeling amongst the members of the Institution that the Royal Family are very important. Such a view is largely shared by Church of Scotland attenders (71 per cent) and football fans (61 per cent), which indicates the extent to which the Royal Family are a popular Protestant and national, even patriotic, image. In addition, a System Three Poll (Scotland) of October-November 1994 (conducted during a strained period for the Institution), concurred with these figures, finding that sixty seven per cent of the Scottish population 'supported' the Monarchy. [37]

Considering the questions connected to 'ascriptive identity', the Irish symbols of Padraic Pearse, the Harp, W.B Yeats, the Wolfe Tones, St Patrick and the Shamrock had almost no significance for Orangemen. Only three Lodge members chose St Patrick and one chose the Harp. This non-identification with such symbols is shared with most other Protestants in the survey.

In contrast, 47 per cent of Lodge members choose the Thistle, 26 per cent the Scottish folk hero Robert the Bruce and 37 per cent decided upon the Bagpipes. These are of course well developed Scottish symbols; although strongly regarded, they are not overly regarded by a large number of the brethren. The Corries were opted for by a very small 7 per cent of the Institutions members; possibly reflecting the popularity of an Orange rather than a Scottish repertoire of songs. But this also ties in with their comparatively weaker single dimensional Scottish identity at the expense of a British one, and their sense of exposing British nationalist songs rather than simply Scottish ones (characteristic of the Corries), which would be perceived as diminishing and undermining the wholeness of their British identity. In addition, Robert the Bruce is of a lesser importance to Orangemen than to Church of Scotland attenders; Orange or more perceptively British heroes are probably viewed with greater esteem.

Two key Scottish historical figures received great recognition. The foremost figure of the Scottish Reformation, John Knox, was chosen by a massive 87 per cent of Lodge members; this number far outweighing the one third of Church of Scotland church attenders and football fans who chose likewise. Such a display of attachment (especially when compared to those of the Church of Scotland) demonstrates the way that Scottish Orangemen consider themselves to be among the chief standard bearers of Scottish Protestantism. The other celebrated figure, Robert Burns (79 per cent), is also extremely popular with the national church goers and football fans (other than Celtic fans). The popular 'Burns Suppers' are a feature of Orange Lodge functions and thus many members find it natural to recognise Burns.

Conclusion and perspective

Given its geographical, social and political limitations, Orangeism is a prominent cultural, religious and patriotic body in, and facet of, Scottish society. However, despite Scottish religious origins, Scottish Orangeism is often perceived as being bound up with Irish issues (though they are consequently also British issues). Initially, indigenous anti-Catholicism only had a partial relationship to Orangeism. Orangeism in Scotland became an adjunct to an already existing anti-Catholic culture. Orangeism is unambiguous, confrontational and bellicose. For many Scots, Orangeism has always been an Irish phenomenon. Historically therefore, it has been relatively easy to castigate, even on the part of others with anti-Catholic feelings. This, in large part, explains its failure to put down strong roots in the northern and eastern parts of the country, areas that have long had their own specific tradition of anti-Catholicism.

Nonetheless, a substantial number of Scots have also adopted Orangeism as their own. As Catholic immigration from Ireland developed in the west-central belt in the 19th century, so too did Orangeism; an ideology and an identity seemingly more relevant as Protestant proximity to Catholics grew. The Orange Order provided an institutional setting for the expression of anti-Catholicism within the most heavily populated area of Scotland. Orangeism gradually became attached 'to already existing bitterness towards Roman Catholics, now particularly focusing on Irish immigrants' (McFarland, 1986, p. 91). Ulster Protestants settled in similar areas to Irish Catholics, and proximity engendered friction and a sharpening of identities for all factions; including indigenous Scots who recognised their affinity with their Ulster brethren. Accordingly, Orangeism has grown in Scotland in two related ways. It grew where Ulster Protestant migrants settled and, in a related sense, as an indigenous Scottish reaction (though clearly not the sole one) to Catholic immigration from Ireland.

Although, Orangemen claim not to be against Catholics as such, but against their Church, this is an empty distinction. The following quotations, taken from a Scottish Television documentary as well as from personal interviews, reflect some of the opinions of Orange-people of Catholics:

a. The Orange Walk is the 'mass anniversary of what we can do against Catholics'

b. 'We're anti-Catholic, and that's it. We don't like them'

c. 'I'm sure God would quite enjoy it' (talking of the Orange Walk)

d. 'He's not God to Catholics; he's only God to Protestants'

e. 'We are keeping the Protestant religion. If it wasn't for us and the likes of us you would have no Church of Scotland....in fact the Church of Scotland ministers have let us down....People aren't going to Church because they are bringing Roman Catholic priests into our Churches'

f. 'Separate schools are all wrong, they lead to bigotry. As well as that, there should be more of the Protestant religion in our schools'

g. 'There is no democracy and fairness here anymore. Power is important in all this, and Catholics have it out of all proportion to their numbers in Scotland'.[38]

These comments typify some of the attitudes of rank and file Orange people. Strikingly, these answers are also quite specific to Scotland. Although it is vital to the Orange identity, none of these interviewees mentioned Northern Ireland. Despite an appropriate version of history being crucial to Orange identity, to the rank and file Orangeman it is everyday and experienced perceptions in Scotland which count most.

Although Orangeism has a profound historical symbolism attached to it, contrary to much disparaging commentary, it is mainly about the present. It does not simply remind Catholics that they (Protestants) are there; 'Orangeism thrives on an apparently contradictory combination of defensiveness and triumphalism, the outpouring of anger'.[39] Despite its various limitations, Orangeism is a popular feature of Scottish life. It is patriotic and a nationalism of sorts. For many people, it is the only or at least, the most substantial statement that they will ever make about themselves and their attitudes to religion, culture and nation.

Almost a sixth of the Scottish population is Roman Catholic, yet Orange perceptions are of a numerical threat and a Catholic social and political assault. This relates to traditional Scottish fears, but is partly an Ulster perception and partly to do with the significant numbers of Catholics in areas in the west of the country. Orange anti-Catholicism therefore has remained most relevant, and indeed most strong, in the Scottish areas of Catholic settlement, where head counts are important, and where siege like mentalities and low level conflict related relationships often dominate. Historically, there was economic, social and political competition in these areas, real or imagined; Ulster like situations were replicated, and Orangeism did directly replace or become an important adjunct to Scottish anti-Catholicism.

The theological antagonism displayed towards Catholicism is clear; that the Institution is anti-Irish is also evident throughout its statements and literature. The Order, and those who identify with it in Scotland, appear to be engaged in a low level tribal struggle against the offspring of Irish Catholic immigrants. Though vehemently denied by the Institution itself, sectarian and ethnic rivalry are intrinsic to the character of Orangeism in Scotland.

Overall, in political terms the organisation and Orangeism itself remain a negligible force in Scotland. Unlike in Northern Ireland, contemporary Orangeism in Scotland does not have the same political orientation in terms of British politics. Orangemen in Scotland are inhabitants of the British state and other local and national politics can predominate.

It is an identity combining a strong emphasis on monarchy and a Protestant perspective on history. This identity is infused with an overriding affinity with Northern Ireland Unionists-Loyalists and, almost invariably, their political orientation is defined as against Roman Catholics. An Orangeman's political outlook in Scotland is defined by these perceptions on the one hand and the realities of British politics on the other.

Nonetheless, with such significant numbers associated with it, and in the context of the identity it conveys, it clearly effects political attitudes and perceptions in many of the working-class constituencies of the west-central belt. Mrs Thatcher's admission of the importance in the constituencies of the loss of some of the Scottish Unionist vote, because of the signing of the Anglo-Irish Agreement, seems to verify this analysis. Orangeism provides the Scottish Conservatives with considerable working class support which they might otherwise not attract (a Protestant identity is one of the main characteristics of the Scottish Conservative vote. See chapters 3 and 5).[40]

However, the nature and concerns of the British political system and how it is shaped by the mass media, work against the overriding occupations of the Orange mind. They help to impart a negative, as well as a perceived anachronistic image and perception, upon many Orange enterprises and interests.

With reference to the survey and Orange literature generally, it is clear that there exists a widespread potential support for the Conservative Party within the Orange movement. However, generally in Scotland there also seems to be a limited hankering for a politics over emphasised with 'sectarian' factors. So long as the emphasis in Scotland is upon 'higher politics' (i.e., British, European and World issues), there seems little likelihood of overt sectarian politics coming to the fore. Thus, the Conservatives are also limited in capitalising on images sometimes viewed in certain areas of Scotland as having the potential to 'over divide' (i.e., images perceived by Catholics as akin to an overly Protestant image of Britain/Scotland).[41]

Orangeism too is assured of its place in the west-central belt's social and cultural make-up, because of the many Orange social clubs that function. The pub or club provides a major social outlet for many people. For many working class Protestants the Orange hall dominates much of their social lives. The Orange social network provides a setting for the transmission of both ideology and identity. Indeed, the existence of this social setting makes Protestantism undemanding for many, replacing as it does church membership and attendance. It is generally held true that non-churchgoing is dominant amongst rank and file Orange supporters, in the same way that it is prevalent amongst Rangers football supporters. Orangeism is also the prime manifestation of a secular Protestant identity.

Orangeism generally exists at a distance from the national Church (unlike in Northern Ireland where it intertwined with the Protestant churches). The Church of Scotland, both as an institution and in terms of its congregation, have for long been characterised in terms of a vision of Scottish respectability. For some Protestants the Orange Order has not always been respectable, though it has long coveted this image. The Order's problem is also reflected in the popular perceptions of its demonstrations being associated with alcohol abuse and sometimes petty violence. This means that the Masonic Order in Scotland rather than the Orange Order has been the respectable organisation for many Scots with anti-Catholic prejudices.

Orangeism in Scotland consists of a particular kind of patriotism. For Orangemen, religious perspectives intertwine and co-exist at many junctures with political and social ones. Despite its limitations, Orangeism is a significant and powerful source of social, cultural and political identity in west-central Scotland. It exists in Scotland as a religious, cultural, political and social counter to all Catholic development; that is the main enemy of Scottish Orangeism today.

Notes

1.   Report of the Committee to Consider the Overtures on Irish Immigration and the Education (Scotland) Act 1918, pp750-761.

2.   See Glasgow Herald reports for the late 19th and early 20th centuries.

3.   The Liberal Party's Disestablishment and Disendowment of the Church of Ireland late in the century also helped convince Orangemen (and indeed many other Protestants) of the Popish influence upon that party. The upsurge in Irish nationalism with the rise in Fenian activity was to further engineer such a mode of thinking. With an Ulster background to many Orangemen, these events were particularly galling.

4.   Glasgow News, November 1885.

5.   See, Laws and Ordinances of the Loyal Orange Institution of Ireland, Dublin, 1896, pp1-2.

6.   Orange Torch, Feb. 1986.

7.   Rev Gordon McCracken in the Orange Torch, July/August 1984.

8.   See The Scotsman and the Glasgow Herald reports of the General Assembly, May 1986.

9.   Orange Torch, Feb 1986.

10. Information from the Orange Institution.

11. Focal Point; 'No Surrender' BBC Scotland, 20/11/90.

12   These numbers were counted by the writer and assistants.

13. An example of this scene is played out every year in the earlier referred to Gartsherrie district of Coatbridge.

14. Figures from Danny Houston and David Bryce. Glasgow Orangeman Mark Dingwall, believes the figure to be much nearer 25,000.

15. The Sunday Mail and the Sunday Observer estimated between 3,000 and 6,000 at the march.

16. County Grand Lodge of Glasgow, contains such premises in Whiteinch, Springburn, Possilpark, Denniston, Partick, Parkhead, Pollockshaws, Bridgeton, Govan, Maryhill, Drumchapel, and in the south-side of the city. Others exist in Dumbarton, Clydebank, Rutherglen, Cambuslang and Kilsyth, and in the new towns of Cumbernauld and East Kilbride. In Lanarkshire, social clubs exist in Caldercruix, Airdrie, Bellshill, Coatbridge, Glenmavis, Greengairs,

New Stevenston, Hamilton, Shotts, Bargeddie, Motherwell and Harthill, as well as Bellshill. Ayrshire also has a number of clubs, in Kilwinning, Greenock, Ayr, Irvine, Johnstone and Renfrew or example; whilst there are other clubs in the Lothians.

17. David Bryce estimated that between 2,000 and 3,000 from Scotland attend the marches in the North every year.

18. Orange Torch, June 1984.

19. This is supported not only via statements issued in the 'Orange Torch' but with reference to the literature distributed by the Institution at the time.

20. Information from David Searight formally of the Department of Government, Strathclyde University. His PhD on the Conservative Party in Scotland was completed in early 1995.

21. Scottish Daily Express, 25/4/90.

22. This example after the killing of eight British soldiers by the IRA near Ballygawley, County Tyrone in 1988. Orange Torch, Sep 1988.

23. Ibid, June 1986.

24. See July/August 1984 for example.
25. Ibid, June 1984.

26. A view expressed to the writer on a number of occasions by many Orangemen and some Protestant Church goers.

27. Interview with Danny Houston.

28. Irish Post 17/2/90 and Glasgow Herald 23/12/89. See also Orange Torch Nov 1989, for a similar view in relation to the Party in Coatbridge.

29. The British National Party regard the anti-Catholic/anti-Irish, anti-IRA culture within Scottish football as fertile ground for their activities. Links have also been suggested with Loyalist paramilitary groups in Northern Ireland. For the latter, see article by Euan Ferguson, Scotland on Sunday, 5/7/92, 'When the empty Orange talk turns to action', Also, 'United Front' The Sunday Times (Scotland), 13/3/94.

30. Herald, 1/7/92. Also letter from 'Commission for Racial Equality' in Herald, 24/6/92, and articles in same newspaper, 15/5/92. 'Sunday Mail' reports on same topic, 12/5/91 and 19/5/91. Also article in the Celtic fanzine, Tiocfaidh Ar La (issue nos 3, May 1992), for response to this activity and Glasgow Rangers fans involvement.

31.   See Bell G: The Protestants of Ulster; Pluto Press, 1976, 1978. Orange celebrations (as well as what might be called Orange ideology) bear a remarkable similarity to those of white South Africans who celebrate the Battle of Blood River in 1838 when a few well armed Boars in ox-wagons held off and killed 3,000 Zulus (held yearly in December) .

32.   An Phoblacht/Republican News, 28/6/90.

33.   Orange Torch, April 1989.

34.   Irish Post, 4/11/89.

35.   Passion Play'; Channel 4 documentary, 1989.

36.   Interview with Danny Houston. The Reverend Stewart Lamont, religious affairs correspondent with the Herald, expressed to the writer his fear of the developing nature of radical and evangelical churches in and around Glasgow. Reverend James Salmond of Holytown in Lanarkshire, and who has one of the most vibrant congregations within the Church, adopts an evangelical/born again approach. He believes that although not working together in any particular fashion, such Churches now make up around one third of the Church of Scotland membership.

37.   See The Herald, 14/11/94.

38.   These comments were recorded in the STV documentary 'The Blue and the Green', (Nov-Dec 1989) as well as being made to the writer in interviews with Orange Lodge members from Airdrie.

39.   Sunday Observer (Scotland), 16/7/89.

40.   See 'Media cheats in Orange card game' Sunday Times, Scotland, 11/10/92. 'In Union there is strength' Scotland on Sunday, 27/9/92. Herald, 3/10/92. Irish Post, 10/10/92. Also James Mitchell 'Conservatives and the Union'.

41.   Ibid.

Other Sources

        Various celebration programmes from Orange parades in Scotland. Literature from the 'Young Cowdenbeath Volunteers'. Ireland's Own article on the Battle of the Boyne, 13/7/90. Glasgow Herald, 23/12/89, for report on celebratory Orange Carnival in Glasgow. Also for article on 'unauthorised collection for the Loyalist Prisoners Fund' 21/3/90. Irish Post article on a row over Glasgow civic reception for the Orange Order to commemorate the 1690 Tercentenary, 17/2/90. Daily Record for article on Orange celebrations in Scotland, 12/7/90. Glasgow Herald article; interview of Steve Bruce by Jack McLean, on his view of the politics and culture of Protestantism. Glasgow Herald review on book edited by Walker and Gallagher, 1990, 26/1/91.

5 Institutional Protestantism and anti-Catholicism

This chapter aims to consider the contemporary view of Roman Catholicism and Catholics on the part of the mainstream Scottish Protestant Churches, with a particular focus on the anti or negative elements involved. The Protestant establishment, or leadership, may determine ideas, policy and such like, or it may merely be responding to the grass roots. Whatever is the case, it is crucial that we examine some of the cultural and social framework governing both the leadership and mass because this largely shapes the way Roman Catholics are seen, and thus, the relations between Protestants and Catholics.

This analysis is important if we are to conduct a more sophisticated analysis of the character of the anti-Catholic dimension of the Scottish Protestant identity. It is more difficult to understand the subtleties involved in Protestant ideology (allowing for a variety of intra Protestant differentials) unless we look more closely at its socio-cultural and attitudinal elements. The social and cultural arguments or perceptions of the Protestant Churches in Scotland in relation to Roman Catholicism, provides a starting point from which to examine the language and ideas of anti-Catholicism. The anti-Catholic dimension of Protestant belief gives rise to anti-Catholic identities.

We cannot concentrate solely upon the Church of Scotland, although it is the dominant branch of Protestantism and regards itself (and is regarded by others), as an important part of the Scottish identity. The other Protestant churches are collectively quite strong and are referred to here. This is not a theological analysis, but it does draw on theological material to effect an understanding of the anti-Catholic dimension in Scottish life. My aim here is to look more closely at a number of the Protestant churches in Scotland. I will look first at some of the smaller churches. Subsequent analysis of the Church of Scotland will, in part, be based on a survey of its members (see appendix).

The Free Church of Scotland

The Free Church began as a consequence of one of inherent schisms that have long characterised Scottish Protestantism. The Church was founded in 1843 under the Principleship of Dr Thomas Chalmers, and today has a formal membership of approximately six thousand people. Including adherents however, the Church has around twenty-three to twenty-four thousand members. Its greatest geographical and numerical strength lies on the Island of Lewis in the Western Isles, where it dominates local culture and where Free Church clergymen are involved in holding local political positions. Although the Church has a substantial membership in the central-belt, its greatest influence lies in the Western Islands and the Highlands. Along with the Free Presbyterian Church of Scotland, the Free Church:

> continued throughout the twentieth century to enjoy the adherence of from half to two-thirds of the Protestant crofting population located mostly in the Hebrides, upholding seventeenth-century Presbyterian standards which ironically never affected that area at the time (Brown, 1987, p. 44).

Cultural and social perceptions

The self-image of the Free Church as the defender of true Protestant Presbyterian values, beliefs, and above all the identity of the Scottish people, is clear in a Free Church General Assembly pronouncement made in 1974, in reference to Roman Catholicism:

> We deplore the efforts of the ecumenical Protestants who have lost faith in the robust doctrines of the Reformation, to 'sell out' to Roman Catholicism and call upon those who have the interests of our land and of its spiritual heritage at heart, to resist the efforts made to abandon 'the faith once delivered to the saints' in favour of a spurious 'unity' inspired by the very enemy of Truth.

The Free Church views society through a similar prism to that of the 16th and 17th century Reformers, particularly those of the Covenanting period. Allied to this, it is clear that the prime enemy is still perceived to be the Roman Catholic faith.

Indeed, the General Assembly of the Free Church, in a similar vein to many of the attacks upon the Roman Catholic Church by the Scottish Orange Order, said in 1969:

> The problems created by Romanist aggression are still with us and are not less menacing because in some quarters the Roman Church is adopting a somewhat new approach to other Churches. The Papacy has been renowned for its capacity to trim its sails in prevailing winds, and the wind of ecumenicism would now seem

to call for some adjustments. That these will be superficial and tentative no one who understands the authoritarianism of the Church of Rome can well doubt.

In reference to the appointment of a Scottish Catholic Archbishop in 1969, the Free Church Assembly (1970) commented, 'that a cardinal should have been appointed to Scotland - the first Scottish prelate since the Reformation - is taken to symbolise the known hopes of Rome to regain here supremacy in the land of Knox'.

Therefore, antagonism is expressed towards the Catholic faith, its leaders and Catholic people generally. Again, in similar language to that used frequently by the Orange Institution, in 1971 the General Assembly spoke of the television coverage given to the Pope:

> However much the BBC may disclaim any Romanist domination we believe the evidence clearly shows that the Roman Catholic authorities have an influence in the BBC greatly out of proportion to what they might claim on the basis of numerical strength in this country.

This argument was also manifest in 1970 in the Free Church's publication, The Monthly Record. The British television programme, 'This is Your Life', introduced by Irish born Eamonn Andrews, was termed; a production managed by a 'well known Romanist' which included too many Roman Catholics.[1]

In 1973, in reaction to ecumenical talks between the Protestant and Catholic churches, the Free Church stated that:

> The Roman Catholic Church is taking the fullest advantage of this changed climate, and her agents are increasingly finding positions of influence in the industrial, educational and political life of this country which they are using for her advantage. It is still true that the price of liberty is perpetual vigilance.[2]

With some reference to the general history of Protestantism in Scotland, but specifically alluding to the Papal visit of John Paul 11 in 1982, the 1981 General Assembly expressed a similar attitude; reflecting a political and social consciousness that is watchful of any kind of Catholic advancement:

> The Coronation Oath of our Kings and Queens for centuries has witnessed the justified fear within our land that Catholic interests and national sovereignty are not compatible....It is incongruous of us as a land to give a welcome to Pope John Paul. We are forgetting or, worse still, repudiating, and entirely reversing the attitudes of our forefathers.

The Free Church in Lewis appealed to the Secretary of State to prevent the Pope coming to Scotland. The church's main worries were, 'that the Constitutional safeguards of our Protestant heritage are not being undermined'; that the visit would become one of more than the mere pastoral nature and that formal diplomatic links were in danger of being established between the Vatican and British states.[3] The British Evangelical Council and the Evangelical Alliance also objected to the visit on similar grounds.

The Free Church eventually accepted the visit as inevitable, in a country they believed was losing its Protestant values. The visit was considered a slight on the national, religious and cultural identity of the Scottish and British peoples. The Free Church argued that the Papal visit, showed that, despite some welcome changes (like the new Catholic emphasis on scripture), 'nothing in the way of dogma has changed and it will serve no good cause to avert our eyes from the facts'.[4]

Since the outbreak of the 'Troubles' in Northern Ireland, the Free Church has expressed a concern with events there; patriotism and religion both playing the significant part in this concern. The Free Church magazine, The Monthly Record, denied the existence of gerrymandering and housing discrimination against the Northern Irish Catholic population in the late 1960s.[5] Clearly, sides were taken early in the Troubles when the Record stated:

> we deeply sympathise with our much-tried brethren in Ulster[6]....We welcome the tougher line that the Government appears now to be taking and pray that God's protecting care may be upon our army units in the unhappy duties assigned them[7]....The people of Ulster are as British as any people who profess loyalty to the Crown.[8]

Like many people in Britain and Ireland however, the Free Church has seemingly become exasperated with events in Northern Ireland and references in Free Church assembly reports have dwindled during the 1980s and 1990s.

Because the Free Church lacks numerical strength, it inevitably has limited everyday relevance to the mass of Scottish Protestants. Nevertheless, the Church offers an institutional setting for anti-Catholicism, despite the fact that much of it is expressed in intellectual and theological, as opposed to popular, terms. The presence of the Catholic Church in reformed Scotland and talk of ecumenicism between the Protestant and Catholic churches disturbs the Free Church. Free Church attitudes to Roman Catholicism remain essentially untouched by any kind of contact with Roman Catholics, but are governed by a strict set of practical principles that are practised and adhered to. Ironically, the Protestant-Catholic 'tensions' of the west-central belt are of little consequence to the Free Church membership.

Professor MacLeod of Edinburgh's Free Church College, believes that the small Catholic communities of the Western Isles are not Irish Catholics and thus share a common Scottish heritage with Free Church people. He also makes the crucial observation that Protestantism dominates in these parts; 'they did not feel threatened by Catholicism'. This meant that there was not the same kind of tensions. MacLeod says that Irish Catholics were different from those of Scotland and England, in that he believed they were less educated and more aggressive in their religion.[9] These Free Church attitudes to Roman Catholicism are important however, because they are relatively close to some of the other churches (for example the Free Presbyterians and the growing Evangelical Churches).

The constant derogatory comment on Catholic Church practices and the Papacy, as well as on the social and political advancement of individual Catholics, displays an aspect of the ethno-religious cleavage that rarely draws comment from those who write on 'sectarianism'. In its adherence to the Westminster Confession and pre-occupation with perceived Catholic social and political encroachments, the Free Church of Scotland has a similar stance to other Presbyterian churches as well as the Orange Institution. Nevertheless, there is no contact between the Free Church and the latter body; the similarities are in terms of ideological stances and the self-definition of their Protestant identity. In Free Church eyes the Orange Institution is bound up with 'Irish quarrels' and a street politics that defies respectability. The secular character, the social drinking and the overtly aggressive political nature of the Orange Institution in Scotland, are factors too important to be ignored as far as the Free Church is concerned. Nonetheless, the Free Church of Scotland has a cultural affinity with the Orange Institution (certainly with reference to Catholicism and in its Reformist character), and despite its distance from the mainstream west-central Scotland cleavage.

Much of the language used by the Church confirms that it shares elements, but only elements, of identity with Orangeism (Lodge membership - Orange and Masonic - is frowned upon by the Church which has an aversion to Lodges and their secret and semi-secret nature. Nevertheless, a few Church members will be members of both lodges). In 1986, the Moderator at the annual Free Church of Scotland Assembly said in his opening speech:

> In 1755 there were no Roman Catholics in Glasgow, our largest city today. In 1786 there were about seventy and by 1830, they numbered 30,000, with 14,000 in Edinburgh. Today Glasgow Corporation is mainly Roman Catholic....As the Irish came pouring into Scotland friction set in between Protestant and Roman Catholic working classes competing for work and housing....When the Pope came to Glasgow the Orange Order made no protest during the visit although it had a small demonstration before it. The 80,000 Orangemen of Scotland were absent. A few hundred others did, however, protest....but the movement has a reputation for drink and Sabbath desecration. We do not have the siege mentality which obtains in Northern Ireland, where the Order is much more virile and the Protestants better informed. The Protestant-Catholic conflict in Scotland today is only shadow boxing. In our land the constitutional and institutional arrangements have led us to think that the land was Protestant. In 1872 the Presbyterian churches handed over their schools to the State, but the Roman Catholics kept their own. The 1918 Education Act incorporated all schools into the state system, but the State, in effect, had to buy the Catholic schools over....The short-sighted Presbyterians had their schools secularised and gained nothing. Educationally this meant that Scotland came to support a huge Irish Catholic educational ghetto, to its own future detriment....Today the

Roman Catholic system is virtually triumphant in Scotland. Being allowed by its constitution to lie and cheat as long as its own ends are realised, its close organisation and its intelligence set-up has enabled it to infiltrate the whole educational framework of the land. This is seen in the bias against Protestantism which has come into history books and television programmes. The Roman Catholic machine has penetrated so deeply politically that no government dare ignore them, hence the all-party agreement in Northern Ireland policies. We are already in the Roman Common Market, and the evangelical sun may be much lower than we think in the ecclesiastical sky[10]

In this extract, the Moderator encapsulates historical and contemporary attitudes towards Catholics in Scotland, in particular towards the vast majority who have their roots in Ireland. The speech also clearly reveals dissatisfaction at the failure of the Orange Order in Scotland to maintain the Protestant values that it promulgates, despite the fact that the two organisations share a similar view on Scotland's 'religious problem'. This is an important statement coming as it does from the Moderator of the Church, a respected figure in wider Protestant circles. It exhibits much of the rationale behind anti-Catholic feeling in Scotland today (as distinct from that which is influenced additionally by Ulster factors).

The Free Presbyterian Church of Scotland

After the Disruption of 1843 in the Church of Scotland, the Free Church of Scotland was set up as a breakaway Presbyterian body. However, as a consequence of further internal problems over church doctrine and practices, another split took place in 1893, which resulted in the establishment of the Free Presbyterian Church of Scotland.
A small branch of Scots Protestantism, the FPs had approximately six thousand members before another split in 1990, with their biggest congregations in Glasgow, Inverness and Stornoway. Other congregations exist in Harris and Lewis in the Western Isles. Although small, the Free Presbyterian Church has contributed much to Scottish Protestant history. This was particularly so in 1989/90 when a controversy involving its foremost public member and prominent elder, the Lord Chancellor, Lord Mackay of Clashfern (see notes), became headline news.[11]
Although most of the media viewed the Free Presbyterian Church's action in suspending Lord Mackay (for attending a Roman Catholic funeral) as archaic, the FP Church argues that it is defender of the true Protestant faith of Scotland. A look at the FP Church should inform us to how it corresponds to other forms of anti-Catholicism in Scotland.

Cultural and social perceptions

The Free Presbyterians, like many other Protestants, view the Bible as their supreme standard, with the Westminster Confession of 1643 being their subordinate standard. They regard the Confession as inspired, infallible and inerrant. As well as taking an oath on the Bible, Lord Mackay had taken his ordination vows on the Westminster Confession of Faith. The subordinate standard regards the Pope as anti-Christ and the mass as idolatrous:

> Attendance at the Romish mass therefore, is sinful because it is attendance at forbidden worship that is idolatrous, blasphemous and dishonouring to Christ. It is further sinful because it involves countenancing a false religion and failure to oppose all false worship....For those in high office to be present at idolatrous worship brings guilt on the whole nation (MacDonald, Middleton and Boyd, 1989, pp. 19-27).

The FPs were to find themselves out on a limb when the controversy over Lord Mackay erupted. The Church of Scotland was moved to comment:

> Lord Mackay of Clashfern is one of Scotland's most gracious and eminent Christians. He deserves all the prayers and sympathy he has received during his ordeal at the hands of a clique in an extraordinarily authoritarian part of the Reformed Kirk. Among their offences is bringing the Presbyterian name into disrepute and providing an opening for malice aimed at all Reformed Christians, perhaps Christianity itself[12]

The national church was disturbed by the furore. However, the Loyal Orange Institution of Scotland (and some other Protestant bodies) were supportive of the Free Church position. Grand Lodge condemned the mass under the same terms as those of the Free Presbyterians.[13]

Ironically, despite the criticism and turmoil, Lord Mackay was unmoving in his strong Free Presbyterian beliefs. Before the furore, Mackay expressed some thoughts on various ecumenical manoeuvrings which seemed to some to be creating improved relations between the Monarchy and the Papacy. Mackay stated that, any Bill which meant Catholic and Protestant relations became formal and the Church of England came under the Papacy, would provide a formidable reason for taking a stance against the Monarchy. He added that; 'the security of the Protestant religion and Presbyterian Church in Scotland' would be severely threatened.[14] Lord Mackay's beliefs reflect a degree of patriotism which is deeply effected by religious identity.

Therefore, the Free Presbyterian Church, the Free Church and the Orange Institution share certain core views of Roman Catholicism. However, like the Free Church of Scotland, the FP Church has an aversion towards bodies like the Orange and Masonic Orders. The FP Church believes that unlike the 'tribals' - those involved in popular Protestantism - they know exactly were they stand in opposition to Catholicism. The forms of protest used by the likes of the Orange Order fails to appeal to the FP Church.[15] Nevertheless, a particular animus against Irish Catholics, a Unionist-Loyalist perception on Northern Ireland, aversion of Rome and fear of Catholic influence in Scottish affairs and of Catholic social and political progress, helps provide a common bond between these bodies.

Talking of media coverage of 'Catholic events' (in this instance, the creation of John Ogilvie as a saint), the FP Church stated in 1977, that there was a danger that an observer; 'could be excused for concluding that Britain was even more Popish than Eire'....and that Protestants should 'awaken to their danger'.[16] Two years previously, Synod expressed the view that:

> there can be little doubt as to Rome's determination to secure positions of influence in the educational sphere and in the world of the mass media. In our own beloved land we have seen her spreading her power.

The Free Presbyterian Synod also expounded the view that:

> It is heartening to note an increase in defections from the Roman Catholic priesthood and to see the necessity for the celibacy of the priesthood called in question. Rome's participation in and exploitation of the sad but explosive situation in Northern Ireland cannot be denied....Furthermore, Rome's desire to gain the West of Scotland must not be overlooked. The 'Ulster Protestant' of November 1973 warned readers that the Church of Rome was strengthening her stranglehold on the West of Scotland and instanced in support of this view the opening of another Roman Catholic Chapel in Baillieston on the outskirts of Glasgow, the opening of a new convent in Bothwell, near Motherwell, and, celebration of the centenary of the Sacred Heart Parish in Bridgeton Glasgow.[17]

These statements reveal themes associated with the arguments of the Free Church and the Orange Order.

At the end of the 1970s in Scotland there was much debate about the constitutional position of the country, this amidst the ongoing devolution proposals. Discussing a resolution on Scottish Independence passed by Synod, the FP Church was apprehensive about the country's future if independence became a possibility. This shows how anti-Catholic Protestants generally can often perceive politics from a religious standpoint. Synod was concerned over the 'threat' to the Protestant faith, and the stability and prosperity of the people:

> In the event of Scottish Independence being realised, there is no assurance that the present recognition of our Protestant Faith, the Protestant Succession to the Throne, or in particular, the position of the Presbyterian Church as the National Church of Scotland, which are entrenched in the 1707 Articles of the Union of England and Scotland, will be preserved in the Constitution of an Independent Scottish State.

Particularly troubling to the FP Synod was the involvement of some Roman Catholics in the movement for Scottish Independence:

> The presence of a strong Roman Catholic population in the midlands of Scotland, composed largely of the influx of Irish

labour over the years, will undoubtedly exercise by its voting power an undue influence upon the proceedings, the composition and the decisions of a Scottish Parliament in Edinburgh in favour of the Roman Catholic Church.

The FP Church advocates a political affiliation consistent with Protestant Unionism, one akin to that of Ulster Unionism. Religion and politics are inseparable at an ideological level. This is a position which is not only associated with Ulster Unionism but with 16th and 17th century Scotland (an era which has helped shape Northern Ireland politics), in which every feature of life contained religious overtones. The politics of the FP Church then is clear:

> We affirm that the prosperity and stability of our beloved land lies in preserving the present Union with England, in which the Protestant Faith and, in particular, the position of the National Presbyterian Church of Scotland are protected by wise and necessary safeguards, and we, therefore, for these reasons, strongly urge that the present Union of Great Britain, which the Lord has honoured and so richly blessed in the past, should not be tampered with but should uncompromisingly be maintained[18]

To a degree, the politics of the FP Church also extend to an affinity with their Protestant brethren in Northern Ireland. During the Hunger Strike period of 1981, the Free Presbyterian Magazine reported the Synod as passing the resolution that it expressed:[19]

> its whole hearted support of the Protestants of Northern Ireland....The Synod recognises the bold and courageous stand of the Protestant leaders in Northern Ireland and prays that all who seek a genuine peace in the Province may be given grace and strength to stand firm against the forces of evil and anarchy.

A copy of this statement was sent to the Reverend Ian Paisley in an expression of solidarity. Three years later, the FPs found cause to affirm these ideas again through Synod:[20]

> We deplore the murderous attacks made by the IRA on innocent civilians and the forces of law and order and the failure of the Roman Catholic Church to disassociate itself totally from the fomenters of unrest....Our prayer for Northern Ireland is that the enemies of liberty and of truth and righteousness may be overthrown; that a just, equitable and honourable settlement may yet be arrived at which will leave the Protestants in possession of their dearly bought religious and civil liberties and Northern Ireland preserved as a integral part of the United Kingdom and under our Protestant throne....Rev Ian Paisley is criticised by the papers and we know that he has gone to the political side, but, if Rev Ian Paisley was not there, I would not like to know what the state of Ulster would be today. We should be behind the man

and praying for him.

The FP Church is against engaging in ecumenical talks with Roman Catholicism in Scotland.

> Let Rome get a grip on Scotland, then it will be farewell to the Evangel, to the Sabbath, to purity and simplicity of doctrine, worship and practice. This is certainly not the time for lowering standards and banners, but for unfurling the banner of Truth so dearly bought in the land of the martyrs and the Covenants. The very nature of the Ecumenical Movement forbids us from having even the most peripheral of connections with it.[21]

Any Protestant move towards greater links with Roman Catholics is condemned out of hand. No truck with Catholicism can be countenanced. The very identity of Scotland itself is perceived to be under threat.

The Scottish Baptist Church

The Baptist Church is part of the mainstream of Protestant churches in Scotland:

> Within Scotland there are 166 Churches located in cities, towns and villages from the Shetland Isles to the Solway Firth. These churches express a common identity through their affiliation to the Baptist Union of Scotland.[22]

One of the main differences between the Baptists generally and the other Protestant denominations is the great stress that is placed upon the act of Baptism itself; the immersion of the believer in water on the profession of their faith in Jesus Christ. Nevertheless, it is the other major distinctive feature which is more important with a view to this particular inquiry.

Baptists agree with Episcopalians that oversight of the church is vested in no individual such as the Pope. They agree with Presbyterians that the very idea of the superior authority of one minister over another is alien to the spirit of the gospel. And they agree with Congregationalists that no bureaucracy external to the individual gathered community has directive power (see Bebbington). Thus any idea of a church establishment conflicts with Baptist understanding of the church as a gathered community of believers owing supreme allegiance to Jesus Christ as head.

The Baptist Church in Scotland has a membership of approximately 17,000, which rises to around 20,000 when adherents are included. The bulk of the membership stretches from the east in Edinburgh and Fife, through the Lothians and Lanarkshire, and into the west in Glasgow, Renfrewshire and the south west. The Baptists are therefore mainly a lowland church.[23]

Their main 'antagonisms' toward the Roman Catholic Church are set out in a recently printed statement by the Scottish Baptist Church. Whilst it asserts that some Baptists in Scotland feel able to communicate with the local

Catholic community from time to time for worship, prayer, discussion or Bible study, they also declare that:

> there are those who regard Roman Catholicism as an evil and corrupt system, would refuse it the name of 'Church', and in some cases would even identify it with the 'great harlot' of Revelation 17, in line with some of the 17th century Reformers. It is probably true to say that some of our people are strongly opposed to any kind of official association with the Roman Catholic Church, although they confess to having good relationships with individual Catholics[24]

Theologically there are areas of 'broad agreement' with the Catholic Church; on the issue of the Person and Work of Christ and on ethical and social questions for example. A special Baptist group was set up in the 1980s, 'to highlight areas of agreement and disagreement, give up-to-date information and help Scottish Baptists to engage in an informed discussion of Roman Catholicism in Scotland today.'[25] The result was a conciliatory work which explained Catholicism from a Catholic standpoint.

The evolution of the Baptist Church meant that they detached themselves from the 'rigours' of the Covenanting period and developed an independence, as state influence began to dominate within the other churches. Given this it seems logical that the Scottish and British nationalist ties, which are so important to the Church of Scotland and the other Presbyterian branches, are not religiously salient for Baptists. Though many Scottish Protestants have a close affinity with Northern Ireland Protestants, questions relating to Northern Ireland are not fundamentally Protestant issues for Baptists in Scotland. Little reference has been made by the Baptist Union to the Northern Ireland troubles and affinity with Protestants in Northern Ireland is a matter for individual Baptists. Simply put, the Unionist identity does not extend quite so instinctively to Scottish Baptists as it does to other Scottish Protestants; primarily because of the other Protestants institutional attachment to Queen, Constitution and country.

Unfavourable rhetoric among Baptists towards Catholics is largely concentrated upon the rule of the Pope. Whilst respecting the faith of individual Roman Catholics, Baptists claim that; 'the authoritarian nature of the Roman Catholic Church, with its insistence on its infallibility', constitutes a major barrier for Scottish Baptists.[26] Added to this, church ecumenicism is approached with extreme caution because of the involvement of Roman Catholics and a fear of 'guilt by association.' [27]

As a consequence, ecumenicism in Scotland was rejected by the Baptist Union and it refused to join the new inter-church body which was created to replace the Scottish Churches Council in 1989. At their Assembly in Edinburgh, Baptists voted decisively against membership of the ACTS (Action of Scottish Churches Together) by 345 votes to 152. It was reported that:

> several Churches had threatened to pull out of the Baptist Union if it had joined ACTS. Objections to the body centred around the involvement of the Roman Catholic Church....The

independent Jock Troop Memorial Church in Glasgow, which is not a member of the union, but has a hard line Protestant stance, issued a statement congratulating the Baptists on their 'total rejection' of ACTS.[28]

Other independent churches, like Pastor Jack Glass's Sovereign Grace Evangelical Baptists were also to protest against the setting up of ACTS.

The Baptists represent a relatively small, but very active, branch of Scottish Protestantism. Although having a number of differences with other Protestant churches, it is Roman Catholicism which disturbs them most.

'Other' Protestant churches

Among the other smaller branches of Scottish Protestantism are Pastor Jack Glass's Sovereign Grace Evangelical Baptists ('Calvinist and Separatist'), who declare in their 'Articles of Faith and Constitution':[29]

> You are now a member of a church which has declared war on all Modernism, Romanism, Ecumenicism and Arminianism, and every member is expected to unfurl the banner God has given him and to display on it the doctrines of Sovereign Grace.

Glass attacks the 'failings of the secular world and tries to achieve some sort of political platform' (Bruce, 1985, p. 198). During the 1980's he maintained a high media profile in leading and having his church members support marches (mainly in the west of Scotland) against the Papal visit to Scotland, ecumenicism, as well as in opposition to Irish nationalist and pro-IRA demonstrations in Lanarkshire and Glasgow. He is also prominent in other protests. For Glass, this is politics practised in the name of religious belief. In truth, more often than not, his media attention has been numerically unwarranted and expressive rather than instrumental.

Ironically, Glass is at pains to point out that the Orange Order in Scotland are 'pretenders of the faith, and defenders not'.[30] Nevertheless, in the past, his street demonstrations have often been supported by the same people who applaud the Orange parades - as well as a notable number of people wearing the football favours of Glasgow Rangers. Meanwhile, the Orange Institution itself believe Glass is 'consciously hypocritical or deliberately inconsistent' (Bruce, 1985, p. 205).

Despite often being engaged in strong demonstrations against the IRA, Jack Glass has a small Church of around one hundred people. They are mainly drawn from Ayrshire, Stirling, and Lanarkshire, with a few from Glasgow. Yet the willingness of thousands of people to publicly side with him in demonstrations (although he received only a derisory vote when he entered the Glasgow Hillhead by-election in 1982) reflects the potency of the religious-political issues he focuses upon.

The Reformed Presbyterian Church of Scotland is another branch 'in the Presbyterian family'.[31] Based mainly in the Lanarkshire towns of Airdrie and Wishaw, and with around fifteen per cent of their small three hundred strong congregation in Stranraer, they also claim the true heritage of the

Covenanters; of Andrew Melville and John Knox, as well as adherence to the 'Westminster Confession of Faith founded on and agreeable to the word of God'. Attitudes towards Catholicism are similar to those of the Free Church and the Free Presbyterian Church.[32]

Likewise, the United Free Church of Scotland abides by the 'Word of God', whilst holding as its Subordinate Standard, the Westminster Confession of Faith. With seventy-five congregations (at the beginning of the 1990s), the heaviest concentrations are in Glasgow and the West with around half in the Lothians, Edinburgh, Fife, Dundee and Aberdeen. A few also exist in Border areas. The United Free Church has over eight thousand communicants on its role, with a number of unaccounted adherents. It is an Evangelical Church which is antagonistic towards the system of Catholicism, as well as the civil establishment of religion. The United Free Church also considers itself to be 'a member of the Presbyterian family of Churches'.[33]

The Church of Scotland

By the mid 19th century, anti-Catholicism for many Protestants, from the period of large scale Irish immigration onwards, was principally anti-Irish Catholic. As the Church of Scotland has been the most powerful and largest body of institutionalised Protestantism since the Reformation, its current perception of Catholicism is crucial for our study of the overall Protestant identity.

The 'formal' membership has been falling since the 1960s (from around one million) to 786,787 in the early 1990s.[34] Although its influence and power has been much lessened (particularly with the growth of secularism) in recent decades, the Church of Scotland remains a meaningful body in terms of its significance for Scottish culture and identity, and occasionally, as a social and political pressure group. According to relevant surveys, most of the population of Scotland claim to be Protestant and the majority of Protestants claim to be members of, or have an association with the Church of Scotland. The front page and in-depth reporting by the quality media of the General Assembly of the Church each May, reflects well the importance of the Church as both a symbol and as an intricate part of the Scottish identity. Even if it is true that the Church is today on the periphery of the affairs of mainstream Scottish society, it still maintains a presence that defies secularism in Scotland.[35]

The aim in this chapter is to analyse both the Church's and its membership's attitudes towards the Catholic Church and Catholics. An understanding of the members attitudes will amongst other things, draw upon the survey which will allow us to compare the attitudes of Church of Scotland members with those of other Protestants and, with Roman Catholics.

As the introductory chapter has reflected, historically, the Scottish Church's antagonism against Catholicism helped shape the Scottish Protestant identity, and its membership was hostile towards any sign of the re-emergence of Catholicism in the country. Considering the change noted in the ethnic and religious complexion of the population in Scotland since the 19th century, a question has to be asked as to how the Church of Scotland

and its membership have responded to this change.

In 1969, a 'Church and Nation Report' stated:

> The Church of Scotland itself can rightly claim to be the national
> Church and to have a unique right to speak with an independent
> voice on behalf of the nation and to be the nation.

Accepting the crucial part that the Church has historically played in the formation of the Scottish identity, it seems ironic that it assumed itself to be speaking on behalf of all the people in Scotland, including those not of the Protestant faith. The Church of Scotland's thinking on these matters also seemed clear in 1923 when their Church and Nation committee approved a paper entitled a 'Report of the Committee to Consider the Overtures on Irish Immigration and the Education (Scotland) Act 1918'.[36] The Report, 'carried out an investigation into the Irish presence after strong representation on the matter from the Presbytery of Glasgow, so it was no isolated outburst but resulted from a ground swell of concern from presumably ordinary Kirk members' (Gallagher, 1987, p. 136). Published in pamphlet form to ensure wider circulation, the report speculated about whether Scotland might not be on the verge of committing 'race suicide', and demanded that means be devised to 'preserve Scotland and the Scottish race' and 'to secure to future generations the traditions, ideals, and faith of a great people unspoiled and inviolate'. The report affirmed the belief that the immigrant community; 'cannot be assimilated and absorbed into the Scottish race. They remain a people by themselves, segregated by reasons of their race, their customs, their traditions, and above all, by their loyalty to their Church, and gradually and inevitably dividing Scotland, racially, socially, and ecclesiastically' (pp. 750-761).

Cooney asserts that as late as 1938, the Church and Nation Committee emphasised; 'the elementary right of a nation to control and select its immigrants' (1982, p. 19). In fact, according to Brown (1991, pp. 19-45), from around the time of the Education Act (Scotland) 1918, until the outbreak of the Second World War, there was an 'official' presbyterian campaign against the Irish Catholic community in Scotland. This campaign was both institutional and popular, and is viewed by Brown as an attempt at 'marginalising, and even eliminating an ethnic minority whose presence was regarded as an evil, polluting the purity of Scottish race and culture' (1991, p. 21).

Such language, which purported to defend the race, creed and identity of the Scottish people, is almost totally gone from the pulpits of the General Assembly. Indeed, Catholicism is seen as being 'almost insignificant' in many cases, given the more threatening spectre of secularism. Robert Kernohan (until 1990 eighteen years the editor of the Churches publication 'Life and Work'), wrote in July 1990, that, 'the Kirk is losing its influence in Scottish life', through 'a kind of national apostasy'.[37] However, such a change also reflects a developing familiarity with, and realism about any perceived threat from Catholics.

Theologically, there are many disagreements with Catholicism,[38] despite some recent progress on such matters as baptism, mixed marriages and the Eucharist. Nevertheless, these differences are not dwelt upon, at least not in

Assembly discussions or Church literature. The Church of Scotland is generally now more concerned with its own well being than with its historical enemy.

Despite this, theological and attitudinal differences can still cause inter-religious problems it is argued here. More importantly, these theological differences go some way to explaining the present day socio-political-religious cleavage that exists in much of Scotland, even at a most 'untheological' grass roots level. In response to events within the Catholic Church regarding the canonisation of a Scottish Catholic 'martyr', the editorial of Life and Work in May 1976 argued:

> If Roman Catholics are in earnest about Church unity they will proceed no further in the business of canonising John Ogilvie....The mediatory role RC's allow to saints, the techniques by which they declare their status, and the venerations which seems to set titled saints apart from the rest of Gods people - all things are unacceptable to Protestants and emphasis on them can only widen a division between Christians.

In the subsequent editions of Life and Work, mainly supportive letters to the editor were printed. The controversy also made the front page news of the Scottish Daily Express, thus reflecting the capacity of religious divisions in Scotland to usurp other news.[39] Added to this kind of occurrence, the Moderator of the Church Assembly, Rev John Gray, found it expedient and necessary to calm grass roots fears and make it clear that his friendly reception to the Catholic Cardinal Gray at the Assembly in 1977, did not imply 'approval of the doctrine or practices of the Roman Catholic Church'.

In 1980 a Papal visit to Britain looked likely. Letters and articles in Life and Work argued that the Catholic Church was a totalitarian system with the Pope as the supreme ruler or dictator. It was also argued that, 'Pope John Paul is a hard line reactionary. He should stay in Italy, or visit Eire, and Knock, again' (this by the chairman of the National Church Association). In addition; 'the Roman Leopard has changed not only its spots but its heart. This is true of some of our Roman Catholic friends. It is not true of their Church'.[40]

Though such language resembles the stricter Calvinists of other Presbyterian churches, as well too as of the Orange Institution, the Church of Scotland's official reaction to the visit reflected a shift in relation to the Roman Catholic Church and community. A change in the cleavage became manifest, though caution had to govern the Church of Scotland's official manoeuvres, lest the leaders spoke with a voice too distinct from that of the grass roots of the Church.

> The visit of the Pope is a pastoral one to his own people....whatever we think about the system of the papacy, it would be unthinkable that the Church of Scotland should not offer a hand of Christian welcome to one who is himself a good and a brave man, as well as representing as a Pole a country for which we have a deep concern. There is no good reason for objecting to the visit nor any justification for using it to stir up

strife and division, far less for turning it into an occasion of violence....To welcome the Pope as an honoured guest and even to hear the Moderator talk with him for a short time does not imply any acceptance of either the claims or the doctrine of the Roman Catholic Church.[41]

This conciliatory statement contains a complex but revealing set of remarks. Clearly the Church of Scotland realised that any reaction to the visit other than passive or welcoming, would be regarded as archaic, and even bigoted in a largely secular Britain, particularly in view of the Pope's popularity as a media figure and his habit of visiting many countries. Generally, the positive response of other countries to Protestant Scotland's reaction was an important influential factor; the Church of Scotland did not want to be connected to the more militant Protestant reaction of Northern Ireland, which had primarily dissuaded the Pope from visiting there in 1979. However, it is also the case that the Church recognised the visit as a simple pastoral one which offered no realistic threat to Protestant fundamentals and principles. In contrast, great respect is also given to the other Presbyterian churches arguments and the Church of Scotland desire not to be seen to be offending its fellow Protestants was also clear in its response towards the visit.[42]

Recent ecumenicism between the Churches, a fear of violence by extremists and an acceptance of the permanent presence in Scotland of a substantial Roman Catholic population, (indicating also a 'changing' perception of the Catholic population of Scotland), were the greatest factors guiding Church reaction towards the visit. Other statements reflect the thin line being trod by the Church in its attempt to appease all quarters:

Surely none of us will want to see anything unseemly or unchristian mar the visit. We must respect the right of others to express their joy and their faith in their own way, whatever our feelings may be.[43]

Such a reaction by the Church of Scotland marks a sea change from the views overtly expressed until the late 1930s. The plural nature of society in Scotland by the 1980s and a world made smaller with the advent of the mass media represented reality for the Church. The Church of Scotland had to respond accordingly. Its voice was the most important one in the Scottish acceptance of the Papal visit. A traditional perception of the Pope coming to convert Scotland was regarded as anachronistic and a reality that he would have little opportunity to be an influential figure overall was recognised. Protestant Scotland was not betraying itself and it had little to fear.

Surveying Church of Scotland attenders

We have already seen in the football chapters and on Scottish Orangeism that Protestants, as compared with Catholics, are more likely to be: Unionists; Glasgow Rangers supporters rather than supporters of another single Scottish club; and Conservative party supporters. Here we examine the attitudes of

119

regular attenders at Sunday services of Scotland's national church and compare them with those of other groups surveyed. These social and political dispositions are important because they give further depth to the various expressions already found in football, Orangeism and in some Protestant Churches. In terms of Catholics, they allow us to look at some of the contrasts between the two communities. Although most of the Church of Scotland parishes in the survey are in the west-central belt, the sample also focuses on a number in the east and north east of the country, as well as upon working class and middle class congregations (see appendix).

Unionist ideas on Northern Ireland have an obvious affinity to Protestants who are Orangemen, to those who follow Glasgow Rangers and Motherwell and, to a lesser extent, to those Protestant fans of the other football clubs surveyed. Brand (1978, p. 129) says that historically, 'there was a great deal of sympathy among Scottish Presbyterians for the Protestant cause in Ireland'. Considering that politically, the issue of Northern Ireland has a limited salience generally in Britain, any Scottish figures which deviate from this can be considered as not only part of an historical legacy, but be viewed as as an indication of a core of common identity in Scotland with regards to the 'Protestant cause' in Northern Ireland, and also, as an extension of the concept of the Protestant-British identity in Scotland.

Like other Protestants surveyed, Church of Scotland attenders (CSA's) today take a relatively strong position on Northern Ireland remaining within the United Kingdom, over 42 per cent support this position. One quarter of their number believe that Northern Ireland should be re-unified with the rest of Ireland, though slightly more do not know what the best solution would be (considered a non-partisan position).

The 1990/91 BSA survey states that in Britain as a whole 55 per cent of those who denote themselves as Protestants favour re-unification. In terms of British political party identification, 61 per cent of Labour, 58 per cent of SLD/SDP supporters, and 48 per cent of Conservatives favour re-unification. Curtice's conclusion that: '....All shades of British opinion believe that the best future for Northern Ireland would be for it to be part of a united Ireland' (in Jowell, et al, pp. 204-212); is again shown to be inaccurate with reference to Protestants in Scotland. Clearly the one quarter of Church of Scotland attenders who favour this position is very much smaller than the BSA figures. The evidence indicates that although 29 per cent 'do not know' which would be the best solution, the proportion who support the status quo or re-unification in the survey are larger and smaller respectively, than among the general British population (BSA, 1990/91). This again suggests that religious identity is more significant in Scotland than in England. In addition, given the concerns of this book, these figures also indicate that within the fabric of the cultural-nationalist identity of many Scots Protestants, there is a stronger element of kinship and partiality towards Northern Ireland unionists than that which is in evidence from other parts of Britain.

Table 5.1
Church of Scotland solution to Northern Ireland conflict

Remain in the UK	42%
Reunify with Ireland	23%
Other answer	5%
Don't know	29%

The position of the CSA's is not as cohesive as other unionist and loyalist groupings, but most do support Northern Ireland remaining within the UK. CSA's also have slightly different views on the withdrawal of British troops from Northern Ireland; 43 per cent supporting this position. One quarter of CSA's oppose a troop withdrawal and the same proportion are in the 'don't know' category. Although they are not as unionist minded as other Protestant grouping's, the CSA's are nearer the unionist stance on Northern Ireland than are the Protestants from Britain as a whole (BSA - 51 per cent for re-unification and 58 per cent for troop withdrawal). Overall, the survey shows that there is a strong indication that like many Protestant football fans, and Orangemen (though not so convincingly), CSA's generally display a degree of empathy with the political position adopted by the Protestant Ulster Unionists. Of course, these views differ even more markedly from those of the Catholics surveyed.

The Church of Scotland has adopted a relatively quiet posture itself on Northern Ireland. Nonetheless, it is unionist and vehemently condemnatory of the IRA.[44] Life and Work made its position explicit during the IRA Hunger Strike of 1981.[45]

For the sake of readers outside Scotland. In the Third World countries and even in the United States it is understandable that Irish troubles and Ulster conflicts are sometimes presented as a problem of colonisation and 'British occupation'. But it is nonsense nonetheless....The rights to life, liberty and the pursuit of happiness are not threatened by 'British occupation', but by terrorism.

Nevertheless, overall the Northern Ireland problem has only impinged upon political debate for the Church of Scotland establishment, when some political event or violent atrocity has forced the issue onto the British consciousness as a whole. Despite its unionist credentials, this aspect of a Church of Scotland cultural or political identity is not a particularly salient one. However, its addressing here does make clear certain links its has with similar identities in Scotland, and in which this expressed issue seems to be a dominant pre-occupation.

Scottish Presbyterians tended to vote Conservative for a number of reasons in the late 19th century. They favoured the Conservatives because the Liberals (by then heading for decline) called for the dis–establishment the Church of Scotland; at the beginning of the 20th century they felt inclined by the growing involvement of Irish Catholic immigrants in the developing Labour Party; and later, they were attracted by the more resilient stance of the Conservatives against Irish Home Rule. Re-affirming to a degree the findings in the previous section, and concerning this issue of Irish Home Rule:

> The opportunity which Irish Home Rule offered the Conservatives was grasped. Links with the Ulster Unionists were forged, close ties with the Grand Orange Order were developed and in 1912 the party abandoned the name 'Conservative', which had proved so unattractive during the previous century, to adopt the name Scottish Unionist Party. This was to remain the party's name until 1965 when 'Conservative' was re-incorporated into the name. From the outset the Union referred to was that with Ireland and even after the establishment of the Irish Free state the title remained (Mitchell, 1990, p. 9).

The link persisted after World War 11, so in the 1955 General Election just over 50 per cent of the vote in Scotland went to the Conservatives (arguably, the Scot's identification with the Party was based more on its connotations as a Unionist than as a Conservative Party), even though Scotland had a proportionately larger working class than in England. Most writers see this as a result of 'the Protestant connection' in Scotland. Kendrick, for example, argues:

> The tendency of the Scottish Protestant working class to vote Conservative was simply one expression of an ideological complex embracing Protestantism, Orangeism and Unionism, with a strong sense of British national and imperial identity. In turn the sense of identity engendered by this complex was embedded in a network of associations at the community level which formed a Protestant working-class sub-culture providing an alternative focus to that based on the labour movement (1989, p. 86).

Kendrick's conclusion raises a question about the national Church's member's adherence to the political parties today.

Margaret Thatcher's years in office saw what many Scots viewed as an attack on Labour held Scotland (Labour held 49 from 72 Scottish seats in 1987 and 1992). That these perceptions were strong in Scotland is illustrated by the strongly anti-Conservative swing that differentiated Scotland from other regions in the 1987 Election. A more personal expression of this view was clear when one Church of Scotland attender at a Glasgow Church was questioned by the writer. She confessed to being a Conservative supporter, but found it difficult to say so in the light of Mrs Thatcher's attitude towards Scotland. In addition to this sense of recent alienation; 'the Church and Nation Committee [has] increasingly came into conflict with the Conservative Party in Scotland' (Dickson, 1989, p. 65).[46]

Table 5.2
Social status: Church of Scotland employment

Skilled manual	14%
Semi or unskilled	9%
Professional or technical	32%
Management or administration	8%
Clerical	24%
Sales	7%
Student	6%

Church of Scotland attenders are generally middle class (Table 5.2) and well educated (with almost one quarter possessing a degree). In addition, they include a high proportion of women (62 per cent), whilst the majority of active goers are over the age of forty-five (15 per cent between 45-54, and 43 per cent over 55). These are all factors which in British terms, are often associated with a Conservative affiliation.[47] Nonetheless, whilst recognising the importance of these factors, it is clear from these figures (Table 5.3), that a highly significant proportion of Conservative Party adherents in Scotland are found within the Church of Scotland's regular membership. Although class may be a factor here (depending on the area surveyed), it is evident also that where Church of Scotland parishes have a working class or working class to middle class make up (for example, St Andrews, Dumbarton; Ibrox, Glasgow; Blairhill and Dundyvan, Coatbridge), there remains a strong Conservative leaning. The argument here is that this Conservative leaning originates with a mind-set which emphasises the Scottish/British patriotic identity as a crucial part of the Protestant one, as well as being part of something that is not associated with Roman Catholics.

Table 5.3
Church of Scotland political party support

Labour	22%	Conservative	34%
Liberal democrats	11%	SNP	11%
Social democrats	2%	None	19%

Clearly, the Conservative Party has strong support from within the ranks of the Church of Scotland. It is also likely that there are a number of 'normally' Conservative Party supporters in the ranks of the 'no party' followers. In contrast, the Church of Scotland does not provide the Labour Party with even half of the regular figure of support it receives in Scotland today. The findings - along with those relating to other Protestant groups surveyed - re-affirm that there is a strong correlation between being a Protestant and being a Conservative supporter.

Adding to a picture of the links between a Protestant identity and unionism, is the historical factor of the Church of Scotland traditionally maintaining a special relationship with the Crown. Indeed, Queen Victoria was herself a formal member of the Church while historically, the Monarch is seen as the Defender of the Faith. Consequently, it is not surprising that almost three quarters of Church of Scotland attenders surveyed feel that the Monarchy is very important (71 per cent). This again confirms the Church of Scotland's memberships sense of a British identity.[48]

A majority of Church of Scotland attenders, like the majority of Orangemen, believe that Scotland should 'remain as it is', or simply be better understood (55 per cent). One third felt it was better to have an Assembly for Scotland (36 per cent), while only 8 per cent reckoned independence as a better option. These statistics contrast remarkably with those in a 'State of the Nation' survey conducted by MORI in early 1991; 51 per cent of that sample said they would like a devolved assembly within the UK, 30 per cent wanted some form of independence and only 16 per cent said they wanted no change.

From this evidence alone, it seems to be the case that Church of Scotland attenders are perceptibly unionist. The evidence does not differentiate between a unionism emphasising Royalty, the Northern Ireland connection, 'class' oriented politics, or even in terms of the constitutional position of Scotland within the United Kingdom. It does stress the links between factors which in other social settings are considered to be, apart from anything else, characteristics of a strong 'Protestant' political and cultural identity. Such figures bear out the British identity which exists alongside the Scottish one in the Church of Scotland. It indicates that the Conservative identification of many members of the Church of Scotland is not simply related to class but is rather an aspect of a broader Protestant identity.

For ethnic origin the vast majority (85 per cent) of Church of Scotland attenders not surprisingly denote themselves as Scottish. The following statistics reflect the importance (singularly and comparatively) of some of the Scottish symbols in the framework of Church of Scotland thinking. Almost none of the Irish symbols were mentioned by the Church of Scotland attenders .

Table 5.4
Cultural symbols identified with (Church of Scotland) (additional material marked a and b are for comparative purposes).

The Thistle	46%	a	47%
		b	62%
Robert the Bruce	46%	a	26%
		b	53%
The Corries	34%	a	7%
		b	20%
John Knox	31%	a	87%
		b	33%
Robert Burns	65%	a	79%
		b	59%
The Bagpipes	41%	a	37%
		b	48%

a = Orange Lodge   b = Football Fans (i.e., other than Catholics)

The most significant figure here is the modest 31 per cent who chose the

124

father figure of the Scottish Reformation. This appears to give some credence to the Orange argument that the Church of Scotland is placing a lesser emphasis on its once unyielding Presbyterian principles, at least in the sense of the practical relevance of the life of John Knox. Nonetheless, there is also a widespread lack of teaching of Knox as an important Scottish historical figure, notwithstanding his contribution to Protestant history and formation. The decidedly high figure for Robert Burns reflects again his popularity for Scottish people.

Because of the high incidence of women (particularly older women), among Church of Scotland attenders, and with relatively few women attending football in Scotland, it is difficult to make conclusions based on the questions raised in the football chapters. One third of CSA's in fact did not answer the main football questions. Of those who did, most CSA's supported teams other than the 'big two' of Scottish football.

Table 5.5
Church of Scotland: team supported

Other Scottish	36%	Rangers	28%
Celtic	4%	Hearts	6%
Aberdeen	11%	Kilmarnock	1%
Motherwell	3%	St Johnstone	1%
Hibernian	4%	Dundee United	5%

Twenty-eight per cent of Church of Scotland attenders identifying themselves with a football team supported Glasgow Rangers. That club is comparatively the most important soccer institution to a significant number of the surveyed Church attenders. However, although Rangers are the best supported football club among CSA's, national Church attenders have many loyalties in soccer terms. Being a Protestant in this institution does not equate with being a Glasgow Rangers fan and often it is the more local side that is supported.

Sixty-six per cent of CSA's believe that Protestants and Catholics have an equal chance of getting a job in Scotland, only 16 per cent believed there was discrimination. Five per cent of those surveyed believed that a Catholic had a better chance of getting a job as opposed to a Protestant, while almost 10 per cent believed that Protestants had a better chance. Generally therefore, Church of Scotland perceptions on this question are not so sharply marked as those of the Orange Institution. As will become clear however, and with reference to the ethno-social cleavage, they do differ markedly from the Church attenders of the Roman Catholic Church and Catholics generally.

Summary

The different Protestant Churches share crucial aspects of social, cultural and political identity. Overall, many members share similar attitudes; they support Northern Ireland in the United Kingdom, related British Unionism, the Conservative Party, similar football teams and the belief that there exists little difference with regards to religion in the employment market, among other things.

Representing a change from the past, anti-Catholic thinking has ceased to dominate within the institutional Church of Scotland. There is a shift in the Church of Scotland perceptions of the Catholic Church. The National Church has become accustomed to the development of Catholicism in Scotland and, as a result, understanding and toleration are evident. In a less parochial Scotland, links have developed between the two main Churches, especially within bodies such as ACTS. Joint statements on popular social and political issues in Scotland have become frequent in recent years. This does not mean however that there is much similarity in the political and social attitudes of rank and file Catholics and Protestants. Prominent members of ACTS recognise that their intentions and activities may in fact be very unrepresentative of their mass memberships.[49]

Such a change in emphasis largely reflects growing secularisation, the Church's own diminishing role within society and the parallel growth of Protestant linked institutions, bodies and groups which have succeeded the role of the Church. These institutions, bodies and groups (Free Masonry, Orangeism, Glasgow Rangers, etc.), have anti-Catholicism as a central feature. Despite the shift in emphasis, overall there is also a clear link between Orangeism, Glasgow Rangers and identifying with the Church of Scotland (and to a lesser extent, other Protestant Churches). These are some of the key institutions within which Protestant identity in Scotland is now shaped, maintained and expressed.

I have also identified the part which other Protestant churches play in the social and political picture of religion in Scotland. We must consider them to gain a more accurate assessment of cleavage and religious identity in society. The beliefs and attitudes, as well as the theological and intellectual promulgations, of the Free Church and the Free Presbyterian Church are rarely considered by commentators on religious tension and sectarianism. For many of the smaller Reformed Churches there is little to indicate any real change in beliefs prompted by a change in circumstances. It is important for our conclusion that we bear this in mind. These institutions perceive Roman Catholicism with great revulsion as well as with a sense of trepidation. Catholicism is the main enemy and it needs to be combated at many levels of society. This is why identity is important in a political and social sense as well as in an obvious religious one. Distinctions have to be made; affinity often has to be established with those of a like mind; and opposition (active, subtle or intermittent) has to be made clear to both the Roman Catholic Church and its members who may be seen to be making headway.

In many rural parts, the smaller branches of Protestantism are the mainstay of the locality and much social, political and moral reference is made to them. This backdrop of the historical antagonism towards Catholicism, engenders its own religious division. In these parts, untouched by Irish immigration, anti-Catholicism is not re-enforced by the ethnic factor. Nonetheless, this ethnic Irish factor has a degree of importance even in these areas because it has helped shape the character and history of the larger society. That is made clear by the comments of both of these Churches.

For Protestantism in these areas, unlike in the west-central parts of

126

Scotland, football is sometimes unimportant. Such areas are rural and lack the traditional ethnic competitiveness attached to the game in the urban areas. The rural character of the areas also reinforces the staunch Presbyterianism and helps explain the 'failure' of secular religious agencies to make much of an impact. Although there are a large number of football supporters clubs and individuals in the more isolated parts of Scotland, the intensity and daily significance (often clearer in an urban experience) of these identities witnessed in the larger population areas, is not replicated.

However, the intellectual Protestant standpoints taken by the Free Church and the Free Presbyterian Church in these localities, are rarely manifest today in the urban areas. Inevitably, this is one of the main reasons why the mass of the population, at least as it is perceived by and through the popular media, is surprised by the seemingly archaic and disproportionately important positions of the smaller Churches on certain religious matters. This surprise stems from the perspective of a secularised society (this should not be seen to necessarily diminish the religion of the more populated areas; rather religion in such areas has different features and characteristics).

Ironically, although these smaller Presbyterian bodies have an aversion towards the Orange Institution in Scotland, they share similar perceptions of Roman Catholicism. Again it is important to emphasise geographical differences; Orangeism exists largely in the secularised west-central belt, whereas the Free Church has its strength in the more northerly and western areas. Nevertheless, the common language used by the Free Churches and the Orange Order is clear. However, the Orange Order is a more socially active body and its inherent secular demeanour has a more obvious 'popular' appeal. Traditional Scottish Presbyterian respectability is important to Free Church members and the like and the social action of the Orange institution, as well as its street and social club image, have little or no appeal to these traditionalists.[50] Nonetheless, Orangeism and the fundamentalist and evangelical Churches can be seen as both religious and secular lowland versions of the fundamentalist Presbyterian Churches of the north and other parts of the country.

For the Baptists, the Protestant identity is very much an independent one, it is less influenced by many of the questions relating to Catholics generally, and Irish Catholic immigrants specifically. However, as is evidenced by the Baptist reaction towards ACTS, there remains as a mark of the cleavage, an inherently antagonistic attitude towards Catholicism. As for the smaller Protestant churches, they are still dominated by elements of anti-Catholic motivation.[51] In some instances, not only are relations with the Catholic Church almost non-existent, but where individual interaction does take place, it leads to conflict and ostracism (a contributory factor may also be a perception of Catholic insularity and dogmatism).

Despite a clearly different era of relations, Roman Catholicism remains anathema to many in the Church of Scotland. In addition, we must bear in mind that the vast majority of the membership and support of the Loyal Orange Institution, Glasgow Rangers and the like, are also members, or lapsed members of the Church. My argument here is that we must take account of all these strands, institutional, ideological and secular. Collectively, they contribute to a fuller picture of Scottish anti-Catholicism.

The overall conclusion arising from this chapter is that throughout the institutional level of Protestantism, there exists traditional ideological and intellectual disagreement with Catholics. Such is the nature of Protestantism. Catholicism obviously has its points of contention too. However, it is the way that many ideological and intellectual differences merge and inter act with social, cultural and political features that are important for this study. It is here that the essential facets and common hallmarks of anti-Catholicism (as opposed to disagreement with Catholicism) are to be found.

Notes

1. Collection of The Monthly Record of The Free Church of Scotland. In Yearbook form; 1970, p45.

2. Ibid: 1973, p132.

3. Ibid: 1981, p13..

4. General Assembly Report of The Free Church: 1983.

5. Yearbook: 1970, p181 (edt).

6. Ibid: 1971, March (edt).

7. Ibid: 1972, p125 (edt).

8. Ibid: 1973, p53.

9. Interview with Professor MacLeod of the Free Church College, Edinburgh. Also a former editor of the above magazine.

10. July/August 1986: Moderators address to the Free Church Assembly.

11. Approximately a third of the ministers and congregation left the Church in support of the suspended Lord Mackay. They formed the Associated Free Presbyterian Church of Scotland. Apart from the issue of power within the Church and the acceptance of the 'concession' of allowing or ignoring the actions of those such as Mackay, the Associated Church remains largely the same as the once united Free Presbyterian Church .

12. Life and Work: July 1989 (edt).

13. See Orange Torch October 1989 and December 1988/January 1989.

14. Synod of the Free Presbyterian Church of Scotland: May 1988.

15. Free Presbyterian Magazine: May 1987, p3. Also interview with Murdo MacLean of the FP Church.

16. Proceedings of Synod: 1975.

17. Ibid: 1974.

18. Ibid: 1978.

19. Magazine yearbook: 1981, p204.

20. Proceedings of Synod: 1984 .

21. Ibid.

22. 'Baptists: Some Questions and Answers', published by the Baptist Union of Scotland (undated).

23. Information giving in the course of interviews with representatives of the Baptist Union, Glasgow headquarters.

24. 'Our Roman Catholic Neighbours'; published by the Baptist Union of Scotland (undated, approx 1990) p5.

25. Ibid.

26. Baptist Yearbook: 1988, p97.

27. Ibid: pp87-88 .

28. Glasgow Herald: 28th October 1989.

29. Steve Bruce in No Pope of Rome, refers to Pastor Jack Glass as 'Scotland's Ian Paisley', Mainstream Publishing, Edinburgh, 1985, pp191-218.

30. Interview with Pastor Jack Glass.

31. From 'Jigsaw of the Scottish Churches': printed by The Reformed Presbyterian Church, undated.

32. See, 'Summary of Testimony of the Reformed Presbyterian Church of Scotland'; printed by Hedderwick and Sons, Glasgow, 1932.

33. See, United Free Church of Scotland, 'Statement of Principles' 1963: Jubilee Handbook, 1929-1989: Published in Newton Place, Glasgow.

34. Figures from the Kirk's board of practice and procedure: April 1991.

35. See Brand, 1978, p134 and Brown, 1987, p252.

36. Sometimes referred to as 'The Menace of the Irish Race to our Scottish Nationality'.

37. Life and Work: July 1990, pp18-20.

38. See September, 1974, for such examples.

39. Daily Express: 23rd April 1976.

40. Life and Work: May 1980, p34.

41. Ibid: April 1982, pp14-17.

42. Ibid: July 1982, (editorial).

43. Ibid: May 1982, (edt). (It is also worth noting that representatives of the Church of Scotland responded positively to a Catholic invite to attend the elevation of Archbishop Winning to Cardinal in Rome at the end of 1994.

44. Ibid: November 1989, (editorial).

45. Ibid: May 1981, (editorial).

46. With reference to this alienation, it should also be noted that the Conservatives (with a new party leader) experienced a minor (1.7%) resurgence in the 1992 election. This at a time when it endured massive losses around the rest of the country. This may indicate a 'Thatcher factor' in Scotland, whilst it may also show that there exists a 'bottom line' for the Party in terms of its Scottish support.

47. See R.M Punnett, 'British Government and Politics', Heinemann, London, 1984, chapters 1 & 3.

48. The British identity was reaffirmed in 1989 when the Scottish Conservatives prompted the national party to allow official organisation in Northern Ireland. See The Sunday Observer, 7/5/89 and 11/10/89.

49. This was a common opinion expressed to the researcher in a number of interviews as well as being relayed via relevant television programmes.

50. Interview: Murdo MacLean of the Free Presbyterian Church.

51. In an interview with Father Roddy MacNeil of the Western Isles, he told the writer that his brother found it expedient to move to London in his capacity as a policeman. As a Catholic, to remain in the Highlands and Western Isles he would have encountered discrimination against him for promotion.

Other sources

Free Presbyterian Proceedings of Synod, 1969 -. Church of Scotland General Assembly Reports, 1969 -. Free Church of Scotland General Assembly Reports, 1969 -. Scottish Baptist Church Assembly Reports, 1969 -

Bulwark: Monthly publication of the Scottish Reformation Society. 1969 -. Covenanter Witness: Monthly magazine of the Reformed Presbyterian Churches of Scotland and Ireland. Various. Life and Work: Monthly magazine of The Church of Scotland. 1969 -. Scottish Baptist Magazine: Monthly, from the Scottish Baptist Church. 1969 -. Scottish Protestant View: Scotland's Own Protestant Newspaper: Edited by Pastor Jack Glass. Various. Steadfast: The Record of The United Free Church of Scotland. (monthly) Various. The Free Presbyterian Magazine: issued monthly by the Synod committee of The Free Presbyterian Church of Scotland. 1969 -. The Glasgow Presbytery: Church of Scotland Newsletter from the Glasgow Presbytery. 1969 -. The Monthly Record: of the Free Church of Scotland. 1969 -.

On the Lord Mackay affair and other matters relating to the Free Presbyterian Church.

Bulwark, May/June 1989, The Lord Chancellor And The Mass pp22-23. West Highland Free Press, Comment, Brian Wilson, 2/6/89. Protestant Newsletter, issued by the National Union of Protestants, Summer 1989. The Independent, 'Uncompromising stand threatens village unity', 8/8/89. Christianity Today, 'Presbyterians Divide' 20/10/89. Readers Digest, 'Lord Mackay Wins His Case', January 1990. The Scotsman, 'Alive and Kicking in the Land of the Frees', 4/11/88. Daily Record, 'For God's Sake: Lord Mackay booted for going to Catholic funerals', 5/11/88. The Times, 'Lord Mackay suspended by Free Church', 5/11/88. Sunday Telegraph, 'Church wrong to suspend Lord Mackay', 6/11/88. The British Beacon, Monthly from the International Council of Christian Churches, article supporting the FP Church's disciplinary action. Glasgow Herald, editorial of 24/5/88. Evening Times (Glasgow), 26/5/89. The Scotsman, 26/5/89. Pittsburgh Post Gazette, Article on the affair, 27/5/89. Sunday Mail, 28/5/89. Belfast Newsletter, 'Mackay a victim of sharp prejudice', 31/5/89. Statement By The Synod Of The Free Presbyterian Church Of Scotland: May 1990. Supportive letter from the Free Presbyterian Church in Adelaide, Australia, 4/10/89 (FP Church archives).

General

Our Roman Catholic Neighbours', published by the Baptist Union of Scotland, undated, 1980s. Also, 'Baptists and Free Masonry', 'Baptists - some questions and answers', 'What is a Baptist Church?

(number 3 in Baptist Basics Series), and, 'Who are the Baptists'? Free Church College, Prospectus, 1990/91. United Free Church Of Scotland: Statement of Principles, October 1963. United Free Church Of Scotland: Jubilee, Handbook, 1929 - 1989. Reports to the General Assembly of the United Free Church of Scotland, June 1990. The Glasgow Herald, 19/6/91, for, article and survey on Conservatism in Scotland over and beyond the Thatcher years.

6 Identity and Catholics: the immigrant community

In 1755 Alexander Webster estimated there were 16,490 Catholics in Scotland, or just over one per cent of the population. According to McHugh, there was only 35 priests in mid eighteenth century Scotland (1982, p. 60). After the Reformation, Catholicism persisted in small population pockets in a peculiar strip of land stretching from the Western Isles of Barra and South Uist, up the Great Glen to the Enzie in Banffshire and parts of Aberdeenshire on the east coast. The economically discarded Catholic peasants of the Western Highlands and Islands, began, after 1770, to emigrate either to the New World or migrate to the industrialising Lowlands. Those who remained Brown asserts, continued to be, 'distinctive in religion and culture both from their Protestant near neighbours and [later] from Lowland Catholics' (1987, p. 45).

The dominant cultural and political Protestant identity of the Scottish people led to the remaining Catholic population in the country maintaining a somewhat low profile. This low profile, and indeed the subservient nature of contemporary Catholicism was evident during the period of the passing of Catholic relief bills in 1788. Throughout this time of crisis, Bishop George Hay protested that Scots Catholics were innocent and loyal, thus emphasising the abstruse nature of the native Scottish Catholic church (Cooney, 1982, p. 14). This attitude would be indicative of some of the problems that would arise as Irish immigration began in the 19th century, when the character of the Catholic church in Scotland was subsequently altered.

Nevertheless, the last decades of the 18th century did witness some relief for Catholics in the form of low level toleration. '....Bishop Hay showing his gratitude by making it a duty for clergy and laity to pray for the Hanovarian Monarch' (Cooney, 1982, c14). Indeed, the growing allegiance of Scottish hierarchical Catholicism with the British state was also manifest in the 1780s, when in pleading to Rome for more priests, the Scottish Bishops declared they would prefer not to have Irish clergy. This attitude may have referred to an Irish tradition of opposition towards their British rulers, a tradition on occasion, assisted by rebellious priests; and a trait that was viewed as dangerous to the position of the native church. The anti-Irish and conservative nature of some of the Scottish born clergy would re-occur over the next two decades and would extend into Roman Catholic life in the 20th century.

The desire of the Hanovarian regime to encourage Highland Catholics into the services of its army was one of the motives for this new toleration. Indeed, much relief seems to have been designed with such intentions in mind. In an Irish context, the British government actually financed the Catholic seminary at Maynooth, a mechanism designed to shield clerical students from the influence of Irish nationalist thinking. Thus, toleration and relief were often found to have a more covert rationale.

Scotland underwent extensive agricultural changes in the years after the union of 1707. Vast improvements added to the growing industrial demand for the products of the land which in turn meant a colossal manpower was required to harvest it. Migrants from Ireland responded to the annual demand for reapers in the late 18th and early 19th centuries, access having recently become easier with the establishment of a cheap steamboat shuttle service across the Irish sea. The seasonal inflow resulted in around six to eight thousand work-hungry Irish peasants going to Scotland yearly throughout the 1820s, with the numbers steadily increasing to approximately twenty-five thousand over a season (Handley, 1964, c16, Devine & Mitchison, 1988, p. 47).

By the early part of the 19th century the 'Irish Navvy' had become a permanent feature of the industrial life of Scotland. Harbours, canals, roads and railways were products of the industrial revolution, and the Irish provided a substantial element of the migratory labour force required for its development. Irish labour was frequently recruited within Ireland by the agents of British industry for these purposes.

A considerable proportion of the early immigrants from Ireland were Protestants, the descendants of the English and Scottish colonists who had settled in Ireland years before. It appears that this section of the immigrants had little difficulty in settling down in Scotland and indeed re-integrating with their kith and kin (see Walker, 'The Protestant Irish in Scotland', in Devine, 1991, pp. 44-66). Protestants from the north of Ireland came to Scotland for employment. Thus, many of the historical animosities that existed in Ireland between colonised and coloniser, most overtly witnessed within Ulster in Catholic-Protestant distinctions and tensions, were now transferred into a Scottish context, where already anti-Catholicism was part of the wider culture.

The Scottish Catholic Church could not cope with the sudden rise in the number of Catholics in the country. Even by the time of the great exodus from Ireland during the Famine there were little more than half-a-dozen priests to minister to growing Catholic needs in the west of Scotland (Gallagher, 1987, c10), when possibly over one hundred were required. Smith argues;

> By 1845, Ireland had been conquered not once but several times, the land had been confiscated and then redistributed over and over again, the population had been brought to the verge of extinction after Cromwell's conquest and settlement, only some

half million Irish survived - yet an Irish nation still existed, separate, numerous and hostile (1962, p9).

Nevertheless, the ultimate consequence of colonialism in Ireland was the 'Great Famine' of 1845-49. By the 1840s, Ireland was a country ridden by poverty, though an exception to this condition was to be found in the colonised eastern half of the province of Ulster. Here a relatively better standard of living was evident. In 1845, Ireland experienced a potato blight - as did other parts of Europe - which attacked the sole diet of the people. The condition of colonial Ireland, as well as the incompetence and disregard with which the Famine years policies were carried out with regard to the country, decimated it's population in two ways. Those who could emigrated; around 1,300,000 to the United States alone between 1847 and 1854, and possibly almost 3,000,000 between 1841 and 1861. Well over one million people perished in the most abhorrent of circumstances due to hunger itself, whilst hundreds of thousands died aboard the emigrant 'Coffin Ships' or within a short period of their arriving in a new land, often the victims of typhus. The effects of colonisation on Ireland are reflected well in one of the statistics of the time. During the Famine years, Ireland actually produced food in abundance. An agricultural census showed that the value of the produce of Ireland in 1847 amounted to almost £45,000,000. Handley believed this to be sufficient to feed more than twice the population of the country (1964, pp. 157-177).

The same writer estimates that 100,000 of the immigrants settled down in Scotland during that particular period. Although accurate statistics were not kept during these years, the 1841 census denotes 126,321 Irish-born in Scotland, a figure which underestimated the Irish presence for it never included the children of those born in Ireland. By 1851 under similar census conditions, it recorded 207,367 Irish born in the country; around seven per cent of the population (Handley, 1964).

The Irish who arrived in Scotland were overwhelmingly from the lower ends of all social status and employment classifications. Much of this was inevitable, given the reality of their condition in a new and alien environment. Their state of desperation meant they took any employment available. In consequence, they lacked in social and political power. Discrimination, reflected in 'No Irish Need Apply' notices, invariably developed both overt and subtle forms when applied against the offspring of immigrants, often identified by their Irish names or their area of residence (for in general terms, the Irish often collected in the same villages, towns, and districts of cities).

Most of the Irish immigrants who settled in Scotland, either directly or eventually, became resident in the west central belt, particularly in Lanarkshire and the greater Glasgow region. In addition to not having the churches to deal with the growing influx, the Catholic Church in Scotland had no hierarchy and was wanting in organisation and finance. Only after 1840, when the numbers of Irish settling permanently in Scotland increased, did the slow process of chapel-school building (for them and by them) begin in the industrial districts of Glasgow, Renfrewshire and Lanarkshire.

Most prominent amongst the religious leaders designated for the Catholic immigrants was the Rev Andrew Scott (later Bishop), from the Banffshire region of the north east of Scotland. In the formal religious sense, few complained about Father Scott, a priest who laboured in his own country to a foreign flock. However, he had little time for and indeed disapproved of the Irish nature of the incomers Catholic faith, and he objected to many of their political activities, either on behalf of O'Connells Catholic Association or on other Irish issues (see early chapters of Handley, 1964, and Gallagher, 1987).

Bishop Scott was attacked from within the Catholic Irish community for neglecting their interests in favour of the small contingent of Scottish Catholics. On one occasion he is reported to have replied to such an attack;

> If yer nae please' twi' the way I dae for
> yer guid, what dinna ye tak 'a sail tae
> Rome, and see hoo ye come on at the Vatican,
> if ye ken whaur that is![1]

The claim that the now overwhelmingly Irish Catholic Church in Scotland were not being consulted or allowed to share in the temporalities of the Glasgow mission was echoed in immigrant papers in London and elsewhere (Scott-Moncrieff, 1960, p. 143), 'Paddy sows and Sandy reaps' (Handley, 1964, chapters on Free Press), being a popular phrase in the (Catholic) Glasgow Free Press in the mid-19th century. Eventually, the attacks directed towards the native church on behalf of the aggrieved immigrants became so vituperative that a rebuke from Rome itself was seen to be in order.

The timidity of the native church, and their fears of the virulence bestowed upon them by virtue of the Irish presence, is best shown in the way it was unenthusiastic over the restoration of the Catholic hierarchy in Scotland in 1878, feeling best the future lay in the existing pattern. One example of these fears and the xenophobia of the Scots church, was brought to the surface by the events surrounding the choosing of the metropolitan see or chief. Lord Bute, the leading Catholic layman in Scotland, and in fact a 'convert', choose Edinburgh as opposed to Glasgow. One writer concludes that Bute would in fact have ultimately preferred St Andrews, the centre richest in ecclesiastical tradition, but where only two dozen Catholics actually existed within its reaches (Gallagher, 1987, p. 46).

The Irish had to encounter more serious problems however. Discrimination towards the immigrants and their offspring for example, can be perceived in the fact that; 'in a community corresponding to 250,000 people in 1880, there were only six Catholics studying at Glasgow University, five in medicine and one in law' (Gallagher, 1987, p. 23). Some of this of course reflected the education of Catholics. The few educational opportunities for the immigrant community led to further impoverishment and 'contributed' to Irish restriction to manual employments.

This short chronicle of the Irish Catholic experience in Scotland gives context to the political and cultural nature of that community today in Scotland.

The Scottish born Irish?

> There are no issues which raise the intense feeling which was associated with the Irish question in the past, except among an unrepresentative minority who profess some religious identity in connection with attendance at Mass.[2]

> It is a reflection of the fact that Celtic has been, for too long, a substitute religion for a large section of the Glaswegian male population that might class itself, however loosely in terms of church attendance or in understanding of theology, as 'Catholic'.[3]

> For many of them the only link with Ireland is supporting Glasgow Celtic, flying the Tricolour and singing patriotic songs at Celtic Park. Most of them forget about Ireland for the rest of the week[4]

Although these comments are largely impressionistic, they emphasise one thing about the Irish and Catholic identity which has apparently not changed in over a century, that is the important role that the Celtic Football Club play's in that identity. Indeed, it might be asserted that these identities would be fundamentally different if Celtic did not exist. Ireland, politics, culture, religion and discrimination, all take on more meaning for the Catholic community when Celtic are considered. Nonetheless, such commentaries also reveal the paucity of any accurate explication of the contemporary Irish identity in Scotland.

The first quotation from Ross invites us to examine the modern Catholic political identity in relation to its historical nuances. The other assertions are linked directly to the contemporary Irish ethnic identity in Scotland, while they also pose the question as to its present constitution.

It is argued, that for some Catholics, Celtic represent the sum total of their connection with their religion. It provides the platform on which many relate to the community to which they belong and, just as importantly, the one to which they do not. For a number of Catholics it is more meaningful in terms of their everyday lives than formal religious practice. Nevertheless, 61 per cent (see chapter 3) of Celtic fans attend mass at least once per week, which indicates a high degree of Catholicity among the Celtic fans. Therefore, the second comment is inaccurate in its claim that Celtic are simply a substitute religion. The Catholic Church in Scotland believes that around 35 per cent of Catholics are weekly mass attenders[5].

The historical image of Celtic Football Club as a fundamental part of the Catholic (and Irish) mind-set, and as their representatives in the field of sport and popular endeavour, is clearly shown to be relatively unchanged today. Almost four in five of 'male' Catholic mass attenders surveyed, from all classes, ages and educational backgrounds, mentioned Celtic as the football team which they supported. Even among the fewer women football supporters, over three in five named Celtic as their favourite soccer side. Overall, the connections between practising Catholics in Scotland and the Celtic Club are seen to be very strong. Similarly, other organisations are popularly seen as having an affinity with Celtic; so 96 per cent of the members of the Irish Republican political solidarity movement and the Irish cultural bodies surveyed named Celtic as their favourite football club.

An historical examination of their political concerns and affiliations is crucial to any understanding of the development of the immigrant Irish Catholic community. This is interesting because it informs us about the characteristics of that group in a contemporary setting. Historically, two political issues have been important to the immigrant community and both help shape the religious cleavage in Scotland. First, the issue of Ireland in British politics has always been a divisive question and marks an important cleavage between football fans in Scotland, in particular between Celtic supporters and a number of other clubs' followers. Second, as will become clear later, the controversy over the existence of Catholic schools within the state system, is also symptomatic of the Catholic-Protestant cleavage. At the same time, the strong attachment of Catholics to the Labour Party has been a crucial feature of Scottish politics and the cleavage within it. Each of these deserves fuller treatment.

Catholics and politics in Scotland: an historical perspective

In view of the state of the country which they felt they had been forced to leave, it is not surprising that Irish immigrants, wherever they went, were often preoccupied with events back home. An interest in political events back in Ireland provided a way to retain a link with 'the oul country', and this at a time when it was virtually impossible to spare the money or the time to visit home.

The Irish nationalist political experience had long 'encompassed an easy, indeed natural, fusion of religion and politics' (O Tuathaigh, 1985, pp. 13-36). Given that Irish nationalist political aspirations were antagonistic to British and Protestant interests in Ireland, any immigrant Irish nationalist political belief and action was inevitably going to encounter opposition in Britain. However, as already noted, the Scottish Catholic Church had since the Reformation encouraged a low profile in Scottish life. It had no interest in Irish politics. As Ross says, the norm for several decades was:

> a policy of reassuring Kirk and Government that they had nothing to fear from Roman Catholics....Bishop Hay had indeed been accused by a Catholic member of 'The Friends of the People' of being nothing less than a recruiting agent for King George. Bishop Gillis, Vicar-Apostolic of the Eastern District from 1834 to 1864, was devoted to monarchy whether in the person of the exiled French King Charles X or that of Queen Victoria. Such loyalties were not shared, understandably, by many Irish Catholics (Ross, pp. 30-55, in McRoberts, 1979).

The dominant bishops and priests of the native church were from the north-eastern part of the country, where, 'appointment and genealogy went hand in hand' (Cooney, 1982, p. 39). The only thing that they had in common with the incoming, numerically larger, Irish Catholic community, was Catholicism itself; though even here both communities had noted cultural differences. (see Handley 1943 and 1947, Gallagher 1987 and Cooney 1982 for a number of such references). As Aspinwall argues; 'Bishop Scott was to tell the Poor Law Commission his flock was too Irish' (1983, p. 242).

Gallagher (1987) traces the development of Catholic immigrant political activity. For most of the nineteenth century the majority of Irish immigrants had a political objective - the broad nationalist one of redefining in some way Ireland's constitutional relations with Britain - which lay outside the range of objectives accepted as legitimate by British public opinion. Such Irish 'deviance' was resented (O'Tuathtaigh, 1985, p. 28).

During the 1870s the Irish Home Rule movement began to grow in Britain. Its branch in Glasgow, known initially as the Home Government Association, was after 1880 called the Irish National League. It was to develop into one of the strongest branches in Britain. The League was able to mobilise the bulk of votes in strongly immigrant neighbourhoods up until the First World War. 'Its support was usually placed at the disposal of the Liberal party which introduced Home Rule Bills into parliament in 1886, 1892, and 1912' (Gallagher, 1987, p. 68).

Although the politically solid and highly disciplined Irish did not mould the politics of west-central Scotland, and though almost half of the British electorate was still disenfranchised until the early part of the twentieth century, the issue of Ireland was at the forefront of the immigrant political consciousness. It was also crucial to the development of the Scottish Labour Party:

> without the Irish question, it is hardly likely that so many un-
> skilled workers [and who made up the vast bulk of the Irish
> community] would have got involved in politics (Gallagher,
> 1987, p. 78).

The radical, anti-establishment content of Irish nationalist politics meant that the Irish were amongst the most important sections of the general population for the evolution of the Labour party. They were at the forefront of the mass of the working class ripe for class politicisation.

The War in Europe was greeted with the call from the Archbishop of Glasgow, John Maguire, for Catholics to go to the front and fight against the 'evil' Germans. Archbishop James Augustine Smith made a similar call from his Edinburgh diocese. In Ireland, nationalist politician John Redmond made a similar plea on behalf of small nations and the cause of Home Rule for Ireland. Subsequent Irish Catholic involvement on the side of Britain in the First World War was substantial. Religious and national inhibitions on both sides became of secondary importance in the face of a perceived common enemy, and, as with the cause of women's emancipation, hopes were high of a new place in Scottish and British society for the Catholic community. Such sentiments, together with the growing ideas of social justice and equality, offered a fertile soil for the parliamentary Labour party.

However, this new submergence into the experiences of the indigenous populace was overtaken by critical events at home. Although the Easter Uprising of 1916 was condemned initially by many Irish at home and abroad, the execution of the leaders by the British soon resulted in a growth of admiration for the 'heroes' of Easter Week. By 1918 Sinn Fein, a mass, separatist and more radical party, had displaced the Home Rule party as the main spokesman for nationalist Ireland.

In Scotland, the number of Sinn Fein clubs increased from twenty to eighty (Handley, 1947, p. 298) and a large number of IRA battalions were formed in the west of Scotland (Gallagher, chapter 3). The influential Charles Diamond, editor of the Catholic Herald and the Glasgow Observer, supported the Irish-guerrilla war campaign which took place between 1919 and 1921. A climax came in 1921, when the pro-Irish independence Archbishop Daniel Mannix of Melbourne, banned by the authorities from meeting the Irish in Glasgow, spoke at an open-air rally in Coatbridge (Whifflet) which was attended by 50,000 people (Gallagher, 1987, p. 93).

This period probably marked the zenith of active nationalist support in Scotland. However, the years 1922-1923 saw the eruption of the fratricidal conflict of the Irish Civil War. The Irish in Scotland became confused and war wearied as the fight in Ireland became less clear-cut.

> the spectacle of Irishman killing Irishman greatly weakened Irish political and cultural movements in many British cities where these activities had reached a high pitch only a short time before (Gallagher, 1987, pp. 94-97).

The political parties to emerge in the new and independent Free State of Ireland had much less need to create an anti-British dimension than had their forbears in the Parliamentary Party and Sinn Fein. To a large extent, Ireland was dropped from the British political agenda. Along with the recent extension of the franchise, this meant that a new era of politics began to impinge upon many aspects of the immigrants and their offspring's lives. Although Irish people all around Britain were to become involved in, for example, the Anti-Partition League, Ireland ceased to stir the same level of activity as in pre-partition days. Immigration from Ireland to Scotland was to decline dramatically after the First World War and the immigrants began to acquire new political allegiances which were the product of their everyday circumstances.

Irish political consciousness: the immigrants today

In the wake of the 1987 IRA bombing at Enniskillen, in which a number of civilians were killed, a Glasgow Herald article emphasised; 'the tacit support for the IRA that you can read off virtually any wall in Glasgow and which you can hear, chanted from the terraces of Celtic Park, or wherever Celtic players take the field'.[6] In an article in the Scottish Catholic Observer in 1986, the same writer spoke of the pro-Hunger Strike graffiti on the walls of Coatbridge in Lanarkshire.[7] More generally, a number of clubs and pubs in the West-Central belt have regular Irish 'rebel sessions', in which the most popular songs of the evening will inevitably be those which reflect support for the ideals and goals of Irish nationalism, the Irish Republican Army and Sinn Fein.

Since the early 1980s, politically inclined bands like The Wolfe Tones,

140

The Blarney Pilgrims and The Irish Brigade have had thousands of young people attend their concerts in west-central Scotland, listening to their pro-Irish republican songs. Other socio-political artists like Christy Moore, have in recent years also developed a very strong following in these parts of Scotland. Irish popular bands like The Waterboys, The Sawdoctors and The Pogues also elicit a powerful and frequently identifiably Irish following. Indeed, pro-IRA chants are occasionally heard at the Glasgow concerts of the best selling band The Pogues, Irish symbols are regularly seen and in 1990 some Union Jack flags were ceremoniously burned in an expression of political and cultural defiance.[8]

During the 1930s, the Ancient Order of Hibernians dominated in the Irish cultural-political street marching scene. However, after a number of disturbances associated with the parades they imposed on themselves a ban which effectively lasted until the 1960s; 'overnight there was an end to the era of Irish marching bands', and Irish street demonstrations as such have never returned.[9] Today, the Hibernians have a limited membership. There are five hundred members attached to the Hibernian social clubs in Carfin and Port Glasgow. There are also over one hundred active Hibernians in Coatbridge, Hamilton, Airdrie and Dundee. Their main marches are twice a year; St Patrick's Day and an annual demonstration in June. A number of marching bands are also attached to each of the divisions.[10]

Although the Hibernians again emerged on the streets in the 1960s and 1970s, the time lapse in activity proved a watershed for the movement and the wider Irish community. In addition, many young Hibernians, as well as other potential members, became disillusioned with both the political inactivity and 'conservatism' of older and more traditional members, especially in view of the events occurring in Northern Ireland and, in particular, the Republican prisoner campaign in Long Kesh/The Maze.[11] As a consequence, and in direct response to the Hunger Strike of 1981, the Republican Band Alliance (RBA) was set up in Glasgow in July of that year[12]

Unlike the Hibernian bands which took their names from saints and more traditionally recognised Irish heroes (e.g., St Patrick's Flute Band and the Robert Emmet Accordion Band), the fifteen to twenty band Republican Alliance adopted names which have strong associations with the latest IRA campaign (e.g., Andersonstown Martyrs from Glasgow and the Crossmaglen Patriots from Wishaw). Although made up primarily of Catholics, the RBA, unlike the Hibernians, claim no obvious religious 'practice or ethos' so as to reject their opponents labelling them as sectarian, though this may also say something about the religiosity of their membership.

The survey found that 90 per cent of RBA members were Catholic. One third attended mass weekly (similar to the average for Catholics in Scotland), whilst 50 per cent attended sometimes and 20 per cent never. The vast majority, 84 per cent, of Band activists were found to be under 34, while again a majority (88 per cent) of the membership were male. Almost all of the RBA members were to be found in skilled or unskilled manual employments and only two were professional or technical workers.

These bands (averaging around three-dozen strong) take part in local parades commemorating favoured Irish political events and figures, like the Uprising of 1916 or the Hunger Strikes of 1981. Often they travel to Ireland

and England, to give support and solidarity at similar events.[13] Given this, it is unsurprising that the survey found that 92 per cent of RBA members believed that Northern Ireland should reunify with the rest of Ireland, while 95 per cent believed that British troops should be withdrawn from the area.

The RBA states that it supports the Irish nationalist community in 'occupied Ireland', whilst it has as its main aim the raising of political awareness among its young band members. Politically it is highly active, supporting not only republican events but perceived anti-imperialist ones, including pro-Palestinian events in the 1980s. Some of the band members see it as an opportunity to live out an Irish identity (See Tables 6.1 and 6.2) which emphasises Republicanism and anti-British imperialism. For a few others however, it is also a Scottish phenomenon, one that again has a strong anti-British and anti-English dimension.[14]

Table 6.1
RBA origins

Irish	58%
Irish and Scottish	4%
Scottish	33%

Table 6.2
Cultural symbols identified with (RBA members)

(Note: few members choose any of the Scottish 'symbols'. Robert Burns a significant symbol among all groups of non-Catholics, was favoured by only 4 per cent of RBA members)

Pearse	75%	Harp	25%
Wolfe Tones	52%	St Patrick	44%
Shamrock	56%	Yeats	---

Table 6.3
RBA political party support

Labour	47%
S.N.P	10%
Others or None	42% (including Sinn Fein)

The RBA is marked out by its Left and working class character.[15] Indeed, one Catholic Bishop in Scotland condemned the Bands, calling on Catholics not to be fooled by the playing of traditional tunes because these bands were 'belting out a hard left wing message'. In addition, he added, that he was not condemning the 'truly traditional bands of either the Orange Order or the AOH'.[16]

Such criticisms have been customary when the RBA or any of the individual bands have marched, or when they have been confronted by loyalist/Orange groups. Actions like this represent a particular feature of a political sub-culture which is based upon street demonstrations and confrontations. In this regards Scotland's largest selling newspaper, The Daily Record, has been unambiguous and has vehemently criticised the RBA. The Record considers the republican marchers as a sectarian menace on the streets.[17]

Confrontations between demonstrators and counter-demonstrators led to a number of violent incidents in the 1980s; in Dumbarton, Glasgow, Coatbridge, Edinburgh and Wishaw. Such events have parallels with other conflicts between young left and right wing demonstrators which have increased in frequency around Britain, particularly in areas of England where 'racism' is seen as a problem. Including marchers, the events in Scotland usually attract crowds ranging from two hundred to two thousand people.[18]

Republican marchers have been widely condemned from all sides of the Scottish community, not least from within the Catholic Church. In 1988, Tom Connolly, Press Officer for the Archdiocese of Glasgow stated:

> In attempting to arouse sectarian or nationalistic emotions they are a threat to the good order of the community and as such should not be permitted.[19]

Similarly, Bishop Devine of Motherwell believes that the bands were; 'importing sectarian strife into areas and recommended that Catholics should have nothing to do with them'.[20] Strathclyde Chief Constable Andrew Sloan, expressed his concern that the increase in annual walks by Protestant and Catholic organisations, was dividing the community.[21]

As far as issues relating to Northern Ireland generally are concerned, the Catholic hierarchy in Scotland has taken its cue from its equivalents in Ireland.[22] In turn, a number of journalists working for the Catholic press in Scotland have supported the views of the Scottish hierarchy, and the popular press. The outcome has been a series of articles, generally in response to IRA outrages, which have given prominence to appointed Catholic spokesmen. So, among recent headlines have been: 'Abandon the IRA';[23] 'No place in the Church for the IRA';[24] and 'Church leaders condemn IRA's bloody actions'.[25]

Considering the history of the Irish community and its media in Scotland, it might be expected that apart from condemnation of violence as such, these newspapers would offer different or more open comment on the situation in Northern Ireland. Certainly, in the past Catholic newspapers challenged British interpretations of the Irish problem (a good example is to be found in Gallagher's account of the career of Charles Diamond, in, The Uneasy Peace, 1987). Even now the Catholic press will occasionally print a letter which questions such an interpretation as well as the motivation of the Catholic hierarchy. So, for example one reader argued:[26]

> The purpose such articles serve in intention is to distance the IRA from Irish and Catholic support in Scotland and Britain. Nevertheless, their primary effect is to give legitimacy to the British presence in Northern Ireland, along with everything that entails. It also demeans Ireland's right to self-determination....When we begin to look at the roots of the problem between Ireland and Britain; when we are prepared to

analyse both the causes and the motivations for the related violence; when we stop condemning no one but the IRA; and when censorship is broken down to allow free speech and round the table discussions; only then can the righteous judge.[27]

However, the Catholic press in Scotland has changed dramatically since the time of Diamond and at no time more than in the post 1969 'Troubles' period. There are few other references to Ireland except when Irish related bodies, cultural groups or the Irish Tourist Board contribute articles or advertisements. The Catholic press therefore is not unlike the general British Press in matters Irish. Overall, there is a great emphasis on things 'Scottish'.

In fact, the newspapers carry periodic criticism of Catholics who express an Irish identity, especially if it is seen as being at the expense of a Scottish identity. This can be seen to reflect a lack of clarity in Catholic social and cultural identity. It also indicates the complexity of modern Catholic or immigrant Irish culture in Scotland.

After one such newspaper attack upon the Irish in Scotland, a number of readers answered back:[28]

Not for a long time have I witnessed the heritage of possibly 90% of Catholics in Scotland being so overtly dismissed and disregarded, if not indeed attacked....Most of my own social experiences here in Scotland are still very much of an Irish kind.[29]

How close one wants to stay to one's roots is of course a personal decision and the ethnic Irish certainly don't need any lectures on 'valuing Irish ancestry above a Scottish birth'. It is hardly the function of a Catholic paper nor indeed of the Church to tell people where their loyalties should lie. Too many people in the Church in Scotland are ashamed of, and want to hide our Irish ancestry, this is why we never hear them decrying those of Italian or Polish descent who are not all that bothered about a Scottish birth either.[30]

The problem of Irish identity is in part a continuing legacy of the controversies between the native Scot's Catholic clergy in the 19th century and Irish Catholic immigrants. However, in more recent times, it is more significantly connected with interpretations of the 'Troubles' in Northern Ireland, as well as popular British/Scottish perceptions of things Irish (see conclusion).

Although many, if not most, politically minded Catholics immersed themselves in Labour politics (See Table 6.3 for RBA) since the partition of Ireland, few have involved themselves in further political activity in relation to Ireland and the present troubles. Clearly, this results in large part from the time lapse between the creation of the Free State and the eruption of the present troubles; for almost half a century trouble in the area was contained and unreported.

Undoubtedly however, many people are also deterred by the seemingly constant violence attached to Northern Irish politics or by the atmosphere of fear which has paralysed political debate on the issue (see conclusion). As far as the RBA is concerned, the first band wasn't to take part in a major Glasgow Irish demonstration concerning the Troubles until over ten years after they began.[31] In addition, an atmosphere of fear was generated in the RBA when it was reported that the Prevention Of Terrorism Act and Special Branch were being used to infiltrate and subdue band activity in Scotland and the RBA's travels to Northern Ireland.[32]

A high point of support for modern Sinn Fein in Ireland was reached in the wake of the 1981 Hunger Strike and this was reflected in a growing activity in Glasgow. However, a major Sinn Fein recruitment campaign was never embarked upon in Glasgow, the organisation wanting a tight body of people given pressure from Special Branch. The small organisation's time was mainly taken up with the selling of Republican propaganda (for example outside of Celtic Park, and in the known Irish bars of Glasgow), raising money for prisoners welfare groups and organising demonstrations. Basically, they viewed themselves as a support base for the Party in Ireland.

In 1986 Sinn Fein decided to dismantle their organisation in Britain. At that time, Glasgow had only two dozen activists, though they had also a larger body of supporters. Since 1990, Sinn Fein in Ireland have attempted to bring together the pro-Republican groups in the west of Scotland (Green Cross, the left-wing editors of 'Irelands War', the Prisoners Committee and the Band Alliance) to form the Republican Co-ordinating Committee. Their task has mainly been one of fund raising for Sinn Fein's election campaign's, for Republican prisoners and selling Republican publications.[33] Nevertheless, the fact that they operate in a world of political sub-cultures in Scotland, reflects how detached, abstract and negative Irish political activity has frequently become for the offspring of the Irish immigrant community.

Much debate and some activity in this sphere is in fact left to left-wing politicians and activists. The Labour Committee on Ireland (founded in March 1980) has a branch in Glasgow, whose aim is to force the issue of Ireland onto the mainstream political agenda. They also support other Irish political issues, for example campaigning against the strip-searching of women Republican activists and the PTA. However, although the Labour Committee contains quite a few activists of Irish extraction, it is more noted for its left-wing credentials than its Irish ones.

Apart from RBA marches for the 'H-Block Hunger Strikers', 'Free the Guildford Four' and the 'Time To Go' campaign, and other related low level Irish nationalist and 'republican' activity, there is little contemporary evidence of the once vibrant political activity in the traditional Irish areas of the west of Scotland. In fact no Catholic initiative on the 'Free the Birmingham Six' campaign (which attracted people from all walks of life as a 'human rights' as well as Irish issue) was organised until its last year (1991).[34] The key point is that while Irish identity and pro-Irish political attitudes can be important for many Catholics in Scotland, pro-Irish political activity is much less manifest, a development which will be further addressed in the concluding chapter.

Catholics, culture and British party politics

In the 19th century there was strong Irish attachment to the Liberal party mainly because of that party's adherence to Irish Home Rule and Conservative hostility to Ireland and Catholics in general (See J.F McCaffrey, 1979, p. 140-155, in McRoberts, 1979). However, although the Catholic Irish were often ignorant of the social and political facts of life in the industrial cities and cowed by the conservatism of many of their priests, they gradually emerged as a major factor in the nascent Labour party (Walker, 1972).

For the first time it seemed possible to change harsh social experiences via a more accessible politics. As McCaffrey puts it:

> The continuing debate in the letter and newspaper columns of the Catholic press in the 1900s demonstrates that there was a growing interest in the new politics of the twentieth century in a new, more outward looking way (1983, pp. 275-300).

John Wheatley was crucial to the development of a labour consciousness amongst the immigrant Irish and their offspring. He was Irish born, originally a prominent Irish Home Ruler who progressively moved to labour politics. Wheatley formed the 'Catholic Socialist Society'. Its aim was; 'to win Catholic workers over to the Labour Party by demonstrating that belief in socialism and adherence to Catholicism were not incompatible' (Gallagher, 1987, p. 78). Despite initial problems, as a committed Catholic, and with some assistance from Charles Diamond of the Catholic Press, he overcame Church hostility. His role was primarily as a mediator between the Labour movement and the Church. His success has prompted one commentator to argue:

> As far as can be seen, this is the only instance in Europe of a formal Catholic socialist movement emerging from within Catholic ranks and not being condemned but, in fact, tacitly accepted by the ecclesiastical authorities (McCaffrey, 1983, pp. 275-300).

The Catholic community's transition to Labour was not easy, partly because the party itself was in a state of flux (see Gallagher, 1987, p. 89). However, conditions favoured Labour; Ireland was a less important issue after Partition and the question of Catholic education was largely settled by the 1918 Education (Scotland) Act. The Catholic press, the priests and the broad community increasingly viewed working class Catholic political interests as being tied up with the Labour Party.

In 1922 Labour received 31.2 per cent of the vote in Scotland compared with 28 per cent in England. As Gallagher says; 'its good showing was undoubtedly due to the strong endorsement of the Catholic working class' (1981, pp. 21-43). Nonetheless, out of a total of twenty-eight Scottish Labour MPs, the immigrant Catholic community produced only three, including Wheatley. Despite contemporary criticism from the Orange Institution in Scotland, that Labour was a Catholic dominated party:

until the 1979 general election, the number of RC Labour MPs from Scotland was proportionately less than the Roman Catholic percentage of the population - and far less than the percentage support Roman Catholics regularly gave to the Labour Party (Gallagher, 1981).

In addition, as McCaffrey points out, until the 1950s:

Catholic MPs were few in Scotland, only three, so far as one can judge, from the electoral guides in 1919-39 and only more numerous for the 1960s onwards. Even at the local government level, while they were more numerous, election results indicate they were fewer than their proportion in the population (1983, pp275-300).

Although Catholics saw Labour as a political vehicle to assist them raise their standard of living and to gain a degree of equality in Scottish society, this did not reflect in their representation at some levels of the Party. Clearly Catholic representatives had the capacity to alienate Protestant voters. Despite this attachment to Labour, and as an indicator of the underlying aspect of religious identity in Scotland, Gallagher notes that Labour were quite well aware that in Scotland:

religion was not a negligible factor in the formation of political preferences. Labour party activists were aware of its potential for trouble and it is the case that very few RCs were nominated for marginal seats until quite recently.

The 1959 general election in Coatbridge and Airdrie indicated one reason for this pattern. As Gallagher (1981) points out:

a previously solid Labour seat, almost fell to the Conservatives after Labour had nominated a Roman Catholic candidate. Many Protestant workers obviously voted for the Conservative candidate who was the sister of a football star who played for the Protestant soccer team of Glasgow Rangers in the 1930s. She lost by only 759 votes (see also, Scott, 1987).

The 'religious factor' was also experienced in Glasgow around the same time; 'As late as 1955, the Conservatives carried seven of the fifteen Glasgow divisions'. Ritchie and Dyer note that this was not only a victory for a perceived middle class party but this process was also one of 'the alignment of cultural defence' (i.e., of Protestantism).

Although the Labour party has always been numerically dominated by non-Catholics, and despite the fact that many working class Protestants also voted Labour this century, Catholics saw Labour as the Party to best defend their interests. Brand believes that Catholic attachment to Labour in the 1970s was extremely high.

Table 6.4
Catholic attachment to Labour in early 1970s

1970 Election	85%
1974 (Feb.)	79%
1974 (Oct)	79%

Brand also notes that the level of support in 1974 persisted despite a sustained nationalist/SNP attack and pressure on the previous Scottish consensus. Certainly Catholics moved to the SNP at a much slower rate than did Protestants (see also, M.C Clarke and H.M Drucker, 1976). Table 6.5 provides more detail on the relationship between religion and voting in the 1970s (Brand, 1978, pp151-153).

Table 6.5
Religion and Labour in the 1970s

1970 Election	C of Scot	Other Prots	R.C.s
Conservative	41.6	57.1	11.0
Labour	47.6	37.5	84.7
Liberals	0.7	0.0	0.6
SNP	10.0	5.4	3.7
1974 (Feb.)			
Conservative	38.2	31.3	11.0
Labour	34.1	37.8	79.3
Liberal	3.7	6.7	2.8
SNP	24.0	24.4	6.9
1974 (Oct)			
Conservative	34.1	40.0	12.5
Labour	35.8	33.3	78.9
Liberals	3.4	10.0	0.7
SNP	26.7	16.7	7.9

These figures show the allegiance of Catholics towards the Labour party (and a commensurate lack of identity with the other parties). Given that the Labour Party has its strongest electoral base in the west central belt and that this is where the vast majority of Catholics live, it is clear also that Catholics voting Labour is a vital ingredient for the continued domination of the Party at a Scottish level. Invariably, this has a relevance for the strength of the Party in Britain as a whole. Although other factors, particularly class factors, are involved, the figures also show clearly that ethnic and religious identity have been important factors in the formation of political allegiances in Scotland.

Given that most Celtic Football supporters, as well as activists in the RBA movement are Catholics also, it is not surprising that our survey shows that 85 per cent of Celtic fans and almost half of the RBA members (Table 6.3) respectively, identify themselves as Labour party adherents. Similarly, 66 per cent of Catholic Church goers (CCGs) surveyed supported the Labour party. After three quarters of a century the Catholic connection with Labour remains at the centre of Catholic political consciousness in Scotland. In this regard, the Catholic offspring of Irish immigrants are at variance with much of society in Scotland.

The inevitable corollary of this strong support, in particular for the Labour Party, is that few Catholics, in any of the groups surveyed, support other parties; only 6% vote Conservative and 8 per cent SNP. A strong antagonism towards the Conservative party is indicated, and this is a significant element of Catholic identity.

Brand also remarks that, 'where there is a large Catholic population, the nationalist proportion of the vote is likely to be lower than elsewhere' (1978, pp. 152-153). In 1978, he calculated that only 6.9 per cent of Catholics voted SNP compared to 48.4 per cent of voters who were linked to Protestant denominations. Brand thus arrives at figures for Catholics which are very similar to those found here for the 1990s.

As well as non-identification with the Scottish National Party, it is also clear that many surveyed Catholic Church goers do not identify with traditional Scottish symbols. This would therefore help account for some of these Catholic attitudes (Table 6.6).

Table 6.6
Cultural symbols identified with (Catholics)

Pearse 9%	The Corries 19%	The Harp 11%
The Thistle 32%	St Patrick 45%	Robert Burns 23%
W.B Yeats 7%	The Bagpipes 29%	Robert The Bruce 23%
The Shamrock 33%	Wolfe Tones 18%	John Knox 0%

The responses of Catholic Church goers to the Irish symbols is different to that of the Celtic supporters or RBA members. Only St Patrick receives general support. Other symbols have a lesser resonance for the larger Catholic community, although, of course, they have much more significance for them than for the non-Catholic population. In addition, Catholic Church goers, like other Catholics, rarely identify with Scottish symbols, even Robert Burns. Overall, the Catholic community does not obviously define its identity with reference to these symbols.

Nonetheless, an outstanding feature of the immigrant consciousness remains clear. They support a re-united and independent Ireland. Almost 70 per cent of CCGs stated that they wished this; only 10 per cent opting for the status quo. In addition, 70 per cent of CCGs said they would support the withdrawing of British troops from Northern Ireland; with only 13 per cent opposing this. Clearly, there is a unanimity amongst Catholic or Irish designated groups on this issue. Even though Irish political activity today is very limited when compared to the past, political support for Ireland remains a characteristic among all generations of Irish immigrants.

The nationalism of the 'Irish' political mind-set in Scotland has relevance for the issue of the constitutional future of Scotland. Despite a clear Catholic antagonism towards the SNP, specifically Irish groupings are amongst the supporters of Scottish independence as a political option. Of the groups surveyed, Irish Republicans are by far the most 'radical' here; almost three-quarters of that group believe Scotland should be independent, while 41 per cent of the members of the Irish cultural bodies believe this also. However, more significantly, there was no great difference on the issue between Catholic church goers and Celtic fans and any of the other groups surveyed (apart from some football clubs supporters). Many Catholics have traditionally feared Scottish independence viewing it as containing the potential to subvert or subsume their Catholicism. Some even see the creation of an independent Scotland as a first step towards a Northern Ireland kind of situation, where the Unionist-Protestant population dominated their Catholic counterparts for the half century after partition.

Overall however, Catholics have a solid attachment to Labour, for both historical reasons and because many Catholics have for a number of years, been at the forefront of trade-union and local politics. Such things engender a grass roots attachment that says as much about the working-class nature of the vast majority of the Catholic population of Scotland as anything else. The perceived radicalism of 'socialist' Labour attracts many Catholics who, in the tradition of John Wheatley, view the Labour arena as the secular political extension of their core views on social justice and as 'an option for the disadvantaged'.[35] This is a tradition which reflects their own roots, regardless of the ability or will of the Labour Party to carry out such changes.

These roots are vital to understanding the Catholic attachment to Labour in Scotland. In most other European countries, Catholics are often seen as being right wing in much of their politics. In some countries Socialist parties have often been virulently anti-clerical. The presence of John Wheatley as an Irish Catholic Socialist in the early part of the century ensured this wasn't a factor in the evolution of Scottish Labour. The powerlessness of the Irish immigrants in Scottish society and their antipathy towards the traditional British parties, which they viewed as having been instrumental in the oppression of their country, together with the fact that Labour were much less associated with the institutions and symbols of British (and thus Protestant) ascendancy and domination, all contributed to this attachment of Catholics to the Labour Party.

In contrast, the Conservative party are viewed as English, more British, unsympathetic towards Catholics and oppressive in terms of Ireland. They are perceived as supportive of the establishment, which is also Protestant in nature and has little regard for ordinary people.[36] In the Catholic mind also, the Conservatives are viewed as the traditional friends of 'Protestant Ulster'. The Conservative social and political identity is seen to be an exclusive one in terms of class and religion. These cultural nuances, along with the perception of 'voting with your own kind' (and not simply in class terms), are amongst the strongest factors which sustain the Catholic-Labour attachment today.

Despite Orange accusations of 'Romanmasonry'[37] in for example, Glasgow and the Monklands (Orange accusations had by the 1990s developed a claim and counter claim basis on a much wider scale),[38] and in reference to Labour's Catholic politicians in Scotland, there is no evidence of bias by Catholic politicians on behalf of 'their own' ethnic or religious community. Indeed, Catholic councillors are sometimes characterised as playing down their own religious identity. Labour dominated areas of Scotland are not known for obstructing popularly perceived anti-Catholic or Orange activity. Catholic councillors within the Labour party have apparently gone out on a limb to accommodate such expressions (see Gallagher, 1987, p329).

Notwithstanding the pro-Irish independence/re-unification posture of most Catholics, including Catholic politicians (See, Levy, Keeting, Evans, Geekie, Brand, 1989), Ireland is largely an undebated subject in mainstream politics in Scotland. It is recognised by some people as having a capacity to polarize much of the electorate if it entered the main current of political debate (see conclusion). With Northern Ireland 'contained' in terms of the Scottish and British political agenda, the other issue that appears capable of increasing the level of contemporary political argument based upon the religious cleavage, is the continuing controversy over the existence of Catholic schools within the state system.

Catholics and the school factor: the background

Until well into the twentieth century, the absence of good educational facilities and opportunities to use them, was a prime factor inhibiting even the brightest working-class Catholics before they became the masters and mistresses of their own destinies. Before 1870, when much of education was under denominational control, the hardpressed Catholic clergy lacked the resources to provide the same standard and range of education as the Protestant schools, which were themselves coming under increasing criticism for their inadequacy. Catholic education was very rudimentary, school buildings were of inferior standard and the meagre resources at hand were barely able to provide the three 'R's and religious instruction to a minority of Catholic children (Gallagher, 1987, p. 57).

The first modernising change to education came in 1872 when the Scottish Education Act created the new school boards. Catholic religious and laypersons became involved, being voted onto these boards in Catholic areas. Until the end of the First World War, School Boards were of great political importance to all of the immigrant community. The Presbyterian Churches were sufficiently reassured over the religious safeguards provided for in the new schools to allow their schools to transfer into the new system. The RC authorities however feared that the faithful would become detached and de-Catholicised within this new environment. They refused to enter the more financially attractive but still nascent secular system:

> With negligible exceptions the School Boards of Scotland resolved to provide religious instruction in all their schools at the cost of the rates in a form acceptable to Protestant Churches generally, but refused to make corresponding provision for the Catholic minority among their rate payers (Struthers, from Fitzpatrick, 1986 p. 31).

In addition, Catholics still had to contribute to the now Protestant dominated or 'non-denominational' schools via the rates.

As the national system expanded, Catholic education fell further behind as money was the determining factor of a basic education. The efforts of Catholics to build schools, buy equipment for them and provide teacher's, together with the efforts of the poorly paid teachers to raise the next generation of Catholics, became a key element in the immigrant consciousness.

Immigrant Catholics in Scotland began to integrate into the Scottish community via their 'political' involvement with the question of education. Therefore, in 1872, education became a significant political concern for the Catholic population. It is also from this time that it began to manifest itself as a primary aspect of the religious cleavage in Scotland.

As Struthers argues; 'although in Scotland the School Boards were free to approve of Catholic or Protestant instruction in the schools, in practice it was a Protestant system that emerged'. Almost everywhere, the new School Boards 'ignored the fact that the Act allowed them to maintain, if they so choose, schools in which the Catholic religion could be taught' (Struthers, from, Fitzpatrick, 1986, p. 31). The new schools were seen as either an instrument for advancing the interests of the Church of Scotland, or, at worse, a force for promoting the growth of apathy and leading ultimately to 'the possibility of secularism dominating National Education' (Treble, 1979, pp. 111-139, in McRoberts, 1979). Lay Catholic, as well as clerical, commitment to a religious upbringing for their children via education, gradually led to direct involvement in the larger political process; a process which reflected the contemporary ethno-religious cleavage present.

Catholic education 'survived' in Scotland, although the new national system despite being at a developing stage, 'constantly outstripped the most strenuous efforts of the Catholic community' (Fitzpatrick, 1986, p. 31). Education became compulsory in Scotland and the Catholic authorities task was to find a way to build and staff schools up to a standard were they could attract some of the government grants which were available to them. With the assistance of the various religious orders who engaged in the teaching profession, and despite the communities limited concern with educational excellence (i.e., a rudimentary education was seen to suffice and 'getting on' meant getting a job), Catholic schools developed. However, the increase in the Catholic school population, the shortage of well qualified teachers, inadequate buildings and equipment and the continuing low level of Catholic advancement, irrespective of discrimination, meant that 'by 1918 the Catholic schools of Glasgow [and Scotland] were fighting a losing battle' (Skinneder, undated). The system was near to breaking point by the end of the First World War (Fitzpatrick, 1986, p. 39).

Pressure to improve came from inside and outside the church which recognised its own inefficiencies. In 1900 Archbishop Eyre of Glasgow (1878-1902) called for:

> the raising of our own Elementary Schools to an equal financial position with that of the Schools that are under the management of the School Boards, so that they may have what our neighbours have (Treble, 1979, pp. 111-139).

However, as far as Catholics were concerned, the issues involved in Catholic education were, to a great extent, settled with the 1918 Education Act of Scotland. For Ross, the Act provided:

> a landmark in the development of the Roman Catholic community in Scotland. securing as it does freedom of religious education (while bringing Catholic schools within the state system of education) and freedom from the kind of financial burden which the English Roman Catholic community carries (Ross, 1979, pp. 30-55).

Teachers became better paid. Catholic doctrinal teaching was ensured, as was the influence of the RC authorities in appointments within the schools. The chance of a state, post-elementary education increased for Catholic pupils and Catholics themselves were now largely freed from all the burdens involved in financing both their own and the state schools. Ultimately, the newly constituted Education Authorities had to accommodate Catholic wishes for a Catholic school where this was justified by numbers.[39] Henceforth, Catholic education, became embedded in the state system.

Importantly however, the Catholic authorities had many reservations about the Act and further political elements were added to the schools debate. They felt that the gains of 1918 could still be lost in the face of the overt hostility of many people in Scotland. These fears were clearly manifested when the Glasgow Archdiocese chose:

> to lease rather than to sell the existing stock of Catholic school buildings to the Ad Hoc authorities and to undertake the construction of all new property which was required to meet future Catholic educational requirements, at its own expense (Treble, 1980, pp. 27-50).

This would ensure they could remain in Catholic hands if the need arose to withdraw from the state system. In the Archdiocese of Glasgow it was only in 1928 that the Act was fully implemented. By then the smooth working of the Act convinced the trustees of its intentions and they decided to transfer completely to the local authorities.

Religion, school and politics: opposition

The Education Act was passed while the country was preoccupied with the outcome of the First World War, and this may have prevented an immediate backlash occurring. It is also relevant that it was introduced by Robert Munro of the then declining Liberal party and passed into law by a coalition government. This meant that although Labour supported the Act, and thus increased their support among the Catholic community, they were not seen by militant Protestants at this time as being 'too pro-Catholic'.

Nonetheless, with Catholics often becoming scapegoats for the harsh social and economic times then occurring in Scotland, for Gallagher; 'the schools question breathed life into the No Popery movement to an alarming degree in the two subsequent decades' (1987, p. 104). The schools question was to become symptomatic of the hostility towards Irish Catholics. In 1935, the Glasgow Herald[40] reported a Church of Scotland minister as saying:

> The indignant opposition to the provision of Section 18 of the Education (Scotland) Act, 1918, is that public money is being expanded in educating an increasing section of the population, in the main Free Staters or their offspring, in a faith and a loyalty hostile to the tradition and religion accepted by the vast majority of the Scottish nation....Why should we feed, clothe, and educate these people who everywhere plot and plan for the downfall of Great Britain.

Here, national identity is indicatively juxtaposed with anti-Catholicism (see also Finley, 1991, pp. 46-67, and Brown, 1991, pp. 19-45, for other elements of this debate). This is crucial to an understanding of the cleavage and the nationalist connotations of religious identity in Scotland.

Gallagher believes that this minister; 'was only expressing what a large number of ministers and their congregations elsewhere shared, if in a somewhat modified form' (1987, pp. 138-139). Certainly, the almost non-existent hostility towards the Episcopalian Church (although comparatively small) whose voluntary schools were also transferred under the 1918 Act, seems to bear out the fact that it was the Catholics who remained the target. One of the most prominent manifestations of general anti-Catholicism, but primarily of the feelings against Catholic schools, was the emergence of Alexander Ratcliffe's 'Scottish Protestant League' in the 1920s and 1930s.

The popular Ratcliffe and his thousands of supporters saw Catholic schools as sectarian (Fitzpatrick, 1986, p. 84). The party was to gain much political success. In the seat of Stirling and Falkirk in 1929, he gained 21.3 per cent of the vote. In 1931 he was elected to Glasgow Corporation. In 1933 his small Scottish Protestant League had four councillors elected in Glasgow, acquiring 67,000 votes in both working-class and lower middle-class districts. This represented almost one quarter of the votes cast (the Moderate Party also drew up an electoral pact with the SPL in 1934. In addition, he was to have close ties with Loyalists in Northern Ireland).

In Edinburgh, anti-Catholic demonstrations and violence reached a highpoint during the mid to late 1930s. Although not specifically concentrating on Catholic schooling, such ideas were inevitably included in John Cormack's Protestant Action programme given that it was to call for the expulsion of Catholics from Scotland. Again, the even greater political successes gained by Cormack's Party were based upon both working and middle-class support.[41] In addition, the 1930s was also to see some of the founders of the Scottish Nationalist Party express similar antagonism towards the 1918 settlement (see Finley, 1991, pp. 46-67). Gallagher argues (1987, p. 197) that until the end of the 1930s the issue of Catholic education was the chief priority of the Catholic political lobby in the west of Scotland and this would appear to be in line with the importance that many elements in society were placing on it.

According to the Rev Andrew Douglas a member of the Church of

Scotland's General Assembly Education Committee in the 1970s:

> With the passage of time, and the graver concerns of World War Two, controversy died down. It became an almost annual habit for the highest court of the Kirk to agree that 'the time was not opportune' to raise the question of the separation of children of school age simply on the grounds of the religious preferences of their parents.

Nonetheless, Douglas had the matter re-opened. He:

> proposed that the Kirk declare itself opposed to segregation in schools, and in favour of a national integrated system without respect to denominational interests. The motion, accepted by the Committee, was submitted to the General Assembly and approved (1985, pp. 94-95).

For Douglas, and presumably for many of his adherents; 'only educational factors ought to determine the nature of the provision to be made' (1985, p. 95). It is seen here as an undue privilege and not as a right. Ironically nonetheless, Douglas argues that 'sectarianism in schools is not the cause of division. Religious bigotry has a longer history in Scotland than the situation created by the Education Act of 1918'. He also adds that 'segregation tends to perpetuate the less admirable features of sectarianism in society'. (1985, pp. 95-97).

The Free Church of Scotland is against Catholic schooling, though they also fear secularisation,[42] which has diminished Christian (i.e., Protestant) teaching in schools in general.[43] The Free Presbyterian Church can be seen to take a similar line, whilst the Orange Order in Scotland has opposition to Catholic schools at the top of its social and political agenda.

Like other protagonists engaged in the argument, the Orange Institution view Catholic schools as sectarian and divisive, whilst they favour 'integrated education'. David Bryce, the Order's Grand Secretary, believes that, in the wake of such a religious amalgamation, the number of Catholics in Scotland would steadily fall. Bryce also believes that Catholic schools turn out generation after generation of Labour party supporters; a party for which the institution has an antipathy for.[44]

The Orange Institution, in common with many institutions and individuals in Scottish society, have long evoked the argument of 'Rome on the Rates', convinced that Catholics in Scotland are favoured and are an unfair burden on the general tax payer. However, there is no evidence to this effect.[45] Nevertheless, it is how critics perceive the issue that is important here. The Orange Institution supported a 'State of the Nation' resolution at the 1986 Boyne Celebrations. They pointed to what they saw as the favourable treatment of Catholics and argued that non-denominational schools (referred to as Protestant) were about to suffer in favour of maintaining Catholic schools and that the very existence of Catholic schools were 'a grievous burden on the people of Strathclyde'.[46] The Orange Institution argues that it wishes to end Catholic schooling for the 'benefit' of Scottish society; so that young people would come together in toleration and togetherness. So, 'Rome on the Rates' and 'Religious Apartheid' have become the most penetrating of cries for this community.

The political parties

Since the 1980's the issue of Catholic schooling in Scotland has re-emerged as a major element of Scottish political debate. This has been provoked by traditional arguments, but particularly by questions concerning falling school rolls. This, in turn, has led to discussions over school closures, as well too as to changes in the curriculum itself regarding religious teaching. Although the Catholic authorities accept that new conditions have ushered in a period of rationalisation of schools due to falling school roles, they are not prepared to give way on what they believe is a fundamental right; that Catholic parents are able to send their children to a 'reachable' Catholic school.

Organisations like the Orange Institution in Scotland can do little but argue against Catholic schools. The views of the Scottish political parties are more significant for their future. Their contentiousness was brought to the fore in 1970 when the Glasgow City Labour Party passed a resolution that; 'segregation of schools on religious grounds be terminated but that provision for religious instruction be continued in accordance with individual belief'.47 Although the resolution was not binding on the Labour council group (then in opposition), senior Labour figures were aghast at the decision. Daniel Docherty, the Labour spokesman on education said:

> A decision like this is political suicide....If these people want to lose the next election; this is a sure way of doing it. There will be a riot in the country if this sort of thing is forced through (From Gallagher, 1987, pp. 277-278).

Considering the Catholic community's historic attachment to the Labour party, it is clear that if Labour contemplated challenging and changing the 1918 Act it could lead to their demise in parts of Scotland. Given Labour's dependence on their high proportion of Scottish MPs, this would effectively mean that their aspirations to govern would be adversely affected. Although the party's Scottish conference have often debated the issue, and a number of motions hostile to Catholic schools have been introduced, generally the party are anxious to contain the problems that would emerge from a full-blown schools debate.

In as much as Catholic schools are supported by the people who want them, and despite official Labour policy to phase them out, Scottish Labour accepts the 1918 Act. Tony Worthington, until 1992 Labour party spokesman on education, and MP for Clydebank, says that:

> where there are a sufficient number of Catholics who wish a Catholic education for their children, we accept our responsibility to supply them.

Worthington is quite prepared to defend the 'status quo' and 'not to upset the applecart'. His priority is to improve education generally, including improving access to universities etc; this is clearly a more political and traditional Labour or 'class' position. For Worthington, education would not be improved simply by removing Catholic schools from the state system. Worthington believes that Labour's position is purely 'an acceptance of the facts as they stand'. Although not religious himself, and supporting the eventual amalgamation of schools, he believes that there is value in Catholic schooling to society.[48] Essentially, the views of Worthington reflect those officially stated by Scottish Labour[49] that:

> Religious education should include a genuine introduction to major religious beliefs and children will be encouraged to be aware of the influence of religion throughout the world.

Similarly they say of denominational schools:

> Labour understands and appreciates the circumstances which gave rise to the present situation of separate schools. We do not believe a further extension of separate schooling would be helpful in the Scottish context. Indeed, we hope that changing circumstances will eventually encourage gradual integration through the growth of understanding and mutual respect.

Some Labour politicians however, like former Scottish Shadow Secretary Tom Clarke, are strongly in favour of Catholic schools and hold that Catholic Schools are a right, a spiritual necessity and a contribution to society as a whole. Such grass-roots attachment to the official Catholic position rather than the party's, reflects well the trouble that the party would find itself in if it decided on a more sweeping policy change.

The Scottish Conservative Party's position on schools in Scotland differs little from that of Labour; again their presence is accepted. They too stress that they are more concerned with education generally and propose nothing in the way of upsetting the present state of affairs; though they also believe a degree of rationalisation is necessary for the 1990s. As long as Catholics in Scotland wish a Catholic dimension within the state system, the Conservatives are; 'happy to accept them....If parents wish denominational schools, the Government has no objections'.[50] In 1993, the Scottish Liberal Democratic Party conference voted against Catholic schooling, though it agreed that it could only end after the widest public debate.[51]

With the Catholic communities apparent antipathy and ambivalence towards the SNP, the party has clearly to tread a cautious line with regards to policies and statements lest they alienate them further, especially with regards to that community's strength in the vital west-central belt area. A 1992 pre-election document on education did not refer to denominational schooling thus reflecting this caution. Nonetheless, the SNP are officially in favour of the schools in that they recognise that to dismantle them could be interpreted as an infringement of the corresponding article within the European Convention on Human Rights. The single most prominent attack on those who have criticised or denigrated Catholic schooling in recent years has come from a leading Scottish Nationalist, former MP Jim Sillars. Sillars is not a Catholic, but until 1992 represented many thousands in his constituency. He insists that:

> The charge of divisiveness against the Catholic community is a
> tactic employed by those whose true intention is not integration -
> but the abolition of Catholic schools.

Bigotry he says, continues to exist:

> and pop up in the most unexpected of places, sometime
> disguised as liberal thinking....The day Scotland is relaxed
> enough to recognise separate Catholic schools as the absolute
> right of a community which contributes to the enrichment of our
> national life and ethics, and is therefore not questioned as to its
> rights, Scotland will have arrived.

For Sillars, Catholic schools are:

> a test of whether the non-Catholic majority is able to
> acknowledge the laudable tenacity with which the Catholic
> community holds to its faith in an increasingly secular society.[52]

Despite such affirmations, some Catholic cynics believe Sillars was
playing the 'Catholic card', in an attempt to gain Catholic votes throughout
west-central Scotland and break the mould of the Catholic attachment to
Labour.[53] Indeed, the Catholic Archbishop of Glasgow welcomed Sillars'
remarks but was unsure whether they represented the views of the party at
large (Sillars lost his seat and announced his disillusion with politics).
Cardinal Winning for example, noted that in 1982, the then president of the
SNP William Wolfe, expressed a number of perceived anti-Catholic
statements (Wolfe voiced fears for the Falkland Islanders, mainly Protestant
and of Scottish extraction, who he suggested were at the mercy of the
Catholic Argentineans. Wolfe also criticised those who allowed the Pope to
visit Scotland in 1982. He was later removed from the party hierarchy for
his outburst). Former SNP parliamentary candidate Hamish Watt was also
known to be strongly against Catholic schools in the same period.
Nonetheless, in relation to the other Scottish Parties, present SNP recognition
of the need to maintain Catholic schools is the most conspicuous.

In the 1990s, Strathclyde Region's Education Committee has been at the
centre of these altercations over Catholic schooling, the issue contentiously
re-emerging due to falling school rolls, lack of finance and the perceived
need to increase school size to broaden subject choice for pupils.
Subsequently, the Education Committee has closed down a number of
schools and amalgamated others. However, this has also created a problem
where the local Catholic school has been closed and pupils are left with a
choice of having to travel a further distance to the nearest Catholic school
available or transferring to a non-Catholic school. In other instances, non-
Catholic children may find that their nearest school is a Roman Catholic one.
This may mean that there are more non-Catholics than Catholics in a
'Catholic school' (schools must accept children of any or no faith). Thus the
idea of a Catholic ethos in a 'Catholic school' becomes nonsensical for many

Catholics. Some Catholics view such moves as an insidious way of dismantling Catholic schools. The views of some Labour councillors in Glasgow, who generally view the integration of schools as a social and political goal,[54] gives some credibility to these fears of the Catholic hierarchy and laypeople (See Keating, Levy, Geekie, Brand, 1989).

Catholic defensiveness is increased by the generally held beliefs of the Educational Institute of Scotland (EIS), the schoolteachers' main trade union. A motion passed at conference in 1979 displaying opposition to Catholic schooling, resulted in a large proportion of their Catholic membership threatening to leave the union. In a speech in 1985, the retiring president of the EIS also criticised Catholic schools stating:

> The segregation of children only five years old on religious grounds is wrong, grossly so....In this matter the law is not merely an ass but an assassin....The results....the tribalism of broken heads at Hampden and the broken hearts of couples whose plans to marry in good faith have been defeated by prejudice, are unacceptable to the majority of the Scottish people.[55]

'Archbishop' Winning countered McLachlan's speech stating:

> It shows what the Catholic community have to put up with from people who I believe have no time for religion in schools.[56]

Popular identities and attitudes

The media is an opinion former but it also reflects attitudes and identities. As such, it is important in the context of this work that contemporary newspapers are used to exhibit Scottish society's marked differentiation from the wider British society with regards not only to the schools issue but also to the more general question of religious related issues within society. Such concerns are not seen as issues elsewhere in the United Kingdom, outside Northern Ireland.

In particular, the (Glasgow) Herald letters column in 1990/91 reflected the heated nature of the schools debate with correspondence on a weekly and often a daily basis (though this period was one of particular intensity, such correspondence is ongoing). This reflected increased concern about the issues of falling school rolls, school mergers and school closures. The continual stream of these letters flooding into the Herald also meant that the editor was not simply choosing letters to fill space in his newspaper. The letters originated from people from all social and political strata in Scottish society. Their line of argument is reiterated whenever and wherever the issue is discussed.

The following representative examples of these letters offer evidence of the antagonisms involved. They show the historical importance of religious identity in Scotland in a way that can quite often be obscured, while they also reflect the depth, widespread nature and pervasiveness of these identities. They repeat the themes of many of the people who have argued against

Catholic schools in the past. They connect with similar expressions in the contemporary popular press while they reflect a number of the arguments forwarded by a number of the Scottish Churches as well as by a number of people interviewed for this book. As a result, they are also evidence of how the schools issue is connected to many matters in society which may otherwise seem unrelated. As evidence of the importance, irascible and conflictual nature of the schools issue, these letters should not be underestimated considering the weight of such material.

Can any supporter of segregated education seriously deny that if all the youngsters in Northern Ireland had been educated in the same secular, non-denominational schools, the number of casualties in that unhappy province would have been greatly reduced?[57]

Why should there be such antagonism to our interdenominational system of education system having as its aim integration rather than separation, combined with a purposeful unification of all factions? In perpetuating the ghastly system of apartheid it is obvious what is feared most by the Roman Catholic hierarchy is losing the tenacious grip that is invaluable for indoctrination during the child's tender years. Such a loss would spell a major blow to Roman Catholicism.[58]

I do believe that the religious prejudice which still exists in some quarters, and in many ways is peculiar to the west of Scotland, will disappear altogether within a generation if separate schools are removed from our educational system.[59]

We know why Mr Sillars was so very sure that he was going to win in Govan. He knew he had the support of the most powerful church in the country, a church - as has been proved recently - which no longer trusts Labour. And his opponent in Govan was Labour.[60]

Religion should be left to parents and the church....it is certainly not the business of teachers.[61]

Why can't those who advocate the retention of the dual education system admit that they are both bigoted and hypocritical? They want to maintain their segregationist policies while living under a facade of Christianity. The only contribution the system makes to the Scottish Nation, and to the West of Scotland in particular, is to provide us with a breeding ground of superstition and mistrust. The sooner the children come together, the sooner they will stop growing up to perpetuate their parents hatred.[62]

160

What sort of world do we live in when MPs and councillors sell their souls because they believe in integrated schools but, for fear of losing votes, their implementation of convictions goes by the board?[63]

The answer is simple. The Roman Catholic Church should be given two options; their schools remain within the State system and appointments are made by the education authority; or Roman Catholic schools opt out of the system and are funded by the Church....The situation as it stands is unacceptable.[64]

Once again Scotland's very own 'apartheid' - separate schools with children divided by religion - rears its ugly head....In an increasingly secular society, why should religion, any form of religion, be taught in state schools? Religion is divisive.[65]

Once again we can see two issues return to the letters page of the Herald and once again we can probably predict that the two shall remain separate in the minds of the people of the West of Scotland. I am of course referring to the last Old Firm match at Ibrox, and the continuation of segregated schools....If we are serious about eradicating the hatred which is vented in the name of sport, let's not try to ease our conscience by arresting a few overpaid footballers. The only solution is for a full integration of our schools.[66]

The defence of Catholic schools centres mainly upon a religious and spiritual testimony. The Catholic perspective and argument is again reflected in a number of letters to the Herald.

Catholic schools support their and their Church's efforts to develop their children's spiritual lives, through the delivery of the religious education programme, and by creating opportunities for our young people to pray and worship together within a whole community of faith....Catholic schools reflect Catholic Christian values in a loving and caring atmosphere, as opposed to the values of society at large, which is largely secular....Catholic schools will encourage the development of intellectual abilities, integrity, and respect for the truth.[67]

What is so wrong in wanting our children to learn in an atmosphere where Christian values of love, respect, sharing, and faith are passed on? Catholic schools do not pass on something wrong or evil to children; they attempt to pass on the message of Jesus Christ, which is a message of love.[68]

The non-denominational school can guarantee only that religion will be presented for study and not as a way of life. What worries Catholic parents is that this must encourage agnosticism or even lead to atheism.[69]

Many countries have Catholic schools yet do not have the sectarianism found in Scotland. The divisions are there for complex historical reasons....British society is based on division and those who decry Catholic schools are somewhat hypocritical if they do not challenge institutional bigotry, such as in the Act of Succession.[70]

Any bigotry or intolerance which exists in society emanates not from the goodness of the Catholic school but from the forces of evil as exemplified by the extremist groups in Northern Ireland and some parts of Scotland.[71]

Catholic education regards knowledge as having two sources; divine revelation and human reason. It stresses the role of faith which can enlarge our understanding and take us beyond the fingertips of the mind.[72]

Though segregation is involved in both instances, racial apartheid is characterised by lack of choice and oppression whereas denominational schools are the product of choice and an extension of parental rights.[73]

I have spent most of my 25 years of ministry in parishes where there is no Catholic school and all the children go to the so - called inter-denominational school. At best it is Protestant, and at worst, secular and humanist, in my experience.[74]

Catholic schools are only an 'imposition' on ratepayers to the extent that any school funded by the rates must, by definition, be burdensome, but hardly especially so by reason of being Catholic.[75]

Catholic children can receive a proper academic education, with adequate time allotted to religious instruction by people properly trained to do so. This, I fear, in a predominantly Presbyterian country, would not be achieved in an education system of state schools only where the natural anti-Catholic prejudices endemic of our country would be fostered by those responsible for administering the system, to the detriment of Catholic children.[76]

The evidence here, and from the statements of the Catholic authorities, indicates that Catholics who support their own schools do not see religion as a subject which can be added to, or taken from, the curriculum. Such a view is considered to be a misunderstanding of the rationale of Catholic schools. Catholic schools are based upon a particular view of the relations between

162

the school, the parishes and the family.[77]

The existence of Catholic schools is under strain and this is manifest clearly in the first group of letters. The antagonism or 'realpolitik' of most political parties and figures is also clear.

Perhaps one of the greatest pressures exerted upon the Catholic school identity originates with the popular press in Scotland. Certainly, many Catholics believe that some newspapers are perceptibly anti-Catholic on issues as diverse as Northern Ireland, Celtic Football Club, Irish political activity and the schools issue.[78] Such perceptions have led many Catholics to see much of this comment not only as secularist, but also to view it in a similar way to that of Jim Sillars, a mark of the intolerance and prejudicial nature of Scottish society at large (it is also an important comment on Catholics in Scotland and on their distinctive identity. Also see conclusion). As indicated in the introduction however, such reporting contributes to misinformed and evasive assumptions concerning the origins of religious cleavage and 'sectarianism' in Scottish society. Popular Scottish media reporting on the subject reflects many of the elements used in previous decades.

Such reporting in Scotland's most popular selling regular, The Daily Record, periodically proclaims 'Barred, Kids caught in the storm over Catholic schools', 'We Are United' (a headline repeated on occasion), and 'Its Pupil Power: Walkout kids in schools protest'. One article stated:

> They swim together....they play football together....and last night David became old enough to join his pal in the Beavers. But there is an Act of Parliament that says Douglas, six, and five year-old David could be kept apart during the day - because one is a Protestant and the other is a Catholic.[79]

For some Catholics, this represents an attack on their Catholic religion and identity. The effect of an ongoing and frequently torrid debate concerning Catholic schools, apart from notions of religious identity, secularism and the spiritual dimension of life, are of political as well as cultural significance.

Some of these political tensions are demonstrated in the way that many non-Catholic (as well as some Catholic) teachers in Strathclyde and in the EIS are opposed to the Catholic Church's influence on some aspects of teaching appointments in Catholic schools.[80] In appointments to Catholic schools a priest has to testify 'that the applicant has been known to me for some time and that he/she gives personal witness to the faith in his/her daily life'.[81] The Catholic Church in the west central area has deliberately attempted to make the rationale for Catholic schools clearer to the faithful, in order to galvanise them as a solid force behind the schools. This was something that was previously taken for granted by the Church authorities (recent research shows that as far as the Church attending sector of the Catholic population is concerned, there is massive support for Catholic schools).[82]

In other areas the political overtones of the debate are also clear. In 1991, a Scottish newspaper reported on a letter from a Catholic priest to Strathclyde Council Labour leader, Charles Gray, stating:

A Roman Catholic priest has threatened Strathclyde region's elected leadership with retaliation at the ballot box unless it withdraws plans to close St Mary's primary in Glasgow's East End.[83]

Ultimately, the continuing divisiveness of the issue on the social and political agenda is viewed by many Catholics as a manifestation of the historic Scottish Protestant attack upon the Catholic religion and identity; little has changed for such Catholics. Closure and integration are viewed as instruments 'of covert ideological politics'.[84] Despite growing secular disagreement with Catholic schools within Scotland, some Catholics believe that the anti-Irish and anti-Catholic arguments regarding the schools issue have only changed in presentation, not in substance. They point to the explicit 'anti' nature of the arguments that the Orange Institution and some of the smaller Scottish Churches forward with regards to the schools and view other demonstrations in the same light (in recent years some of this antagonism has taken on a humanist and secular element).

The schools issue is undoubtedly a potentially corrosive one for some of the political parties. Although there has traditionally been a massive Catholic attachment to Labour in Scotland, there may in fact be the first sign of a change in Catholic political allegiance. According to the survey, there seems to be no significant move towards either the Conservatives or the SNP on the part of Catholics. However, the one in five who identified themselves as not supporting any political party, may be an indication of an emerging class of floating voter amongst the Catholic community. Any move of this sort may be a result of social/moral issues becoming more salient for many Catholics.

Indeed, in 1991 the Labour Party banned the anti-abortion grouping, 'Labour Life' because the pressure group's policy went against party policy. Archbishop Winning responded to Labour on behalf of the Catholic Church in Scotland:

> The pro-life credentials of individual candidates and of political parties should, I believe, play a crucial role in deciding who we vote for....We should think long and hard before we vote for someone who is prepared to permit the killing of unborn babies.

The editorial of the official journal of the Archdiocese of Glasgow, Flourish, continued the Archbishop's theme, but in addition, took the political dimension of the argument a step further:

> Is Labour, any more than any other party, best poised to reflect our Christian priorities? The dilemma is evident in its grudging attitude to Catholic schools but it is thrown into sharper relief by its pro-abortion policy - an issue which no Catholic can regard as marginal....Significantly, during voting on that Bill [the Embryo Act], several Labour MPs stood at the entrance to the pro-life lobby making the Sign of the Cross, whilst jeering at others, saying "the Pope says go that way....The time has come for Catholics to make their views known to the party which

traditionally expects their support: the time has come to let it be known that "care" can never mean "kill".[85]

The press, as well as at least one Catholic Labour MP in Scotland (who is in fact against abortion), criticised Winning for interfering in politics and attempting to influence party political choice.[86]

As far as Winning is concerned he is attempting to raise a fundamental issue of Catholic moral and social belief to a higher political platform. Winning believes that if housing, nuclear weapons, education and perceived cutbacks in the NHS are issues of political and moral importance, then even more so is abortion, particularly given that; 'one in five pregnancies in Britain now ends in abortion'.[87] Of course, this belief is shared by many ordinary Catholics and a number of Catholic Labour MPs.[88] The Archbishop argues that he is attempting to educate Catholics to vote not out of habit, but based on what MPs and parties say about issues. Winning argues that Catholics, like anyone else, have a right to use the opportunity 'to shape the parties we have'.[89]

The Labour Party in Scotland remained relatively silent amid the furore.[90] For some Catholics, this may reflect the Party's concern that if such religious related matters became key party political issues, they might lose much of their Catholic constituency.[91] One leading British newspaper commented upon the link in Scotland between these issues and religious identity in society. It pointed out that 'mixing abortion, Labour and the Roman Catholic Church makes a powerful west of Scotland cocktail'. [92]

The 'attack' by Winning and Flourish was not simply an attack on Labour or an attempt to introduce morality into politics on one issue. Since its founding in the late 1970s, Flourish has also emphasised what it regards as the lack of a moral element in the policies of the Conservative Government. Arguments against the Government's perceived cutbacks in the health service,[93] their treatment of the poor[94] and Government sanctions policy on South Africa,[95] have been a recurring theme.

Catholic's letters to the press were generally supportive of the Archbishop; this illustrating a high degree of support for an anti-abortion stance amongst the community itself.[96] Some believed that it was important that the issue should have an important place on the political agenda:

> any political ideology which considers unborn life to be part of the Age of the Disposable must be confronted. Archbishop Thomas Winning, president of the Conference of Bishops of Scotland, has chosen to do so now, not a day too early....It is commonplace for politicians to set the political agenda: this stratagem is a usurpation of the role of the electorate.[97]

Future Scottish Shadow Secretary, Tom Clarke, contributed to the debate by writing for the Catholic Observer, following the publication of the controversial Flourish article. Ironically, Clarke fully supported the Archbishop's stance. He also resurrected a key element in the 'old' Catholic identity by making an appeal to the Catholicism and socialism of John Wheatley, arguing that Catholic hopes and aspirations for 'improving the quality of life' were still to be best found in the Labour Party.[98] Here an issue with direct religious overtones can be seen to possess the capacity to create another dimension to political cleavage in Scotland, as well as to influence a possible re-alignment of voters.

Conclusion

In this chapter it has been the task to place the Irish Catholic identity in its historical setting, whilst looking to see how and why it has changed? Some of the answers to these questions are addressed more fully in the concluding chapter.

Irish political activity in Scotland today is only a shadow of its former self. The watershed which took place in much of the Irish consciousness in the post 1916-23 period, corresponding to the rise of Labour, caused many immigrant Irish to look away from politics in Ireland and set about the task of improving their lot. This invariably marked a step in their integration into the wider community. For some, two generations passed before the renewed Irish troubles rekindled a more political form of Irish nationalism.

However, the emphasis here has been on activity. Irish political activity amongst the Irish in Scotland generally (as distinct from those of a purely left wing background) involves only a few thousand people. Irish political activity is restricted to Irish Republican activities (although a branch of Fianna Fail did exist in Glasgow until the 1960s) and usually this entails a level of support for the Irish Republican Army. Nonetheless, the legacy of the Irish nationalist immigrant mind-set has lasted throughout the period of immigration and cultural integration/assimilation. Support still remains strong (though its salience is variable) for a united Ireland, independent from Britain. The survey figures for all types of Catholic opinion is evidence of this support.

Clear from the data collected here is that for many of the offspring of the Irish, the habit of a family holiday in Ireland every few years, began to disappear with the outbreak of the Troubles (while the outbreak also coincided with the rise of the affordable holiday abroad). The passage of time had already inevitably diluted some of the direct family connections with Ireland for many Irish. However, for many of these second, third and even fourth generation Irish, the Troubles meant contact with relations at home became more infrequent. Invariably, as the Irish identity itself has become affected, so too has Irish political consciousness in Scotland.

A number of other factors are worth noting. Some young people of Irish descent have in the 1980s and 1990s, in a number of instances, begun again the habit of holidaying in Ireland. Empirical observations and discussions conducted throughout the period of this investigation gives a strong impression of younger people appearing less inhibited by the northern Troubles than their parent's and grandparent's generations. A wider literature on the Troubles now permeates some parts of the Catholic community in Scotland. In addition, the 'old rebel' records of fathers and grandfathers have been replaced by other accessible Irish and 'rebel' music in the 1980s and 1990s. This development adds substance to the argument of Isajiw (1974, pp. 111-124):

Much evidence indicates in North America ethnic identities persist beyond cultural assimilation and that the persistence of ethnic identity is not necessarily related to the perpetuation of traditional ethnic culture. Rather, it may depend more on the emergence of ethnic 're-discoverers', i.e., persons from any consecutive ethnic generation who have been socialised into the culture of the general society but who develop a symbolic relation to the culture of their ancestors. Even relatively few items from the cultural past, such as folk art, music, can become symbols of ethnic identity.

In addition, this choice may correspond to their needs created by the specific character of the relations in society as a whole.

The point here is that, despite the undoubted a general Catholic distaste for violence in Northern Ireland and seemingly in contempt of British interpretations of the northern Troubles, an Irish nationalist identity persists among the offspring of the Irish in Scotland. One observer has described part of this 'Irish legacy':

> The common memory of the Irish people is enshrined in these songs - the names of dead heroes and past victories and recollections of old wrongs. Ever recurring themes and motifs keep the past alive, and relate it to present struggles, individual and national. There are young men in the first flush of their youth, sacrificing themselves willingly so that Ireland may be more nearly free....The Irish are constantly alive to history.[99]

Many Catholics in Scotland have a varyingly passionate, but more often passive, emotional attachment to an Ireland united and detached from a British presence. Much of this support is instinctive and inherited; it is not a dynamic identity. Rather, it is part of the Catholic identity. It is part of immigrant Catholic culture; a disposition of mind, a loyalty, an emotion and a political identity.

The importance of the Celtic club as a focus for the Irish identity should not be underestimated. Throughout its history the club has been perceived as a safe and appropriate environment for the singing of Irish nationalist songs. Today, amongst many of the fans, Celtic Park is the context in which they engage in nationalist 'conversations' and exchange/purchase nationalist literature. It has been a prime socialising and politicising mechanism during the Northern Ireland troubles; an arena for the promotion of a nationalist sub-culture. Apart from the Catholic Church itself, the Celtic club has become the most important medium for cultural expression. The majority of those who follow Celtic, either passively or actively, are the Irish who are in a sense most proud of their origins, and who are least prepared to subvert their identity amidst the hostility experienced. This was evidenced in the past in the way that the Celtic club became the focus and symbol of the Irish in Scotland. It is evident in the present, as indicated by the survey data, by the fact that Celtic fans are more likely to identify themselves as Irish than are Catholic Church goers (although there is obviously an overlap in membership). Thus the intensity of being Irish is both raised by, and expressed through, the Celtic Football Club. Celtic is therefore of major importance to vast numbers of Catholics; they are a socialising agent into a unique form of Irish cultural activity.

By emerging as the major focus for much Irish and Catholic secular activity, Celtic inadvertently have also contributed to the demise of other more intrinsically Irish cultural activities. Celtic absorbed much of this activity and consciousness to the point that for many people it became the only obvious manifestation of an Irish identity. As a result, the language, music, and inherent sporting traditions of Ireland have only had a fluctuating degree of success in the relevant parts of Scotland. Celtic have the paradoxical capacity to stimulate and enhance the Irish identity and consciousness, whilst also assisting in aspects of its demise.

Regardless of the patriotic clothes worn by the offspring of the immigrants, this characteristic should not be emphasised at the expense of other factors of Catholic life in Scotland. For over half a century the main political concerns of the Catholic Irish has been borne of their everyday circumstances and aspirations. Over the past three generations the immigrant community have submerged themselves in Labour Party activity or support. Thus they have integrated into mainstream political life in Scotland.

An important feature of this pattern has been the communal nature of the support; that both working and middle class Catholics have voted Labour. The party invited and then shaped the traditional political rebelliousness and radicalism of the Irish (see, Hickman, 1990, for references to Irish radicalism and its perceived dangers to the British establishment in the 19th century). The Irish also made an impact upon Labour thinking; the influence of John Wheatley was particularly important. Ironically too, despite this Catholic Irish attachment to Labour, the party have, since the outbreak of the Troubles, essentially followed a bi-partisan policy with the Conservatives with regards to Northern Ireland. Northern Ireland has not been an important question, or has been avoided, on both the British political and the Labour Party agenda.[100]

The existence today of a one in five 'floating voter' means that the Labour-Catholic marriage may be entering a trial period, as issues such as abortion and Catholic schools have came increasingly to the fore. There is no indication that Catholics will switch their allegiance to the SNP or the Conservatives. Rather, the key point is that issues important to those with a strong Catholic identity, are emerging onto the mainstream political agenda. Abortion is often seen as a pre-eminent Catholic issue (though the FP Church and the Free Church are also anti-abortion, whilst the Church of Scotland has a fluctuating policy), and positions taken by parties and individual MPs are likely to have an important influence on future Catholic voting patterns.

This social and moral alienation of many Catholic Labour supporters, may mean a fundamental shift in certain west central constituencies of Scotland where Catholics are most concentrated. In a similar vein, the disputes over Catholic schooling also threaten Labour's dominance in Scottish electoral politics. Labour could find itself split on the issue and faced with a traditional Catholic support who's demands they can no longer meet.

For Irish immigrants in Scotland, the Catholic education established for the community remains one of the linchpins of distinctive Catholic identity. Although Catholic education has, academically, been absorbed within the state system, it has retained a distinctiveness in reference to ethnicity, ethos, spiritual awareness, belief and practice. The contribution which defenders of Catholic schools claim they make towards the upbringing of young Catholics is inadvertently supported by the Government Department of Education, who in 1991 advertised the general teaching profession, stating:

> You can't overestimate a teacher's contribution to a child's development. School helps to shape future adults. Not simply in terms of careers but in less obvious ways too. Attitudes, outlook and self- confidence, for example, are all affected by a teacher's skills.

The Catholic identity and view of religion gains substance from the existence of Catholic schools in Scotland which are strongly supported by Catholic parents. Certainly, such support, as evidenced by the amount of young Catholics who attend these schools, also undermines the claims of critics such as politicians on the Strathclyde Education Committee, who in 1990 stated that Catholic schools were falling apart from within and were enjoying a lessening support from their own community.[101]

Perceived attacks on Catholic schools can come from various sources. Elements of Scots society resent the presence of Roman Catholicism in the country and the schools are viewed as the prime reason for its persistence. There are also arguments from the secular lobby whom are themselves influenced by the ideas of some Protestants as well as people of no religious beliefs. The Catholic community have also been subject to the rigours of the secular press.[102]

Certainly, Catholic schools must be considered as amongst the most salient features of the Catholic Irish identity in Scotland today (though there is little or no Irish content within the schools themselves). This is primarily because they would not exist in 'Protestant Scotland' except for the factors of Irish immigration, but also because most of their occupants are the tangible product of that immigration.

Notes

1. See Handley, 1964, Chapter on Free Press controversy.

2. Ross A: The Development Of The Scottish Catholic Community, 1878-1978; in D McRoberts (ed.), Modern Scottish Catholicism, 1878-1978, Burns, Glasgow, 1979, pp30-55.

3. Hugh Dougherty; Glasgow Herald, 9/2/90.

4. Tommy Main; Irish Post, 15/8/87.

5. Interview with Archbishop (elevated to Cardinal at the end of 1994) Winning of the Glasgow Archdiocese; 21/6/91.

6. Glasgow Herald, 13/11/87.

7.   Scottish Catholic Observer (S.C.O); 21/3/86.

8.   Herald, 18/3/91 and Strathclyde University Telegraph, 4/5/89. In a similar vein, popular 90s bands Runrig, Deacon Blue and Hue and Cry, have been viewed as having celebrated Scottish nationalist and cultural identities, and, as a result, often attract a largely corresponding audience to their concerts.

9.   Irish Post, 19/3/88.

10.   Interviews with Benny Kangley of Port Glasgow Hibernians, and Tommy Paton of Carfin Hibernians, 14/6/91. Also see A.O.H programme for annual demonstration, Saturday, June 27th 1981.

11.   As a consequence of their overt Republicanism, from the late 1970s, the James Connolly Band from Glasgow was ordered by the Hibernians not to participate in their parades.

12.   Labour and Ireland; No 15, pp11-13; and Irish Post, 19/3/88.

13.   See Irish Post for example, 9/12/89.

14.   Jimmy Wright, a leading member of the RBA, and a member of the James Connolly Flute Band from Govan in Glasgow, is prominent in Scottish left wing Republican circles. Wright's strong feelings, as well as connections with the Scottish Republican Socialists in the 1980s, led to him attempting to have the Scottish saltire flown alongside the Irish Tricolour, by every Irish republican band. This caused a degree of turmoil among the bands who were motivated by mainly Irish ideas, and had little affinity with Scotland. A compromise was reached, after some bands threatened to leave the Alliance, and which basically stated that bands could opt to fly the Scottish flag if they so wished.

15.   Whilst carrying out the survey amongst the Jim Lynagh Republican Band in Dumbarton, an impromptu meeting was held, in which one activist encouraged the others to collect in the following days, and to forcibly prevent Poll Tax officers from entering the home of a non-paying protester.

16.   Flourish, July 87.

17.   Daily Record, 4/5/88 and 28/5/91.

18.   See, Lennox Herald, 18/4/86; County Reporter, 23/4/86 Also for counter demonstrations against the Orange Lodge. See, Lennox Herald, 15/4/88 for Republican marches in Dumbarton, and Sunday Mail and the Sunday Observer (Scotland), for similar troubles in Edinburgh. The latter article also refers to the growing involvement of the BNP in anti Republican activities.

19. Flourish, May 1988.

20. Flourish, July 1987.

21. Airdrie and Coatbridge Advertiser, 1/8/86. Also see 19/9/86.

22. This was more or less confirmed by Archbishop Winning during interview.

23. S.C.O, 27/7/90.

24. S.C.O, 13/10/89.

25. S.C.O, 26/8/88.

26. In 1991, sales of the Scottish Catholic Observer was approximately 20,000, while Flourish was between 14,000 and 16,000.

27. S.C.O, 3/11/89.

28. S.C.O, 19/10/90.

29. S.C.O, 2/11/90.

30. S.C.O, 16/11/90.

31. Interviews with ex-member of Glasgow 'Sinn Fein', June 1991.

32. Irish Post, 4/3/89.

33. Files, letters, communications and minutes of meetings, of Glasgow Sinn Fein, 1981-85.

34. Interview with member of the Glasgow Birmingham Six committee, June 1991. See also a number of references in the S.C.O in early 1991; for example 22/3/91. Previous to this, Flourish commented on the issue on a couple of occasions.

35. The theme of Catholic social values was referred to by the SNP leader, Alex Salmond at his parties annual conference at Inverness in September 1994.

36. This was a common theme to arise in the course of a number of interviews conducted among Catholic subjects of the questionnaire.

37. Orange Torch, July/August 1986.

38. Interview with David Bryce, 15/1/90. At a local level in the Monklands there is a degree of argument going on at present relating to nepotisic employment practices. However, most informed opinion

stress that where there is any truth in this, it is a negative custom but one unaffected by religious considerations. It is also a problem found in other Labour councils as well as a number of Conservative ones in England. In an attempt to establish the facts behind the controversy, an independent enquiry, paid for by the local council, was to give its findings in early to mid 1995.

39. A contested case in Stirlingshire 1924-30 provided the practical example for future developments in this aspect of the Act. See references in Douglas, 1985, p94; and Gourley, 1990, pp119-131.

40. Glasgow Herald, 8/5/35.

41. For Ratcliffe, see Gallagher, The Uneasy Peace, 1987, chapter 4. For Cormack, see Gallagher, 1987, Edinburgh Divided, Polygon.

42. The Free Church's General Assembly of 1967 stated that education cannot be utterly secular.

43. Free Church Monthly Record, editorial, March 1986.

44. Interview with David Bryce.

45. The only authoritative reference which gives some credence to the financial side of the argument was reported by Barclay McBain in the Glasgow Herald, 3/5/91. However, this is open to interpretation.

46. Orange Torch, September 1986.

47. Glasgow Herald, 10/3/70.

48. Interview with Tony Worthington, 18/6/91.

49. Quotes from contemporary document of the Labour Party in Scotland.

50. Interview with Craig Stevenson of Conservative Party headquarters in Ednburgh, 14/6/91.

51. Herald, 27/3/93.

52. Flourish, May 1991.

53. This is more obviously shown in the line taken by the Orange Institution in Scotland; i.e. June 91.

54. For example, see interview with Ian Davidson, Chairman of Strathclyde Region's Education Committee, in Flourish, May 1991.

55. Times Higher Education Supplement for Scotland, 14/6/85.

56.   Evening Times, 6/6/85.

57.   Glasgow Herald (unless stated all letters are from the same source), 20/5/90.

58.   10/5/91.
59.   24/4/91.

60.   7/5/91.

61.   14/12/90.

62.   14/12/90.

63.   15/11/90.

64.   5/11/90.

65.   14/9/90.

66.   18/11/87.

67.   15/5/91.

68.   18/3/91.

69.   1/5/91.

70.   27/12/90.

71.   14/12/90.

72.   30/11/90.

73.   16/10/90.

74.   S.C.O 22/1/88.

75.   18/11/87.

76.   18/11/87.

77.   A degree of debate has also been apparent in recent years within some Catholic circles over the continuing validity of Catholic Schools. The debate has had a new element added to it by a demand for Muslim or Muslim influenced schools in Glasgow, and indeed in other parts of Britain. See Sunday Observer (Scotland) 30/7/89, 18/3/90, 6/5/90; and the Glasgow Herald, 19/6/91, 20/6/91, 22/6/91.

78.   A general impression given during interviews. Also reinforced in the course of new research being carried out by the author based on the attitudes of parishoners at a Catholic Church in Hamilton.

79.   Daily Record, 17/5/88, 18/5/88, 13/1/89.

80.   Glasgow Herald, 1/11/90.

81.   Sunday Observer (Scotland), 23/12/90. Also relevant document published on behalf of the 'Catholic Education Commission of the Bishops' Conference of Scotland, February, 1991'.

82.   Glasgow Herald, 15/4/91. Also, interview with Archbishop Winning, 5/7/91. See footnote 96.

83.   Glasgow Herald, 1/5/91.

84.   See Glasgow Herald, 10/1/91. Not only is this view manifest in the Catholic media, but it was an attitude displayed by some Catholics who were subject to the questionnaire.

85.   Flourish, July, 1991.

86.   Jimmy Wray, Glasgow Provan, stated; "I hope that people will vote for the party they want to vote for....the Roman Catholic Church should not be able to dictate who they should vote for": Glasgow Herald, 5/7/91.

87.   Interview with Archbishop Winning, 5/7/91.

88.   Interview with Fr Noel Barry, Editor of Flourish, 17/7/91.

89.   Interview with Archbishop Winning, 5/7/91, & Flourish, July, 1991. A number of Catholic Labour MPs subsequently phoned the Flourish office to give their support to the Archbishop.

90.   Glasgow Herald, 5/7/91.

91.   See Glasgow Herald, 8/7/91, article by Brian Meek.

92.   Glasgow Herald, 7/7/91.

93.   Flourish, March, 1989.

94.   Flourish, May, 1988.

95.   Flourish, 1990.

96. See Flourish, 29/4/89, for results of a Gallup Poll which considered such questions among Catholics. Again, this attitude has been reinforced by current research focusing on the parishoners of the Hamilton parish of St Marys'.

97. Glasgow Herald, 11/7/91.

98. Scottish Catholic Observer, 19/7/91.

99. Article by Carey Schofield on 'The Kilburn Irish'.

100. A member of the Coatbridge Labour Party informed the writer that the moment the issue of Ireland was introduced, the discussion was deliberately and quickly moved to another area. The Party in this district is numerically dominated by Roman Catholics.

101. In the Motherwell diocese approximately three thousand Catholics are born every year. 90% go on to attend Catholic primaries (some of the 'shortfall' can be accounted for by everyday factors like deaths and migration). In 1990, twenty-five of the resultant pre-secondary school pupils did not go to a Catholic secondary. In the Glasgow diocese, which Catholics have traditionally seen as being more vulnerable to demographic change, 96.3% of Catholic children went on to a Catholic secondary school. From interview with Bishop Devine of the Motherwell Diocese, 22/7/91. Also, information from Fr Noel Barry of the Glasgow Archdiocese

102. Ibid.

Other Sources:

Burnett Roy: Time to get out of Ulster for the sake of Scotland; in the Sunday Observer (Scotland) 13/8/89. McGarrigle Joe: St Patrick's Day in Glasgow; Donegal Democrat, 31/3/89. Irish Post, 8/6/91, 16/5/87, 28/3/87, 9/12/89. CARN, Magazine of the Celtic League: Interview with the Republican Band Alliance, Winter 1987/88, No 60. Ireland's War, September 1988, No 28. Sunday Tribune, article on The Wolfe Tones in Glasgow, 1983. Glasgow Herald, Review of Christy Moore, 22/10/85. Files, letters, communications and minutes of meetings, of Glasgow Sinn Fein, 1981-85. Also Sinn Fein Bulletins, November and January 1983 and 1984. Literature - various; from, The Republican Band Alliance, Birmingham Six Campaign, Glasgow, Time To Go, Glasgow, Guildford Four Campaign, Glasgow.

7 Identities

America has been consumed since its birth by the troublesome question of race, and for decades sport has constantly served as the most visible expression of its racial tempest, mirroring society's darkest prejudices.[1]

Identities

This book emphasises the historical importance of religion and its concomitant identities to Scottish society. It also stresses the role which football plays in relation to religious and political identities (the above quote shows Scotland is not unique as far as the socio-political role of sport is concerned). Religious identities cannot be reduced to questions of religious commitment. Rather, this work indicates the ethnopolitical, ethnosociological and ethnocultural nature of these identities.

Many previous attempts to explore religious identity in Scotland have been constrained by both the abuse and over-use of the term sectarianism. However, sectarianism is only one aspect of religious identity. In particular, concentrating on sectarianism emphasises only the negative aspects of religious identity. Its use has often been limited to looking at black and white, positive and negative, images of society. It frequently posits one group in opposition to the other. Using the concept of identity and exploring its ethnic and religious manifestations, has enabled us to appreciate features of religion in Scotland which are otherwise ignored.

The concept of identity is not imbued with the traditional moral judgements of the past. It is a more open concept, less vague and evasive, allows more subtlety and assists us in adding to our knowledge of religion in Scottish society. Although the key concept here has been identity, an important secondary concept has been that of ethnicity. The definitions used here of ethnicity have also allowed us to move away from the narrowness associated with the term sectarianism, whilst raising the possibility of analysing some of the identities involved.

Religion is a badge in Scotland. Of course, it is important in its own right for many people. However, it is also a badge recognised as standing for particular traditions, cultures, sub-cultures and, sometimes, national identities. In addition, a great number of social organisations and social practices in Scotland are constituted on a religious basis or are influenced by religious identities. In much of Scotland, as in Northern Ireland; 'relationships are rarely reached in ignorance of the religion of each party' (Darby, 1978, p. 161). In fact, the major social division in Scotland is based on religious identity.

However, as many social factors have developed and changed in the 20th century, so too have these identities. Invariably, this has resulted in the evolution and diversification of much of the nature of the historical cleavage. In part, this socio-political change has paralleled the development of football in Scotland in the late 19th and 20th centuries. In this book, both the descriptive element and the survey/analytical one reflect how, as in Spain, Northern Ireland and in major parts of the English game, Scottish soccer has become politicised as well as socially and culturally symbolic. Frith and Hornett's argument (1988, p. 16) that: 'people's sense of themselves has always come from the use of images and symbols', implicitly recognises this development. However, it is separate from the grander political concerns which only effect the majority of people in a way mediated by, and through, politicians and the media. It is not the politics which the media and politicians see as determining who does what, where and when in British democratic practice. Indeed, allowing for the presence of a complexity of factors, it is a politics that has little to do with economistic interpretations of social and political relationships, but more to do with common perceptions of cultural hegemony that sees one of its manifestations in the football arena.

The concern here therefore is with a politics which revolves around perceptions of history and linkages to the religious and cultural identities which produce this cleavage in Scottish society. This strata of politics and identities does not exist below or above the more usually addressed class or regional identities in Scotland. In fact, they co-exist with them and through them.[2] They can dominate or become subservient to them, depending on the social context experienced by either the individual or the group concerned. Rokkan and Urwin make the same general point, stressing that:

> individuals can possess more than one identity, and several layers of identity can exist....whether these multiple identities are benign or antagonistic depends in each instance upon the particular political [and social] concatenation of events. (1983, p. 114)

Although there is some ethno-religious motivated voting in Scotland (clearly manifest in the Monklands By Election of mid 1994), it is a mistake to reduce the political nature of religious cleavage to the question of a relationship between religion and voting. People can express their politics in a variety of ways. Political ideas and attitudes, for example, could have been asserted through not buying South African goods because of a dislike for Apartheid in that country. A vast number of people also took to the streets throughout Britain to protest against the community charge in 1990/91.

Chapter 6 has also indicated how moral issues such as abortion have the potential to become significant political issues also.

Likewise, ethno-religious political attitudes in Scotland can often be more manifest in street demonstrations and counter demonstrations, in group affiliations and activity and in sport; particularly in the field of Scottish football. People in Scotland do not 'think religion' and then vote on that basis. This book has reflected that the state and its institutions are not the only vehicles or focus for political attitudes, identities and activity. The political importance of religion does not lie solely in voting patterns. Rather, voting primarily reflects what might be termed socially related economic attitudes (health, employment, trade unions, etc.). Religious identity has never fully translated into a political cleavage in Scotland but as this book shows, it does contain crucial political resonances. Religion then is not simply reflected in politics, indeed, it often contains much more of a cultural meaning than a political one. Nonetheless, the wider connotations of religious identity are crucial to the political culture and sub-cultures of Scotland.

Little has been said concerning possible gender differences in terms of religious identity. Although women are less involved in football than men, they often retain a passive attachment to the club supported by the male members of their families. They are often the ones who contribute to their male children's upbringing by buying them football favours, etc. Also, women do have a significant impact on other Protestant and Catholic cultural activities. A high number of Orange adherents are women and Irish music followers tend to be equally distributed between males and females. Generally, this study has avoided gender questions. However, these are questions which could provide the focus of future work developed from this book.

Overall, 5 main points emerge from this work:

1.   Although the term sectarianism has major limitations, it also has a relevance for religious identity in Scotland.

2.   Football is a crucial element of religious identity in Scotland, and national, cultural, social and political expressions become more explicit in the Scottish football arena. As a flexible vehicle, football in Scotland allows for the reinforcement of various ideological associations.

3.   Anti-Catholic culture runs deep in Scotland. This book has located it in its historical context, explained its wider ideological underpinnings and reflected its complexity and variability in modern society.

4.   The term 'sectarianism' has had the function of shrouding the character of the Irish immigrant experience and identity. It has also served a long term ideological purpose in its debasement of the Irish identity.

5.   Identity is a much more useful concept than sectarianism for our understanding of religious cleavage and cultures in Scottish society.

Sectarianism

Sectarianism is clearly an inadequate concept through which to address many questions of religious identity and cleavage in Scottish society. It conceals and distorts the nature of these questions because it is partial, in a number of senses. As I indicate in this section, sectarianism is just one aspect of identity in Scotland. Also, and the point will be developed at a later stage, the term can be used to serve an ideological purpose, seeking to marginalise the Irish identity in Scotland. In fact, such an emphasis often equates with an inability to recognise the origins and nature of sectarianism. The emphasis upon sectarianism stresses only the negative aspects of religious identity and its links with politics, culture, football and national identities. In doing so it reduces our understanding of the content and significance of ethnic and religious identity.

Nevertheless, there is clearly a relationship between sectarianism and identity. Sectarianism is an aspect of religious identity in Scotland; an aspect of religious identity clearly reflected in attitudes and behaviour. Fundamentally, sectarianism in Scotland is considered here to be discriminatory social and economic practices, subtle and overt antagonism and often opposition, towards either the indigenous Scottish Protestant population or the immigrant Irish Catholic one. Sectarianism has a wide resonance throughout Scottish society. For many people in Scotland, as in Northern Ireland, religious identity involves a complex interaction between religious, social, cultural, historical and political factors. These factors form a matrix of variables which define the depth, category and pattern of the cleavage. Sectarianism is thus an aspect, but only an aspect, of religious identity. An over-emphasis on the term covers up the nature of sectarianism itself, its origins, history, development and wider connections and implications.

Used in its traditional manner, sectarianism seeks to portray Protestant and Catholic individuals, groups and communities, as each other's mirror images; certainly with respect to cleavage. This negates the value of much of the content of these identities. It has also resulted in a social and political image which is largely incomprehensible; it can only be understood by utilising such a term as identity.

The popular, academic and media use of the term sectarianism indicates also a lack of recognition on the part of Scottish society of its inherent anti-Catholic traditions. The usage fails to acknowledge that for many people, religious cleavage in Scotland divides the dominator and the dominated. Scottish society has yet to recognise the Irish content of the identity of its largest immigrant group. In addition, this is connected to both the colonial dimension of the cleavage and the social, cultural and political strength of the indigenous Scottish Protestant identity, particularly its anti-Catholic dimension.

Nevertheless, the day to day dynamics of sectarianism are largely restricted to the more populated central belt. Here, close proximity has also regularised and ritualised much of the cleavage and this is a further reason why it has been ignored in some analysis. In much of the eastern part of Scotland day to day life is more secular, so religious practice or identity is seen as having lesser relevance. There are more 'neutral' activities in these parts of Scotland and the ubiquitous effects of religious identity are both less significant and less apparent. In contrast, in west central Scotland almost all of the elements and dimensions of religious identity can converge.

In west central Scotland, residential areas are often known by their Protestant and Catholic labels. Such nuances are important to self and other defined religious labelling. In these areas, religious labels are frequently availed of to determine peoples cultural and political preferences. The potency of communal awareness has no parallel in the UK apart from in Northern Ireland. Codes of identification associated with pubs, names, clothes, residency, football teams supported or played for, whether one holidays in Ireland, even grammatical peculiarities are readily recognisable and can indicate your identity.[3] These features of religious identity can be important markers placing people in a certain social and political context. An image is often acquired then of a person or a group of people. The school attended, whether Catholic or non-denominational, also serves to identify individuals. The result of such thinking can be reflected in non threatening individual and group behaviour, but also, in prejudice, bias, discrimination, parochialism, bigotry and general, but always varying, levels of division and cleavage. The latter group are characteristics of Scottish sectarianism.

Tajfel (1978) and Davey (1983) stress that more variability in behaviour will be in evidence in situations of an interpersonal nature. In contrast, the nearer the social situation is to the intergroup level, the greater the readiness to be prejudiced or sectarian, or to conform to group cohesiveness and exclusivism. The fact that these identities can be ignored in some social and political contexts in Scotland indicates another major difference with the Northern Ireland situation, where similar identities are all-encompassing. Life in Scotland has a fluidity which is absent in Northern Ireland. The vast majority of services for example are generally used with no reference to religion, which indicates that in Scottish society there is a capacity to transcend the cleavage in a way that cannot be done in Northern Ireland. Significantly, Protestant and Catholic communities have also evolved rituals of avoidance and interaction which have, in the main, produced an ethos of self containment. More importantly, in such circumstances the communities tend to distance themselves from anything that does, or might, disturb a sometimes 'uneasy peace'. Tajfel's view is appropriate here, as he argues that:

> The complex dialectical relationship between social identity and social settings is stressed, in the sense that the salience of a particular social identity for an individual may vary from situation to situation and indeed from time to time within the same situation.(see Introduction, and Tajfel, 1978, p. 283).

Nevertheless, sectarianism in the west-central belt can be narrow and tribal. It is none the less real for all that, as Elliott and Hickie argue: 'If men define situations as real, they are real in their consequences' (1971, p. 71). Sectarianism where it does apply, achieves its exclusivist effects and distortions via sub-cultural practices and the worst effects of community stereotyping and identification. As Curtis argues (1988), such stereotyping can be seen to have its origins in the indigenous view of Irish immigrants in the last century (See also Miles and Muirhead, 1986, pp. 108-136).

One example of the sectarian dimension of identity and cleavage can be seen in the football arena - though it is important to stress that differentiation expressed in the football environment can often be fundamentally at variance from a negative expression of sectarianism. Football in Scotland is a way of displaying antagonism, separateness and distinctiveness; that is identity. It is for this reason that it is a mistake to ignore the importance of football as an important indicator of social and political attitudes. In Scotland, identity has, in part, been displaced into the rivalry between football teams, and the hostility which can result from the conflict of identities are experienced in their sharpest forms in the football arena. Ideas concerning proximity, salience and circumstance are also important to football. For a number of people, football raises the intensity of these identities because in this environment they are not subsumed. Football is a competitive situation by nature and in Scotland extra-religious features are drawn into, and limited by, that competition.

In other mediums sectarianism can be displayed in a less obvious manner. For example, there is a common Catholic perception that a significant number[4] of golf and bowling clubs discriminate against Catholics[4] In addition, the survey material indicated that identifiable and frequented Protestant and Catholic pubs in Scotland are an important phenomenon, but one 'largely' limited to the west-central belt. In contrast, scores of Masonic clubs and pubs are evident around all of the country.[5] However, despite all this, sectarianism is modified by a significant degree of social mixing, a fact indicated by the survey.

As we have already seen, a perception of discrimination against the employment of Catholics is evident, although this appears to have been reduced. Crucial to the opening up of new avenues of employment for Catholics, has been the growth of multi-national companies. In addition, since the 1960s, greatly increased advancement by Catholics (and of course of women and the working class generally) in the education and social spheres has assisted the break-down of numerous barriers.

Sectarianism is also clearly in evidence on the days of the major Orange parades in the towns and villages of west-central Scotland. Minor disturbances are regular features of either the parades, but more so, their related social activity. Catholics affected by the marches perceive them as triumphal and intimidatory. This is a major difference between Orangeism and other forms of anti-Catholicism. Orangeism is a demonstrative and bellicose identity. Orangeism also remains, unlike many other expressions of Protestantism, but like football, an almost entirely working class phenomenon. In contrast, the Free Masons are substantially drawn from the middle and 'aspiring' working classes. For that reason also, Orangeism is kept at a distance by many other 'respectable' Scots. Indeed, Orangeism's popular images; the dress and demeanour, abuse of alcohol, violence, aggressiveness and frequently an emphasis on events in Northern Ireland by Orange demonstrators, can be negatively reported in the media, as well as commented upon by its Protestant detractors.[6] However, in such reports, there is little focus on the Protestant nature of their anti-Catholicism.

Sectarianism has political resonance in Scotland in the behaviour of so called fascist and racist political groupings. They have 'tended to agitate upon the Irish question' rather than on the black/white question as in England (Muirhead and Miles, 1986, pp. 108-136). This is an implicit recognition of the strength of anti-Catholicism and anti-Irish feeling in Scotland and its colonial context (a source of pride for the BNP and National Front). As the European Parliament reported in 1990, the BNP is flourishing in Scotland.[7]

Little reference has been made to Catholic anti-Protestantism. Sectarian Catholics do exist. They are typically narrow minded, bigoted and exclusivist. As such, they can have the term accurately applied to them. However, if we saw racism in the USA and South Africa as simply a problem 'between' black and white, rather than a problem largely of white dominance and white ideological, economic and political power, it would be a fundamental misjudgement. It cannot be understood outwith its historical contexts. Though there are clear theological disagreements, there is no anti-Protestant history in Scotland and there are no specifically anti-Protestant bodies that sectarian Catholics can join. Indeed, there is no demand for such bodies from Catholics.

Unlike Catholics in Scotland, Protestants can join (or support) explicitly anti-Catholic bodies or organisations. The very existence of organisations and institutions with strong anti-Catholic identities, indicates the close relations for some Protestants between ideology and their everyday life and experience; i.e., their identities. Cultural domination is a sub-text for these bodies. Post-Reformation Scotland has always contained powerful anti-Catholic identities, whilst the Protestant identity also became the dominant one in the context of the British-Irish colonial relationship. The vast majority of economic, work and sporting institutions have invariably been in the control of, or run in the interests of, Protestants - although undoubtedly, one could identify instances of Catholics discriminating against Protestants and Catholic exclusivism also exists in other limited spheres of Scottish life.[8]

As a term sectarianism has often been corrupted in Scotland, and this corruption tends to see both sides - Protestants and Catholics - as responsible for the cleavage. It fails to recognise both its origins and the context. Often one group is simply defined by its relationship to the other. In Scotland however, sectarianism is not in fact a social hang-up, rooted in 'irrational prejudices and tribal animosities'. Sectarianism in Scotland is largely the outcome and consequence of both the historically inherent anti-Catholicism found in Scotland and the repercussions of a deep Scottish involvement in the building of Empire and the Ulster plantation. This has had inevitable effects upon the British/Scots identity itself. In addition, there exists a much less significant Irish Catholic reaction to these factors and which has contributed towards the cleavage.

Football and religious identity

For many people football provides an appropriate, or even a safe, environment in which to make known otherwise repressed or unarticulated political attitudes, cultural affinities, national allegiances and prejudices; a focus for identification. In particular, the examples utilised from Spanish football shows that football in Scotland, particularly because of the presence of Celtic, is not unique in its use as a focus and a medium for national, political and ethnic identities. Barcelona's club motto of 'more than a club' could easily be transferred to Celtic, due to the seeming ability of its fans to support it independent of the team winning or losing matches.

The prestige afforded by victories in the football arena cannot be underestimated in terms of its value for many in the Roman Catholic community. The birth of Celtic Football Club allowed Catholics to integrate and participate more significantly and more rapidly into mainstream Scottish life. It is plausible that the increase in social and political confidence of the Catholic community in Scotland from the 1960s (referred to by such as Gallagher, 1987) was partly assisted by a new self assurance emanating from the phenomenal Scottish and European success of the Celtic club during this period; a time when the club was a dominant force in football.

Celtic are a substantial cultural activity, representing a symbol of a community otherwise indefinite and differentiated in its own Irish identity. For the Catholic/Irish community, Celtic are the greatest single ethno-cultural focus because they provide the social setting and process through which the community's sense of its own identity and difference from the indigenous community is sustained, in and through a set of symbolic processes and representations. Rokkan and Urwin's idea of identity as 'myth, symbol, history and the institutional' (1983, p. 67), has clear resonance in the Celtic affected aspects of the Scottish football scene.

Again like the Spanish example, support for Celtic, Glasgow Rangers, Motherwell, Hearts, Dundee, Falkirk and a number of other clubs, expresses or reinforces the more basic divisions, distinctions and solidarities in the extra-sporting world.[9] For Rangers and Celtic fans in particular, games are often viewed as opportunities for para-political expression. Football in Scotland has became the major environment for celebrating and confirming ethnic differences. Rivalry between the fans of both clubs corresponds in a sense to the much larger religious and colonial rivalries that are centuries old. Celtic, Rangers and, to a lesser extent, other clubs in Scotland, are in solidarity with the communities which they represent. This book has demonstrated that social, ethnic and political identities are important to Scottish football. The evidence presented here, in addition to the other wide ranging ethno-religious references, reflects the central part football has in ethnic and religious identity in Scotland.

Football is also a reflection of the changing identities in Scotland and of how and when these identities can manifest themselves. So, for example, Celtic Football Club have obviously only become a focus for the display of Irishness since the club was founded; drawing towards itself many of the emotions, sentiments and passions which might otherwise have been displayed elsewhere. Certain dimensions of anti-Catholicism developed within Scottish football in response to this social, cultural and political development. As these events occurred there was a gradual change in both the identity of the Irish and in the character of Scottish anti-Catholicism. A Celtic match against a number of other clubs involves the; 'ceremonial reaffirmation of memories of past [and present] hostilities and unfinished business [and] is a powerful strategy of identity building' (Rokkan and Urwin, 1983, p. 89).

Ironically, Celtic and Rangers also provide a metaphorical lid which keeps in place and in check some of the negative, aggressive and violent manifestations of these identities. It helps 'exhaust the tribal animosities', as one commentator stressed.[10] The psychological satisfaction which people gain from football victories, related media coverage, social events, wearing the respective team colours and identifying with the emblems and symbols which represent hundreds of years of history as well as everyday realities, is immense. Indeed, these manifestations should not be underestimated, for they frequently allow the conflictual or confrontational aspects of these identities to be displaced, that is re-positioned into the football arena, thus reducing the chance that they will undermine the operation of a plural society. The creation and development of such cultures has thus been a feature of Scottish football. In particular, Celtic Football Club help sustain a counter culture, which is Irish nationalist and Catholic in nature, and which is opposed to the perceived dominance of Scottish/British Protestant culture.

However, distinctive Protestant and Catholic cultures (including their respective secular versions) exist within the same socio-economic environment, in which the they share common experiences. The key point is that both Protestant and Catholic cultures in Scotland are now multifaceted rather than monolithic and they meet and consort at various social and political junctures. Despite the strength of religious identity in Scotland, the two communities share powerful elements of a common culture which often pushes ethno-religious tensions to a sub-cultural level. Therefore, the cleavage has limitations. Whereas in Northern Ireland almost every issue is seen from either Protestant or a Catholic perspective, all social relationships in Scotland are not pervaded by a consciousness of the religious dichotomy. Unlike Northern Ireland, Scottish society, because of the nature of its social and political links to English society and its greater integration into the 'outside world', has inadvertently succeeded in containing and diluting much of the cleavage. Although the nearest analogy for Scotland is Northern Ireland, in that it represents a social context in which many of the same ideas and symbols are involved, there have been fundamental differences in the two countries historical, cultural and political circumstances.

Scottish anti-Catholic culture

Protestant anti-Catholicism is a feature of Scottish society and has remained so for more than four centuries. Support for a number of football clubs reflects this anti-Catholic culture, whilst it resonates with the religious and political concerns of the country since the Reformation. The history of Scottish anti-Catholicism is crucial to its contemporary understanding, for only in that context can the social, cultural and political perspectives of many Protestants be understood. This is one of the reasons why the analysis of

Protestant anti-Catholic ideologies, attitudes and perceptions of Catholicism, has been important here.

We can see from the evidence that antagonism towards Catholicism does not necessarily entail pro-Orange or pro-Rangers attitudes. It is therefore a flawed analysis that believes that it is an undifferentiated phenomenon. Too often commentators have defined anti-Catholicism as synonymous with Glasgow Rangers, Larkhall, an Orange parade or Scottish Loyalist paramilitary activity. These are important features of Protestant identity for very large numbers of people, but a concentration on them fails to recognise the wider context of anti-Catholicism or religious identity generally. The important links with history and the wider society become submerged in such a superficial approach which emphasises sectarianism. Despite this often popular perception, it is clear that such tendencies or identities are only the most demonstrative of those enmeshed in the complexity of the cleavage. For example, the anti-Catholicism of the Free Church and the Free Presbyterian Church has no popular appeal.

I have described and analysed anti-Catholic statements, letters, symbols and football chants, in their socio-political context. Anti-Popery, an aversion for many Catholic practices, beliefs, institutions, a rejection of Irish Catholic immigration and its legacies, and an historic fear over the perceived aims of the Catholic faith provides the background out of which the system of beliefs and orientations of anti-Catholicism developed. The evidence here shows that many anti-Catholic's emphasise, indeed are pre-occupied with, the aspects of Protestant ideology which relate to Catholicism. In some cases (for example with non religious Rangers supporters), they are the sole aspects which make up secular Protestant identities in Scotland. Therefore, such thinking represents an historical bloc; a configuration of attitudes and ideas focusing around a central tendency of Protestantism. It involves various sub-blocs, which reflect different combinations of these attitudes and ideas which maintain the general configuration of the fundamental historical bloc. It also provides an ideological underpinning and is at the root of the psyche which leads secular Protestants to incorporate these aspects of Protestantism as the dominant factors in their cultural make-up. However, the emphasis on anti-Catholicism will vary depending on the church, the individual, the community, the location and the circumstances involved.

Protestant anti-Catholic culture or sub-cultures in Scotland are widespread and pervasive. However, they have little direction and often lack substantial goals. They have more to do with being an identifiable Protestant, not being a Catholic, and with how Protestants perceive their heritage, culture, nationality and present day society. Anti-Catholicism is not a monolithic bloc, rather it has a whole series of expressions and implications. Even if religious practice is not as important in the lives of many Protestants in Scotland today, for many, the domain of the Protestant identity, as well the negative attitude towards Catholics and Catholicism, provides a measure of central tendency, a value system and a sense of self.

There are many different elements and strands to anti-Catholicism; ethnic, tribal, Ulster related, football, sports, institutional Church, Orange, Masonic, Unionist, regional, ideological and theological. There are clear differences between these, but they can also overlap. If one is not a Protestant in Scotland, as distinct from being a Catholic, one is, to a large proportion of

185

the population, a deviant.[11] 'Protestant' is a positive reference for many Scots whilst 'Catholic' is a largely negative one. The ideologies of anti-Catholicism also leads to, and feeds, discrimination, stereotyping and xenophobic beliefs. As a result, prejudice becomes the 'habitués of social and ideological relations' (see Bell, 1990, p. 149) which governs the lived experience of many who hold these attitudes. In Scotland, anti-Catholicism is an identity in itself. As such, it has become for many 'secular' Protestants, the dominant or most visible aspect of their Protestantism.

On the question of doctrinal matters, Catholic schools, Catholic progress in Scotland and in relation to the politics and cultures of Northern Ireland, many Protestants share a broad ideological spectrum of ideas. One writer believes that along with common worship, common hatred is one of the 'strongest social cements' (Sheed, 1991, pp. 91-115). Celtic Football Club are viewed as an overt manifestation of the presence and the 'march' of Catholicism in Scotland; as representatives of the ethnic group and identity of the negative group which Protestants have historically faced.

It is essential however, to appreciate that ecumenicism has made some headway in the Church of Scotland since the 1980s. This has assisted in diminishing aspects of anti-Catholic feeling, as well as reducing the more negative perceptions of Protestants on the part of Catholics.[12]   As Protestantism weakens in an increasingly secular society, anti-Catholicism has changed in form and force. This process has often been determined by such factors as geography, increasing cultural familiarity, the outside world, the changing Irish identity in Scotland and events in Northern Ireland. The anti-Catholic riots of the 19th century have long gone and the worst aspects of discrimination in employment have diminished. However, the decline of discrimination is more due to changing employment patterns (and particularly the rise of the multi-national in Scotland), than to any tangible change in indigenous attitudes. Heskin's view of the state of affairs in Northern Ireland has resonance for Scotland (1980, pp. 30-31):

> Ulster Protestants....could express negative attitudes about Catholics both on public occasions and in private, with impunity. O Neill's new direction [in the 1960s] slightly tilted the scales in favour of social punishments for the public expression of such views and, in the international gaze of world opinion since the onset of the present troubles, the balance of attendant rewards and punishments has been radically altered, representing a force for change in Protestant opinion.

Anti-Catholicism has therefore become less publicly acceptable in Northern Ireland. Anti-Catholic discrimination in employment for example, once clearly overt and publicly acceptable in Northern Ireland, has now become less obvious. Nonetheless, a key point in our understanding of how anti-Catholicism can visibly change (or disguise itself) with circumstances is that discrimination has been documented as largely unchanged in the post-Stormont era.[13]

So, although anti-Catholicism in the area of employment in Scotland has diminished since the 1960s, the survey and interview material suggests that it is still a force in the 1990s. An overwhelming number of Catholics from the groups surveyed indicated that they had experience of discrimination, or at least believed that discrimination against Catholics was common in Scotland. This was given further credence by the quite high number of Protestants - around one in five - who concurred. Other evidence indicates discrimination and disadvantage effect Catholics. When commenting upon the high proportions of Catholics in Scottish prisons for example, one writer asked: 'Could it be that our leaders are scared of the larger question of a religious underclass suffering more than its share of unemployment, poor health and foul housing'?[14]

The large size of membership and support for perceived anti-Catholic institutions in Scotland is an important statement. Some sporting clubs, much Scottish Free Masonry, etc., are largely secular embodiments of anti-Catholicism. There is no a full analysis of Free Masonry in Scotland. It may very well be a 'sexist and power seeking organisation' (Finn, 1990, pp. 160-192), but it also has undoubted anti-Catholic connotations in Scotland. There is certainly a widespread belief among Catholics in Scotland that there is an inter-relationship between Freemasonry, Protestantism and self-advancement. In addition, with a cross-class membership in the region 100,000 to 150,000, higher proportionally than England and Wales, it is a powerful body in Scottish society. Such figures are more in line with the 55,000 Free Masons in Northern Ireland,[15] a society with polarised political and religious identities.

One writer on Scottish Freemasonry has concluded that: 'there can be little doubt that many masons are anti-Catholic....and Masonic lodges can become conduits for anti-Catholic sentiment' (Finn, 1990, p. 182). The strong inter-relationship between Freemasonry, Glasgow Rangers and other Scottish clubs, reflects another dimension of the intricacies of Scottish life. For Finn:

> the Masonic bond helped band diverse Protestants together in mutual antagonism towards Catholics, but masonry has also truthfully reflected the strength of that prejudice buried deep within Scottish Protestant culture (1990, p,182).

The argument here is that it is not upon Masonry itself, but upon its interaction with local culture (despite fundamentalist Protestant antagonism towards it) that much anti-Catholicism depends.

Class and regional factors do cut across religion and help to explain different patterns of anti-Catholicism. So Ulster Unionist type politics and the Orange Order are particularly strong among the west-central Scottish Protestant working-class. In contrast, the Free Presbyterians and the Free Church are strongest in the north-west of the country and are not noted for their interest in Northern Ireland question. Significantly, the Masons are strong throughout Scotland. Many other people in Scotland however, may be more accurately described as being antagonistic towards Catholics, suspicious of them, and offended by their alien origins and their differing cultural practices.

Anti-Catholicism also shows itself to have a relevance for British national identity in Scotland. Ulster Unionism is the political expression of the mind-set of colonising Protestants in Ireland. As is shown by the survey evidence, the Ulster Unionist position on Northern Ireland's continued attachment to

Britain is supported either by the vast majority or high percentages of the members/numbers of all the non-Catholic Scottish groups surveyed. This is in sharp contrast to the wider population in Britain. Throughout the Protestant groups surveyed, it is clear that 'Unionism' is a strong force in Scotland (and across the political parties). Unionism in Scotland though should not be confused with Englishism or Englishness. It is a particularly Scottish and Protestant perception of the nature of Britishness. It incorporates a strong sense of Scottishness, and often in the working-class west-central belt it involves an affinity with Ulster Protestants. This is less the case in other areas and among Protestants who are more likely to be alienated by the unedifying and demonstrative nature of working-class Unionist-Loyalist support.

The survey indicates that the importance of Northern Ireland as a part of the UK and as an integral aspect of the Protestant identity, is much less in eastern Scotland. This result, together with the weak support for the Orange Institution in these parts, reflects the lack of Protestant and Catholic migration but, it also shows that anti-Catholic antagonism in these parts is less affected by an affinity with Northern Ireland Protestants. A major factor in the east therefore has been a lack of Protestant proximity to Catholics; this has resulted in far fewer tensions and a detachment from the more overtly divisive experiences of the cleavage in the west-central region.

If we are to understand the overall picture of religious identity and anti-Catholicism in Scotland, we must appreciate that religious identities are less focused and, on the whole, more subordinate to other influences in eastern Scotland. Nonetheless, sectarian and/or prejudiced anti-Catholic expressions can be witnessed via east of Scotland football clubs. The argument here is that in the east of Scotland, despite a growing secularisation, Protestantism generally is still bound up with much of the population's self perception and identity. Untainted by Irish influences, geographically lacking in any significant number of Catholics, this Protestant identity often retains a negative attitude toward Catholicism. This negative and antagonistic disposition can have a class dimension, it can be theological and ideological and thus have more of a religious content, or it can be nationalist and patriotic in sentiment. For many in the west of Scotland, where Protestants and Catholics live in close proximity, the Protestant identity is defined by its anti-Catholic content and is asserted in the everyday nuances and idioms of dominant culture and sub-cultures. In the east, many of the differences with the dominant west-central codes of anti-Catholic practice are exemplified in the vast number of Masonic Lodges existing there (Finn, 1990, p. 187).

The Irish Catholic identity

The Irish Catholic identity in Scotland today is a complex one. Catholics in Scotland have an identity in relation to both Ireland and Scotland which varies in intensity and emphasis depending on circumstance and environment. 'Irishness' has, for a large number of people, become privatised and is reduced in many cases to support for Celtic, St Patrick's celebrations calling children by Irish forenames and retaining suppressed political feelings on political relations between Ireland and Britain. The formative influences of the Irish identity have changed. This community can be either Irish or Scottish in certain settings, but on the whole they find it difficult to define and articulate their identity. Like many others in society, Irish Catholics in Scotland can possess more than one identity and even several layers of identity. On the whole, the Irish in Scotland are a bi-cultural community; retaining a fluctuating and multi-dimensional identity. Part of the reason for this however, is that there exist few structured means of expressing 'Irishness'. There are few vehicles of expression adequate to its self-consciousness. It is an identity often insecure and with little sense of future.

The survey material showed that although most church going Catholics believed their roots to be Irish, a high proportion of them reported their heritage as Scottish.[16] Identity itself can often be a source of confusion, inconsistency and even anxiety. Individuals may find it difficult to define the content and origins of their identity. Bearing in mind the loss of identity inevitable via incorporation into the host society, as well as the existence of a variety of identities existing side by side, the inability or desire not to articulate an Irish background should be seen mainly as a result of anti-Catholicism in Scotland as well as the consequence of exposure to a dominating and antagonistic indigenous culture and identity. But also, as will be explained, it is the result of Scotland-Britain's relationship with Ireland over a period of hundreds of years.

Irish identity in Scotland has been shaped by the immigrant's experiences. Many of the Irish, like immigrants in other countries, thought the best way to survive was to keep a low profile. Celtic Football Club has assumed the dominating presence in the Irish cultural scene. In fact, Celtic reflect a definition of the Irish identity that is unique among the Irish diaspora. Celtic are a politicised club in the same way as Athletico Bilbao, San Sebastian and Barcelona in Spain. Through their politicisation and their evolution as a dominant aspect of Irish Catholic secular culture and identity, their presence has stimulated a reaction in other clubs in Scotland, particularly Glasgow Rangers. For many Catholics, Celtic, like themselves, have also been disadvantaged. The relationship between Celtic, Scottish football and other elements of Scottish society, has thus for that community become a microcosm of the larger society.

Because Irish/Catholics of Scotland do not differ in any critical physical way from the indigenous population, and because of their 'integrative' history, it is not usual to consider them as an ethnic minority. Such terms have only become commonplace in the late 20th century and after the vast majority of Irish immigration to Scotland had taken place. However, in accordance with the discussion of identities in the introduction, this work marks them out as an ethnic community. They are 'a group with a common cultural tradition and a sense of identity which exists as a subgroup of the larger society'. In addition, and as the evidence presented here shows, as an ethnic group, they differ with regard to certain cultural characteristics from the other members of their society. (Isajiw, 1974, pp. 111-124). The Irish in Scotland have integrated into the host society, but they have also retained a viable identity of their own.

Although the concept of ethnicity applies to the Irish in Scotland, it must be remembered that few communities are completely watertight. Indeed, the evidence in this book shows that the Irish and Catholic community, as well as being a distinctive one, is also splintering. This reflects in a lessening Church commitment and a loss, or contraction, of an articulate or clearly definable Irish identity.

LeVine and Campbell (1972) suggest that groups should be seen as cores of interaction and cultural affinity with contour lines of variation stretching almost imperceptibly into other groups. Again this is true with regards to the Irish in Scotland. Nonetheless, its spiritual and traditional conventions and beliefs, its unique educational arrangements, its massive support for the Labour Party, the desire to see the re-unification of the island of Ireland (which indicates a sub-nationalism - a strong sense of Irishness but with little or no national project) and the presence of Celtic Football Club, all point toward a cohesiveness of tradition, history and belief, distinguishing the Irish Catholic (2nd, 3rd, and 4th generation) as an ethnic grouping in Scottish society.

The Irish identity in Scotland stands out as a Catholic one (see Keyes, 1976, pp. 202-213). A sense of this identity continues to act as a political and cultural reference - even for many Catholics who are unchurched. Although the Irish ethnic identity in Scotland is a tangible one, it is also largely hidden and not articulated. This identity is the result of both historical processes and observable and resultant traits. Keyes states (1976, p208):

> While ethnic groups are based fundamentally on the idea of shared descent [in this case religion is an intricate part of this 'sharing'], they take their particular form as a consequence of the structure of intergroup relations.

In the context of Scotland, these relations have been almost exclusively of a Protestant-Catholic type.

Religious, cultural and national relationships

The period of time that the Irish have been present in Scotland and the number of 'mixed marriages' have led to integration.[17] The multiplicity of political and cultural factors which criss-cross in such a way as to reduce the homogeneity of a particular group is a prime reason for integration. Nonetheless, the greatest influence determining much of the content of the contemporary Irish identity in Scotland, and which is an underlying and fundamental element in the inter-group nature of religious cleavage, is the context of British colonialism in Ireland. In a related sense, Davey states: (1983, p. 8)

> For centuries Britain had a master servant relationship with their colonial subjects in different parts of the world. Not only was the relationship economically and politically exploitative but Britons convinced themselves that the subjugation of other cultures was a moral necessity.

This accords with earlier references to ethnic politics on the football terraces and racial tensions in England. In addition, the moral aspect of this idea, is related to the Protestant religion and the way it was availed of by British colonists in their push into Africa etc. Davey (1983, p. 8) expands on his first assertion:

Now, having laid down the white man's burden, it is still thought natural for whites to expect preferment over blacks, and the disadvantaged position of the non-white immigrant is taken as natural.

If we consider Britain's long colonial relationship with Ireland as persistently undermining Irish identity (religion, culture, language, etc.), subjugation and assimilation must be viewed as being part of that overall process. The legacy of this is seen not only in sectarianism but also in the uncertainty which the Irish in Scotland feel about their relationship to their heritage and origins.

Hickman (1990, p. 257), argues that the wider process of 'incorporation entailed pressure on the Irish to deny their Irishness or to be invisible and silent about their identity'. She sees the efforts by the indigenous Catholic Church in Britain to lessen and restrict the Irish identity of their immigrant Catholic flock[18] as successful to the point at which the Irish joke (in which the Irish are portrayed as stupid and 'thick') is acceptable and there is a widespread association of violence and the IRA with all things Irish.[19] Such stereotyping, together with the media's uninformative reporting of Irish affairs and the existence of repressive legislation which engenders a fear and restricts the opportunities for protest or debate,[20] contributes to the diminution of the Irish identity for the Irish and their offspring in Britain and Scotland. Sensationalist reporting of IRA violence creates and sustains an anti-Irish hysteria, which, in turn, undermines relations and perceptions in many communities.[21] The process of debate is stunted and aborted and the result is a silencing of discussion and political and cultural activity by innuendo and association. People with certain 'deviant' identities therefore become marginalised. Self perceptions of Irishness are thus devalued. All this reinforces a process of conformity and assimilation (rather than integration).

Protestant Church, Orange and popular football expressions of attitudes in relation to Northern Ireland often differ little from those of the popular media in Britain, particularly those reflected in the biggest selling newspapers, the Sun, the Daily Mirror/Record, the Star and the Daily Express. The Scottish broadsheet, The Herald, also reflects this consensus via occasional editorial comment as well as through articles from its leading journalists.[22] Again this demonstrates an ideological convergence leading to perceptions which do not allow for the expressions of alternative attitudes. All this means that the Celtic 'environment' is important because it is a 'safe' one for such expressions.

Hickman (1990) demonstrates how British government policy, allied with the intentions of the English Catholic hierarchy, strove to lessen the Irishness and de-politicise, as well as 'civilise', the massive numbers of the offspring of the Irish in Britain. In Scotland, as indicated in chapter 1, this process was reflected in the cases of Bishop Murdoch and Bishop Scott and in the 'The Free Press' controversy.[23]   A conservative, Catholic community, which referred little to its heritage, was one of the social and political goals of the hierarchy. There has always been little or no reference to Ireland in a school curriculum (or indeed in 3rd level education) in Britain/Scotland which stresses a common Anglo-Saxon and Scottish heritage. In the past: 'the teaching of subjects other than religion differed very little in Catholic elementary schools' (Hickman, 1990, p. 176). Thus, if the British and/or Scottish identity was being reinforced via the education system for the indigenous population, it invariably had a negative effect upon the Irish identity, whilst, in the longer term, possibly also undermining Catholicism itself (for there was little account taken of that religion in textbooks etc). The education system has not only helped integration, but has facilitated assimilation.

As far as Britain's relations with Ireland, and later Northern Ireland, are concerned, the Irish in Scotland have on the whole, despite supporting a united Ireland, been de-politicised in terms of Irish political activity. This can be seen in media reporting of this activity in Scotland which emphasises 'sectarianism'. So for example, when the 1981 Irish Hunger Strike raised consciousness among many in the Catholic community, one journalists interpretation of an academic's view of this change was that he saw this as involving the raising of sectarian tensions.[24] Such a characterisation treats legitimate Irish political and ethnic expression as deviant and as one of the causes of sectarianism.[25] It also ignores the roots of religious conflict in Scotland, the indigenous reaction to Irish immigration as well as the ideological framework involved in these.

In terms of the ethnic identity of the Irish and in the context of this raising of consciousness, De Santis and Benkin (1980, pp. 137-143) take the view that:

> Unscheduled external events can periodically serve as reminders
> of ethnic ties and stimulate for a period of time an increase in
> ethnic self-identification.

In this context, it is appropriate to accept that 'ethnicity is highly malleable and responsive to the circumstances in which groups find themselves' (Greenwood, 1977, p. 101).

The colonial aspect of the relationship between Protestant-British and Catholic-Irish identities is crucial to any analysis which seeks to make clear the complexities of these identities. Colonialism cannot exist unless the conqueror sees himself as superior and the conquered as inferior. In this relationship the native will invariably be conscious of his/her low self-esteem and inferiority, if the wisdom of the colonist is held up to be truthful and persuasive. Justification of discrimination will be sought; denigration of the native culture, religion, language and identity is an inevitable outcome.[26]

Curtis (1984, introduction) argues that this has long been a vital aspect of Britain's relationship with Ireland: 'anti-Irish prejudice, from which anti-Irish humour springs, is a very old theme in English culture'. Curtis stresses that this denigration is tied up with British colonialism and its corollary of British superiority and native inferiority. She cites examples of anti-Irish racism as far back as the 12th century and sees this as rising to peaks at the times of Irish rebellion and British oppression. Almost inevitably, this attitude has a relevance for today's conflict in Northern Ireland. In fact, Curtis (1984, p. 79-96) argues that:

> Just as in previous centuries, the Irish are regularly depicted in the press and on television as stupid, drunken and backward.

The writer concludes with reference to the contemporary Irish joke in British society (pp. 86-96):

> In a situation where the Irish are constantly denigrated, and where the war in the North is blamed on Irish 'irrationality' rather than British policy, it is scarcely surprising that the centuries-old, anti-Irish joke has flourished once again....Anti-Irish racism desensitises British people to atrocities committed in their name.

Such a consciousness pervades many references to Ireland by both Scots and British commentators. So, in an apparently innocuous British stamp album, the Great Famine of the 1840s, with over one million dying of hunger and one million being forced to flee, is covered by a small sentence in a paragraph description of Ireland: 'Many Irish left the country during the Great potato famine of 1846'.

A more unreserved derogatory commentary on Ireland was made in 1985 by the editor of the Daily Express, Sir John Junor (the latest in a series of such comments). Junors' remark provoked the following comment from an observer of Irish affairs:[27]

> John Junors remark that he would rather go looking for worms in a dunghill than visit Ireland is but one example of a quite unrepentant anti-Irishness of so much of the Tory press.

Such views have often been explicit in Scotland. One example is particularly apposite for the concerns here. A cartoon published in a Scottish football newspaper early in this century depicted two Old Firm players in a bar playing pool. The cartoon portrayed the Celtic player as 'typically' Irish, dumb with grotesque and brutish facial features. The Rangers player was handsome and with intelligent looking eyes. The cartoon was captioned 'Apes and Aryans'.[28] In Scottish society, and in a similar way to the history of the relationship between colonial black nations and their white superiors, these portrayals are generally viewed as being unlikely and unacceptable today (i.e., not politically correct). Nonetheless, such references are crucial to understanding the background of present day relations.

One observer believes that such prejudice and stereotypical attitudes:

> ....has to do mainly with racism and conquest - a politically motivated form of denigration brought into being by the British imperialists to deride the national identity and aspirations of the Irish people. History has shown that it has always been the way

of empires not only to divide and to exploit but also to attack and pour scorn upon the self-respect of those they sought to subdue by ridiculing their race, colour, religious beliefs and mannerisms. And the harder they found it to conquer a people the more sustained and vicious the denigration imposed.[29]

Davey (introduction, 1983) highlights similar prejudice in the treatment of black/brown immigrants in English society. He argues that:

> their cultures are negatively evaluated and they are under constant pressure to adopt British habits, customs and values which they are assured will make a better way of life for them.

Ex-British Cabinet minister, Norman Tebbit demonstrated such reasoning as recently as 1989, when he suggested a novel type of cricket test. Asian immigrants integration could be tested by asking which cricket team they supported: England or Pakistan/India. He went on to suggest:

> that those who continue to cheer for India and Pakistan, are wanting in Britishness....that the only satisfactory way to be an Asian in Britain was to cease being Asian.[30]

The cricket test, in its form as a 'football test', has also been applied regularly by the Scottish/British press in the 1980s and 1990s as it became common for 2nd and 3rd generation Irish to represent and support the Republic of Ireland in international football.[31] Depreciative comment has constantly characterised the success of the Irish football team. The logic which underpins such an argument was exposed by a respected British journalist:

> the assertion that we are one people, has always been a lie used
> to justify the unjust dominance of one group (whites, Protestants
> or Anglo-Saxons, for example) over the society as a whole.[32]

These examples, which in themselves might be seen as insignificant and normally unrelated comment, could be repeated many times and reflect a well developed broad ideological and attitudinal position.

In British-Irish terms, cultural subjugation must be seen as a process of colonising not only of Ireland, but also its people and its offspring.[33] Significantly, involvement by Scots in the colonisation of Ireland gave Scottish anti-Catholicism a new cultural and political focus, as also did 19th century Irish immigration. In particular, it is significant that Scot's colonists in Northern Ireland were the creators of Orange ideology and identity. British colonialism in Ireland gave birth to Orangeism and as a result, the British were the architects of sectarianism in Northern Ireland. The colonist Scots (linking religion with nationalism) provided this fertile ground. This has been a long historical process, tied up with British colonialism and the Irish identity, as is well reflected in a quote from Sir William Parsons about the Irish in 1625. For Parsons, only the depreciation and destruction of Ireland's cultural traits and identity, could result in the Irish being absorbed into the Crown's realm: 'We must change their course of government, apparel, manner of holding land, their language and habit of life'.[34]

This relationship between colonist and colonised is inadvertently referred to in its Scottish setting as 'sectarianism'. This relationship reflects a cleavage arising primarily from the identities of colonised and coloniser in a fundamentally different setting; Scotland. The relationships between Britain and Ireland and thus Protestants and Catholics, has always involved the domination of one group over another. Conflict has been present from the very first manifestations of this assertion of power, which aimed at eventually subordinating the Irish/Catholics and taking away their means of expression. Conflict is a result of domination. The British/Protestants sought to establish, through the course of the conflict, the foundations of their domination and tried to impose the legitimacy and universality of their norms and cultures on the subordinated group.

Historically in Scotland, the Irish and Catholic identities have been primarily undermined by their unacceptability to society. Irish and Catholic are clearly not the interchangeable terms they once were, though for those of an explicit anti-Catholic disposition, they remain so. Although in some societies identity can be strengthened in the face of antagonism, the conclusions of Hickman and of Curtis suggest that in Britain, large numbers of Irish people have underplayed their Irish, and in some circumstances Catholic, identity. Likewise, while the writer was carrying out the empirical part of this study some Catholic interviewees expressed their inhibitions in calling their children by Irish/Catholic forenames. In some instances, the Irish part of their identity was too difficult for them to recognise, they were inclined more towards a Scottish name or a name that had little to do with a conscious identity. In other cases however, the reason that 'my child would never get a job', or 'I don't want to be bigoted', were forwarded as the rationale for such decisions. For many Catholics in Scotland, the Irish identity is a submerged one. Apart from other factors, such as the length of time the Irish have been in Scotland and secularisation, this is determined by way of anti-Catholicism and the present day, colonial, British-Scottish psychology which denigrates Irishness and at times, Catholicism.[35]

This denigration has largely produced a complex, confusing and multilayered Irish-Catholic-Scottish identity for the offspring of Irish immigrants in Scotland. Despite the strength of the Irish identity in Scotland, this identity becomes less clear if we explore the cultural nuances involved. They are not Scottish in the same ways as the Protestant or secular Scottish community, but they are also unsure of what their Irishness involves. This uncertainty is one of the reasons why it is only in the context of Celtic and football that many people feel confident enough to display this aspect of their identity and reject the cultural and national orthodoxy's. Ironically, this has created a mould which was rejected and resented by the indigenous population. So, a great deal of the disdain and antagonism towards the immigrant community has been channelled into the football environment.

The Irish in Scotland experience a multifaceted assimilation (see Davey, 1983, p. 103), where assimilation proceeds in different ways and at different rates. It is often the case too that less assimilation takes place in certain spheres (i.e., family, religion, Celtic) than in others. Despite both unity and diversity within the immigrant community, Catholics generally engage in positive relations with mainstream society.

Negative attitudes towards the Irish identity may in fact also have damaged the Catholic practice of the Irish community. At the very least, it seems to have reduced Catholic cultural barriers against secularisation (a phenomenon which has generally served to shape and redefine identity in Scotland). This analysis has some substance because the Irish cultural groups and Celtic fans surveyed here, who are the two groups with the 'highest' levels of Irish consciousness, are both seen to contain large proportions of individuals with high levels of Catholic church attendance.

Although it has been asserted here that Celtic have also partly assisted in the diminution of, or change in, Irish culture, this has had less to do with Celtic than with the pressures exerted by the wider society. However, the intensity of feelings which surrounds football in Scotland generally, means that to associate oneself with Celtic, whilst being a member of the Catholic and Irish community, can ordinarily be viewed as sufficing; as far as expressions of that identity are concerned. Related to this point, Elliott and Hickie (1971, p. 22) state that the continued use of symbols often satisfies the interests of those who desire what they think these symbols represent.

This points towards one of the main conclusions of this work. The Irish identity has been reduced in Scotland to highly specific cultural facets (the enduring elements of this identity).[36] Accepting that the effects of secularisation (and related mixed marriages)[37] in recent decades has also been a force for change, such a diminution of the Irish identity is also due to the dominance of Protestant culture. It is important to emphasise that the modern Irish identity has largely been created by the pressures and attitudes associated with Scottish anti-Catholicism and British colonialism in Ireland, that is, from the psychological colonisation of the people, as well as the subsequent social and cultural imperialism involved. Hickman stresses that; 'ideologies of superiority and inferiority always accompany colonisation' (1990, p. 18). In essence, this is a post-colonial cleavage. Despite its variations, the Protestant-Catholic relationship in Scotland today can be viewed as an extension of, and, subsequently a different setting for, the British/Scots - Irish colonial relationship.

In perspective

In the recent past there has been a tendency among some commentators on religious identities and cleavage in Scotland, to misunderstand its origins, its significance and its implications. In Scotland, there exists a broad constituency of Protestants - whether Church going or otherwise - who are overtly or covertly, actively or passively, disturbed by Roman Catholicism, particularly in its Scottish-Irish context. Scottish football's anti-Catholic identity, the strength of Orangeism and Free Masonry, Churches preoccupied with the Catholic presence in Scotland, aspects of anti-Catholicism within the National Church, perceived anti-Catholicism in employment and the impact upon the indigenous population of Irish immigration and the Northern Ireland conflict within a context of Scottish/British colonialism, are the substance of this broad constituency. The roots of ethno-religious cleavage in Scotland lie with this constituency.

It is a cleavage which varies in application, intensity, subtleness or openness, depending on circumstances and geographical location. This work also recognises the limits of ethno-religious cleavage in Scottish society. Anti-Catholicism is not totally pervasive, though if we took each social cleavage in isolation it is clearly a very important one; and certainly for a number of people, the dominant one. Scotland is not a polarised society, but anti-Catholicism is 'a' key cultural and social feature particularly in central Scotland, although its make-up and prominence vary in other parts.

Modernisation, capitalism, welfarism and secularisation have diminished and obscured the cleavage, facilitated its reshaping, whilst simultaneously affecting the national, cultural and religious identities which have long been intertwined with historical factors. The tensions and cleavage between and within the two identities have also become more complicated. One of the main results of this reconstitution and reshaping, has been the compartmentalising of many of the aspects of these identities, but more significantly of the cleavage itself. So much so, that for Catholics, the Irish identity is less clear because of pressure to conform to the dominant identities and cultures; not only to integrate, but to assimilate. Although much of the cleavage has developed into a symbolic one, symbols are crucial to people's identities and even to fratricidal cleavages and conflicts. Perceptions of dominance and power are important. The symbolic element of the cleavage suffices for many people. The importance of symbols in the Northern Irish conflict for example means that: 'the demand is for the other side to give up its symbols or ideology' (Elliott and Hickie, 1971, p. 72). Likewise in the Scottish context, the marginalising or eradication of the immigrants Irishness, can be considered to be a form of 'cultural imperialism' (the earlier used example of the Scottish Football Authorities demand for Celtic to cease flying the Irish national flag is an apposite example). It should also be noted that assimilation, not integration, has been an inherent policy in/or consequence of, colonialism itself.

However, in a quite separate social, religious, and political sense, secularism in the latter part of the 20th century has undoubtedly become the biggest factor in a monumental metamorphoses in Protestantism; previously the essence of the identity of the Scottish people. An important factor for the indigenous population is the contemporary debate over the Scots identity or identities in/of Scotland, which suggests among other things that the historically strong and integrative force of Protestantism as 'the' identity of the contemporary Scot is in question.[38] If new definitions are to evolve, then clearly there must be accommodation for those of a fundamentally different origin and culture.[39] Even if the Scottish identity is to remain an inherently Protestant one in character (albeit without the anti-Catholic dimension), then a similar accommodation remains. This should evolve if Scotland is to be recognised as a modern multi-cultural and plural society. It cannot entail the dominance or imposition of a oneness that fails to recognise difference. With the question of the Northern Ireland conflict possibly being opened up for a more informative debate as a step towards a long term solution, then this may also cease to contribute to the persistence of some of the worst aspects of the cleavage within Scottish society.

Notes

1. William Nach, Sunday Observer, 22/10/91.

2. See Chambers, 1986, p13.

3. Sportswriter Archie MacPherson wrote in the Herald, 22/10/91, 'Trust is a casualty of our environment. Very few take you at your face value and mostly actions and words are interpreted through the sieve of someone's fundamental perceptions of you'.

4. Haggs Castle, Williamwood and Hilton Park in Glasgow, and the Drumpellier Golf Club in Coatbridge, are a few examples of clubs, perceived by a number of Catholics, as having mechanisms designed for this purpose. Such discrimination however, is subtle, for such 'routines' are generally not spoken of and are largely hidden in practice. One of the first popular press references to these practices emerged in a 1993 (12th April) in an article in the 'Evening Times', entitled 'War On Sports Club Bigots'. Although Coatbridge is a predominantly 'Catholic town' the same 'routines' are part of the reality for Catholics who wish to participate in the sport of bowls. Catholics made 'progress' here in that two public greens in the town became available for more popular use in the 1980s and subsequently they have almost become predominantly Catholic in nature - information from interviews with members of various golf and bowling clubs in Coatbridge and Airdrie. Also, during discussions with Dr Calum Brown of the history department at Strathclyde University, he made it clear he was aware of discrimination against Catholics at the Royal Greenock Rowing Club. Two notable journalists have remarked on a similar black experience in the USA. William Nack (Sunday Observer, 23/12/90) asks of Baseball; 'in a game in which 20% of the players are black, why are there no black managers on the field, or no black general managers'. Andrew Stephen's wrote of Golf Club's exclusivism against blacks; 'Die for us, but don't expect to play with us' in the Sunday Observer, 23/12/90. Also, 'Trespassers in a white man's sick world' 26/7/92.

5. See article 'The long march of bigotry', Euan Ferguson, in, Scotland on Sunday, 12/7/92. Such a mode of criticism also relates to Catholic attitudes towards many Irish marches.

6. Sunday Observer 'Review' section, 26/7/92, 'Mountain agony and ecstasy' (p61) for reference to an English writers experience of visiting the Scottish Highlands, going into a Masonic pub, and being asked his religion. The writer reported that all seemed well after he had identified himself as a Protestant. According to the survey data, approximately 50% of all Catholics surveyed stated they drank in a pub with a Catholic label. The majority of Rangers supporters, Motherwell fans and Orange Lodge members (81%) drank in Protestant-labelled pubs. Although some other Protestants (i.e., 25%

198

of Hearts fans) also drank in Protestant pubs, most people surveyed said they did not drink in a pub with such a label, or did not know if the pub was known in this way. In the aftermath of the 1989 Scottish Cup Final between Celtic and Rangers, Tommy Main of the Irish Post (in an interview with the writer) and the Daily Record both reported on a number of violent attacks by Glasgow Rangers fans upon pubs seen as Irish and Catholic.

7. An EC report in October 1991 (reported in the Herald, 18/10/91) noted that in Scotland, which used to consider racist violence as an English problem, racial violence has escalated since 1984 when the BNP opened an office in Glasgow. Also, Dr Stuart Cosgrove, in 'The enemy within', Sunday Observer, 11/3/90, noted the number of reports in Scotland emphasising racism in society and how it was hidden from public viewing - He referred to it as an 'insidious silence'.

8. See Brown, 1987, p234, for short reference.

9. See Goward, 1981, p24.

10. Archbishop Winning, on 'This Is Me Since Yesterday'; BBC Radio Scotland; 5/1/90.

11. Ironically, Protestant church attenders in much of Scotland today are often popularly viewed as 'deviant' by their co-religiosts.

12. With regards to the views of each of the two communities Churches, there remains a high degree of ignorance on the part of both group. For many people hearsay and myth still represents the literal truth.

13. See Irish Post, Dolan, 13/1/90. Also 'Discrimination In Employment In The North Of Ireland' by the Irish Social and Economic Research Unit, nos. 2, Derry, c1990 and 'Equality and Inequality in Northern Ireland' Policy Studies Institute, 1987.

14. 'Puzzle of Prison Catholics' Bill Rankine, Sunday Observer, Scotland, 9/4/89. Also, around the same time, the Chief Inspector of prisons in Scotland carried out a random survey, finding 35% of the inmates Catholic. This was linked to urban alienation etc., whilst one priest commented that the 'figures fitted in with greater poverty and deprivation still experienced by Catholics in Scotland'. BBC Radio Scotland, 'Speaking Out' 12/7/90.

15. Herald, 2/7/92 and 11/6/92. Also 'In The Grip? A psychological and historical explanation of the social significance of freemasonry in Scotland'; in Gallagher and Walker (edts) 'Sermons and Battle Hymns' pp160-192.

16. This confusion (or the miscomprehension of the question) was displayed a number of times when some individuals on reporting their background-heritage as 'Scottish', were further investigated, and asked by the interviewer their names and where their grandparents etc., originated. Lennon, McCann and McHara, three of the respondents (all Irish names, none coming from a mixed religious marriage), were found to have between them, one Irish born parent, at least five known Irish grandparents, whilst McHara was reminded by a friend that his family had come to Scotland from Armagh in Ireland. In relation to this, Hickman argues that since the education of the Irish began in Britain in the last century: 'removing the history of Ireland was a chief means of denationalisation because it created a silence in the narrative of history' (p188) .

17. Around half of Catholic marriages in Scotland are now with non-Catholics, though this figure varies across the country (i.e., it is less so in strongly Catholic areas). Significantly, the figure for Northern Ireland is approximately 9%. For English figures (70%) see, A.P Purnell, 'Our Faith Story' Collins, 1985, p123.

18. See Hickman 1990, as well as Bernard Aspinwall pp91-115, in Devine, 1991.

19. For example, in the wake of the IRA pub bombings in Birmingham, a Daily Express feature on November 23rd, 1974, stated; 'Today in Birmingham, if you are called Sean or Patrick, you do not boast about it' Also see Irish Reporter, issue seven, third quarter, 1992.

20. As an example of this, the British Press Council upheld a complaint in early 1991 against the News of the World, ruling that the paper's assertion that 'the IRA had murdered 2,758 men, women and children since the present troubles in Ireland began was inaccurate and misleading'. The paper was criticised also for not publishing a correction until 15 weeks later. The Council has in fact ruled against a number of newspapers for the same statement. See also the Irish Post 8/6/91 and 16/3/91 for reports on the PTA, and 23/3/91 for report on the media-public atmosphere that allowed for the wrongful convictions of the 'Birmingham Six' in the mid 1970s. See same newspaper 'letters' 13/9/91, Tom Shields Diary, Herald, 29/3/91 and, article by Michael Foley, 'Skin Deep impression of emigration' in the Irish Reporter, Issue 1, First Quarter, 1991. See also The Irish Post, 8/8/92, for issue of Channel 4's reporting of events in Northern Ireland, and reactions towards it; 'Out of bounds for future reporting'? See also, 'Labour accuses police over ban on 'pro-IRA' meeting'; Sunday Observer, 30/8/92.

21. In light of these acts of violence, it must also be acknowledged that some of this anti-Irishness might be viewed as inevitable. Nonetheless, an historical and cultural perspective demonstrates that IRA atrocities are not required to give rise to anti-Irish sentiment.

22. For example, see article by John MacLeod, 20/9/94, p21, 'A Marriage hatched in Hades' .

23. See Bernard Aspinwall, in Devine (edt), 1990, p91. He says that the Catholic Church has acted as a far more integrating force than critics allow. Hickman is also of the belief that the Catholic Church in England/Britain was actually a vital instrument in this strategy (p150).

24. In, profile of Steve Bruce in the Glasgow Herald, 21/9/89.

25. Clydeside 'Troops Out Movement' request that their supporters 'Do not wear or flaunt football favours of no relevance to our campaign....Avoid sectarian or quasi religious gestures which only serve to demean our message and fuel the arguments of our opponents'.

26. See Collins, 1990.

27. Reported by Donall MacAmhlaigh, in Ireland's Own, 5/7/85.

28. The Scottish Referee, 3/2/1905. Similar more recent comment denigrating the Irish has originated from some writers in Glasgow and west of Scotland newspapers. See the Irish Post 27/2/93 for two such reports.

29. Sean O Ciarain, Irish Post, 3/5/90.

30. Quoted by Michael Ignatieff, Sunday Observer, 16/9/90.

31. The examples have been common in the press throughout the 1980s and 1990s. Some recent direct and indirect remarks can be seen in James Traynor's articles already mentioned; Sports Herald, p9 22/8/94 and p9 12/10/92. In addition, see Phil MacGiollabhain in the Irish Post, p35, 27/3/93. Comments made by Detective Inspector Peter Chapman of the English Football Inteligence Unit (World in Action, 'The Nightmare Returns', 29/3/95) also characterised the English game as being virulently anti-Irish; 'The one thing we do find that runs through football is the violently anti-Irish feeling'.

32. Adam Lively, Sunday Observer, 22/7/90.

33. Hickman shows this throughout her thesis though with particular reference to the city of Liverpool. For the Scottish identity and role in Empire building, see B Aspinwall 'The Scottish Religious Identity in the Atlantic World', in Studies in Church History, vol. 18 (1982). Also R Miles and L Muirhead in Scottish Government Yearbook, 1986, pp108-135, 'Racism in Scotland: A Matter for Further Investigation'.

34. Irish Post, 8/12/90.

35. Whilst it also attempts to de-politicise the community in terms relevant to Northern Ireland. See G Bell, 'On the Streets of Belfast and London' p99, in M Farrell (ed) 'Twenty Years On'. Also Dolan, Irish Post, 23/6/90.

36. Ibid. See The Irish Reporter, Issue 1, First Quarter, 1991. See also Hickman (p9) for the higher profile of the Irish in Britain in the 1980s.

37 The research for this book as well as ongoing research into the Catholic community in Scotland reflects that the vast majority of Church going Catholics have Catholic parents. This clearly shows that among Catholics who are falling away from the Church those who marry outside of the faith are very likely either to continue not attending Church, or to stop going.

38. Most of the Scottish quality press has been covering this in latter years. See Arnold Kemp, Herald, 1/8/92 for example.

39. Little mention has been made in politics or any other area of society with regards to accommodating the different identities of the people who now make up Scottish society (the first notable comment in relation to Catholics, originating with SNP leader Alex Salmond in late 1994). With regards to the Irish identity in Scotland, it remains largely unrecognised, ignored and treated as a manifestation of sectarianism within Scottish society. Pat Kane of pop group Hue and Cry, a 'popular' spokesman for the Scottish nationalist cause in Scotland, has in recent years expressed his desire for either the diminishing in stature of, or a fundamental change in, the identity of Celtic Football Club, i.e. the eradication of their Irish identity. Somewhat paradoxically, Kane a former Catholic of Irish descent, sees Glasgow Rangers in their role as a European football power in the early 1990s, as fitting his own ideas of what a Scottish Football club should be like. See 'Scotsman' Weekender, 'Why must Bhoys always be Bhoys?', 14/4/90. See also letters in the Irish Post 16/5/92, 23/5/92 and 22/6/92, for some Scottish nationalists denial of the existence of an Irish identity in Scotland.

Appendix

The sample

The empirical study had several objectives. The questionnaire was designed to elicit the background and attitudes of the respondents. The great majority of the population of Scotland is in the west-central belt; including almost all of the Catholics in the population. For this reason much of my sample was drawn from this area.

A: Groups chosen

Bearing in mind resource limitations, I concentrated upon those groups who were most overtly religious, or who exhibited clear evidence that religion was a key element of their identity. So, I surveyed sections of Catholic Church attenders; Church of Scotland attenders, members of Irish political and cultural groups; and members the Orange Institution of Scotland.

Given that this book is concerned with the importance of football as an aspect of identity, I also surveyed supporters of the Premier division clubs with the biggest levels of support; Glasgow Rangers, Celtic, Aberdeen, Dundee United, Kilmarnock, Hibernian, Hearts, Motherwell and St Johnstone. All together 1813 persons completed the questionnaire.

B: Groups included in the survey

<u>Church of Scotland</u> (total surveyed, 653 persons)

Coatbridge:	Blairhill
Coatbridge:	Langloan Middle Church
Larkhall:	Trinity Parish
Edinburgh:	Murryfield
Ayr:	Castlehill
Larkhall:	St Machins'
Dumbarton:	St Andrew's
Aberdeen:	St Marys'
Aberdeen:	Queens Cross
Airdrie:	Clarkston
Glasgow:	Ibrox
Broxburn:	Broxburn
East Kilbride:	South
Bathgate:	St David's High
Edinburgh:	Currie
Falkirk:	Irving Parish, Camelon
Falkirk:	St Andrews'
Dundee:	Balgay
Dundee:	Menzieshill
Kirkcaldy:	Viewforth
Edinburgh:	St Serfs'
Edinburgh:	St Andrews'
Glasgow:	Old Church
Paisley:	St Marks'
Glasgow:	Burnside
Kilwinning:	Abbey
Glasgow:	Drumchapel Old Parish

Catholic Churches (total surveyed, 521 persons)

Glasgow:	Baillieston: St Bridgets'
Hamilton:	St Marys'
Glasgow:	Govanhill: Holy Cross
Ayr:	St Pauls'
Glasgow:	Tollcross: St Josephs'
Coatbridge:	St Augustines'
Carfin:	St Francis Xavier
Larkhall:	St Marys'
Wishaw:	St Thomas'
Paisley:	St Fergus
Paisley:	St Charles
Dumbarton:	St Patricks'
Glasgow:	Kingspark: Christ The King
Glasgow:	Toryglen: St Brigids'
Glenboig:	Our Lady and St Joseph
Coatbridge:	St Monicas'
Greenock:	St Andrews'
Greenock:	St Patricks'
Clydebank:	St Eunans'
Dundee:	St Francis'
Motherwell:	St Bernadettes'
Stirling:	St Margarets'

Football Fans (total surveyed, 449 persons)

Games attended

Glasgow Rangers	versus	Hibernian:	24/3/90
	v	Hearts:	5/5/90
	v	St Mirren:	13/10/90
St Johnstone	v	Celtic:	6/10/90
Aberdeen	v	Celtic:	2/5/90
	v	Celtic:	1/9/90
Kilmarnock	v	EastFife:	7/4/90
Celtic	v	Rangers:	1/4/90
	v	Motherwell:	25/8/90
	v	Hibernian:	8/9/90
Motherwell	v	Celtic:	25/8/90
Hibernian	v	Hearts:	31/3/90
Dundee Utd	v	Hearts:	28/4/90
Hearts	v	Dundee Utd:	28/4/90

Irish Cultural Bodies (total surveyed, 27 persons)

Gaelic League
Gaelic Athletic Association
Irish in Scotland Forum

Irish Political Solidarity Groups (Republican Band Alliance)
(total surveyed, 52 persons)

Dumbarton: Jim Lynagh
Glasgow (EastEnd): Sons of Ireland
Wishaw: Crossmaglen Patriots
Coatbridge: John 'Bap' Kelly

Orange Institution of Scotland (total surveyed, 111 persons)

Glasgow District (including a few representatives from Lanarkshire and
Ayrshire)
Ayrshire District
Lanarkshire District
East of Scotland District

Churches were chosen randomly to give the greatest possible range and variation. At an early stage, it became clear that at a parish level, the Church of Scotland was more influenced by class than the Catholic Church. It therefore became an important feature of the operationalising of the survey to ensure an even spread of working-class, mixed-class, and middle class Church of Scotland parishes throughout. Priests and ministers of the randomly chosen parishes were contacted for permission to conduct the survey. The majority of them then either placed a notice in their church bulletin and/or noted my visit to their church after the service. As a consequence, at least 95% of people randomly approached responded positively. Approximately two dozen questionnaires were then completed within each selected parish.

A similar approach was also used for the Orange Institution and the Irish bodies. Here contact was made with the respective hierarchies and permission was given to attend a meeting, a practice or a social event, to conduct the survey.

With reference to the football clubs surveyed, no formal contact was made with the clubs themselves. Fans were surveyed in supporter's club's, in pubs and outside of stadiums. Although numbers varied with each location, the most popular setting was that of the football ground. Here care was taken to stand or sit at various ends of the stadiums to prevent the survey being skewed by the presence of a particular kind of fan. Again, the vast majority of those approached to complete a questionnaire willingly did so.

Only those who 'looked' over the age of sixteen were approached on the assumption that the appropriate attitudes and identities could be quite well articulated in the questionnaire by this age.

C: The Questionnaire

The questions asked were determined by the theoretical and substantitive concerns of this book. Hence they dealt with the respondents demographic background i.e.; age, sex, class, religion, geographic area, occupation, education, etc.; ethnic identity; attitudes to well known symbols of Scottish and Irish national identity, religious observance; attitudes to discrimination; attitudes to the Monarchy; attitudes to constitutional arrangements in Scotland; attitudes to Northern Ireland; attitudes on ethnicity; and support for football teams. The questions asked were:

1) What is the name of the town or village that you were born in?
2) What is the name of the town or village that you now live?
3) Would you describe your families background, heritage and national origins (for example three or four generations ago) as being? English, Irish, Scottish, British, Other
4) What is your religious denomination?
Country of birth and religious denomination were obviously important, whilst it was hoped that ethnic identity could begin to be established via question three.
5) Thinking about your workplace (if you are unemployed, retired, etc., please think about your last work), as far as you know, are the people who work there the same religion as you?
6) Apart from funerals, weddings and christenings, do you attend church, or mass, or religious services? (six categories were used from 'once a week or more' to 'never')
7) What were the religious denominations of your parents while you were being brought up?
8) What is your present marital status?
9) What is your husband's, wife's, partner's present religious denomination? Please answer for your last marriage if your partner is deceased or you are divorced etc.
10) What religious denomination did your husband/wife's/partner's parents bring him or her up in?
11) Was the school you attended (either non-denominational RC or other)
12) How old were you when you completed your continuous full time education?
13) Do you have any highers or A levels? If you have, how many?
14) Have you attended a polytechnic or a university and gained a degree? If yes, please state the name of that degree.
15) Which of the following best describes the sort of work you do? And which one best describes the job your father normally does or did do when you were aged 14? (8 categories)
a) Are you self employed or do you work for someone else as an employee?
b) At the position at work, are you (or were you....a supervisor, not a supervisor, etc.)
16) On the whole, do you think that Protestants and Catholics in Scotland who apply for the same job, have the same chance of getting a job, or are their chances of getting a job different?
17) If any, which group is most likely to get a job?
Again much of this is biographical data. However, it was initially felt to be quite important with reference to the relationship between religious identity and job 'chance', or educational 'attainment':
18) Generally speaking, do you consider yourself to be closer to any one political party than another?
19) How about the monarchy or the royal family in Britain. How important

or unimportant do you think it is for Britain to continue to have a monarchy?
20) Let us consider the constitutional and national position of Scotland. If you had to choose a future for Scotland, which one of the following comes closer to your own views?

All of the above questions have an obvious importance to a social and political study of any grouping or community. In addition, the following three questions relating to Northern Ireland have a relevance in view of its influence in certain areas of Scotland.

21) Do you think that the long term solution for Northern Ireland should be for it to (remain in the UK, re-unify, other solution, don't know)

22) Some people believe that Government policy towards Northern Ireland (in either the long or short term) should include a complete withdrawal of British troops. Would you personally support or oppose such a policy?

23) At any time in the next 20 years, do you think it is likely or unlikely there will be a united Ireland?

Questions 24 to 27 are connected entirely to the football aspect of the survey. The Scottish team questions were intended to discover if there was, as was commonly believed, an antagonism or lack of affinity on the part of many Catholics towards the Scottish international side. Something similar applied in the case of question 27 where it was intended to explore the perceived growing degree of support from within sections of that same community for the Republic of Ireland soccer team.

24) Which football team if any, do you support (Even if you do not watch football, who then would you like to see win more than any other team?)

25) Do any of the other members of your family (male or female) support, or even just like, the same team? (all, most, some, none)

26) Do you attend the Scottish international football team's games?

27) Do you support or like any other international football team? If so, write down the name of that country.

28) Which three of the following do you feel something most in common with? Please indicate this by ticking three boxes alongside your choice

Patrick Pearse	The Harp	TheThistle
Robert the Bruce	W.B Yeats	TheWolfeTones
The Corries	John Knox	RobertBurns
St Patrick	The Bagpipes	The Shamrock

These were considered to be symbolic historical, cultural, political figures which might play a part in terms of Scottish or Irish identity. On the Scottish side it was generally intended to discover the attachment to some obvious religious symbols as well as to the religious/cultural ones. The same applied as far as Catholics in Scotland of an Irish background were concerned; what was being tested was the salience, strengths, and weaknesses of the Irish identity amongst this group. Question 29 examined the extent to which religion shaped everyday cultural practices.

29) Do you ever drink in a club or pub that has the label or has the popular description of being a Protestant or a Catholic one?

30) What is your age?

31) Are you female or male?

D: The Pilot Study

A small pilot study involving 15 football supporters and 8 church attenders was conducted. The pilot study established that there were few problems with the questionnaire. The language used and the order of the questions seemed appropriate as interviewee's first dealt with their own biographical material before engaging in some of the questions they might be expected to be more reluctant to answer. The time factor presented a minor problem (generally it took between 5 and 10 minutes to fill out a questionnaire) though it was felt that the questionnaire could not be cut down further as this would affect its utility.

Responses were typically mixed. Some respondents enthusiastically filled out the questionnaire and enquired about it and the results. Others became more 'suspicious' in response to the questions concerning 'job discrimination' 'Northern Ireland' and 'political affiliation'.

E: Other Points

It was important that no one interviewed was acquainted with the interviewer so that no one knew the interviewer's religious or ethnic background. This could quite easily have dissuaded them from completing the questionnaire. In fact, one or two of the situations the researcher found himself in proved quite lively. Unfortunately, names, physiognomy and on occasion, even the colour of a subjects clothes in a particular environment, have the capacity to 'betray' something about a person's background; and thus prejudice attitudes towards them.

Generally the questionnaire was filled out by people who were approached by the interviewer. On occasion however, especially when interviewing the Orange Institution, the Irish bodies and to a much lesser extent the Church attenders, samples were taken from people who volunteered their services. This had clear advantages given the time it took to distribute questionnaires. However, care was taken to make sure that no one sex, age, etc., dominated.

F: Findings and Treatment of Data

The data was collected between the months of April and October of 1990. It was using SPSSx. This analysis is largely based on the presentation of the percentages in the various response categories.

Interviews

Hugh Adams: Glasgow Rangers Director
Fr Noel Barry: Flourish Editor
Dr Calum Brown: Strathclyde University
David Bryce: Secretary of the Loyal Orange Institution of Scotland (L.O.I)
Dr Sean Damer: Glasgow University
Bishop Joseph Devine: Motherwell Diocese
Mark Dingwall: Rangers Fanzine Editor; L.O.I; Young Conservative
David Douglas: L.O.I
Jim Douglas: L.O.I
Dr Tom Gallagher: Bradford University
Pastor Jack Glass: Sovereign Grace Evangelical Church
Tom Grant: Celtic Director
Jeff Holmes: Rangers Fanzine Editor
Danny Houston: L.O.I
Hugh Keevans: Scotsman Journalist
Stewart Lamont: Herald Journalist
Robert Leach: L.O.I
Tommy Main: Irish Post
Patrick McAleer: Irish Cultural Activist
Jack McLean: Herald Journalist
Murdo McLean: Free Presbyterian Church of Scotland
Professor Donald McLeod: Free Church of Scotland
Ian Paisley: MP and MEP
Bill Richardson: Scottish Football Association
James Salmond: Church of Scotland Minister
Norman Shanks: Ex convener, Church of Scotland's Church and Nation
   Committee
Jim Steele: Irish Political Activist
David Thompson: Scottish Football League
Dr Graham Walker: Queens University, Belfast
Archbishop (now Cardinal) Thomas Winning

Bibliography

Allan, J. (1923), *The Story of Rangers: Fifty Years of Football, 1873-1923*, Rangers FC Glasgow.

Allison, L. (1986), *The Politics Of Sport,*: Manchester University Press.

Allison, Wm. (1966), *Rangers: The New Era, 1873-1966,* Rangers FC Glasgow.

Anson, P. F. (1937), *The Catholic Church in Modern Scotland*, Burns & Oates, London.

Archer, I. and T. Royle, (1976), *We'll Support You Evermore. The Impertinent Saga Of Scottish 'Fitba,* Souvenir Press, London.

Arnold, D. (1969), *The Sociology of Subcultures,* The Glendessary Press, Berkeley.

Ashford, N. (1983), 'The New Class: The Neo-Conservative Analysis', *Strathclyde Government Papers,* No 12.

Aspinwall, B. (1986), 'Popery in Scotland: Image and Reality, 1820 - 1920', *Scottish Church History Society Records,* vol xx11, part 3, pp 235-257.

Aspinwall, B. (1982), 'The Scottish Religious Identity in the Atlantic World', in*Studies in Church History,* vol 18.

Austin, W. G. and Worchel, S. (1979), *The Social Psychology Of Intergroup Relations*, Brooks/Cole Publishing, California.

Barrett, D. P. (1962), *The Northern Ireland Problem: A Study in Group Relations,* Oxford University Press.

Bebbington, D. W. (undated), *Baptist Convictions,* Published by the Baptist Union of Scotland.

Bebbington, D. W. (1988), *The Baptists in Scotland; A History,* Published by The Baptist Union of Scotland.

Bell, D. (1990), *Acts of Union: Youth Culture and Sectarianism in Northern Ireland,* MacMillan.

Bell, G. (1976), *The Protestants of Ulster,* Pluto Press.

Benedict, R. (1942 & 1983), *Race And Racism:*, Routledge and Kegan Paul.

Berger, P. (1973), *The Social Reality Of Religion,* Penguin University Books.

Birch, A. H. (1986), *The British system Of Government,* Allen and Unwin.

Black ,E. (1963), 'The Tumultuous Petitioners, The Protestant Association in Scotland', in, *Review of Politics,* 25, pp 183-211.

Boal, F. W. and Douglas J. H. N. (1982), *Integration And Division, Geographical Perspectives On The Northern Ireland Problem:,* Academic Press.

Bochel, J. M. and Denver D.T. (1970), 'Religion And Voting: A Critical Review And A New Analysis', *Political Studies,* Vol XVIII, No 2, pp 205-219.

Bosanquet. N. (1973) *Race And Employment In Britain:,* A Runnymede Trust Publication.

Brand, J. (1976), *The Ideology of Scottish Nationalism:,* Paper for the ECPR.

Brand, J. (1977), *Parties and Politics in Scotland,* Paper for the ECPR.

Brand, J. (1978), *The National Movement in Scotland*: Routledge & Kegan Paul.

Brand, J. 'National Consciousness And Voting In Scotland', *Strathclyde Government Paper,* No 15.

Brass, P, (c1985. *Ethnic Groups And The State:,* Croom Helm.

Brown ,A. and McCrone, D(1991). *The Scottish Government Yearbook.*

Brown, C. (1987), *The Social History of Religion in Scotland Since 1730:,* Methuen, London.

Brown, C. (1988), (1), 'Did Urbanisation Secularize Britain', *Urban History Yearbook.*

Brown, C. (1988), (2), 'Religion', *Urban History Yearbook.*

Brown, C. (1989), 'Religion': in, *Atlas Of British Social And Economic History Since c1700,* in R Pope, (edt), Routledge.

Brown, S. J. (1991), 'Outside the Covenant: The Scottish Presbyterian Churches and Irish Immigration, 1922-1938', *The Innes Review,* Volume XL11, No 1, Spring, pp 19-45.

Brown, T. N. (1976), 'The Origins and Character of Irish-American Nationalism', in, L J McCaffrey, *Irish Nationalism And The American Contribution* , Arno Press, New York.

Browne, E. W. (1983), *Nation, Class And Creed In Northern Ireland,* Gower.

Browne, H. (1983), *Spain's Civil War:,* Seminar Studies in History, Longman.

Bruce, S. (1985) *No Pope Of Rome: Anti-Catholicism In Modern Scotland,* Mainstream Publishing, Edinburgh.

Bruce, S. (1988), 'Sectarianism In Scotland: A Contemporary Assessment And Explanation': pp150-165, in *Scottish Government Yearbook,* edt by McCrone and Brown.

Bruce, S. (1992), 'Out of the Ghetto: the Ironies of Acceptance': pp 145-54, in *The Innes Review,* Vol XL111, No 2, Autumn.

Bruce, S. (1994), *The Edge of the Union: The Ulster Loyalist political vision:* Oxford University Press.

Budge, I. and Urwin, D W. (1966), *Scottish Political Behaviour: A Case Study In British Homogenity,* Longmans.

Burton, F. (1978), *The Politics Of Legitimacy,* Routeledge and Kegan Paul.

Campbell, A. B. (1979), *The Lanarkshire Miners, a Social History of their Trade Unions, 1775-1874,* John Donald, Edinburgh.

Campbell, G. (1989), *Discrimination: The Truth,* Published by the Ulster Democratic Unionist Party.

Campbell, T. and Woods, P. (1986), *The Glory and The Dream, The History of Celtic FC, 1887-1986*, Mainstream Publishing.

Campbell, R. H. (1985), *Scotland Since 1707,* John Donald Publishers.

Canning, B. J. (1979), *Irish-born Secular Priests in Scotland 1829- 1979,* Bookmag, Inverness.

Carr, R. (1980), *Modern Spain 1875-1980*, Oxford University Press.

Carr, R. and Fusi, J. P. *Spain: Dictatorship to Democracy,* Allen and Unwin.

Carter, A. (1979, 1981), *Direct Action And Liberal Democracy,* Routledge and Kegan Paul, 1973.

Cashmore, E. E. (1989), *United Kingdom? Class, Race and Gender Since The War,* Unwin Hymen.

Cashmore, E. E. and Troyna, B. (1983), *Introduction to Race Relations,* Routledge and Kegan Paul.

Catholic Scotland. (1982), *A Profile*: The Catholic Communications Commission, Scotland, J.S Burns, Glasgow.

Checkland, S. G. (1976, 1981), *The Upas Tree: Glasgow, 1875-1975*, University of Glasgow Press, Glasgow.

Church of Scotland Yearbooks, (1990 & 1991).

Church of Scotland, Board of Social Responsibility: *Lifestyle Survey.*, (1987).

Clancy, P. Drudy, S. Lynch, K. O Dowd, L (1986), *Ireland: A Sociological Profile,* Published by the Institute of Public Administration.

Clarke, M. G, and Drucker, H. M. (1976-77), 'Catholic Education in a Secular Society: in Our Changing Scotland', *A Yearbook of Scottish Government.*

Cohen, A. P. (1986), *Symbolising Bounderies: Identity And Diversity In British Cultures:,* Manchester University Press.

Collins, K. (1990), *The Cultural Conquest Of Ireland,* Mercier Press.

Cooney, J. (1982), *Scotland and the Papacy,* Paul Harris, Edinburgh.

Connolly, M and Loughlin, J. (1986), Reflections on the Anglo-Irish Agreement: *Journal of Comparative Politics,* Spring, pp 146-160.

Conway, W. (1970), *Catholic Schools*, Catholic Communications Institute of Ireland.

Coser, A. L. (1956, 1965, 1968), *The Functions Of Social Conflict,* Routledge and Kegan Paul.

Coulter, F. (1988), *Sport And Anti-Social Behaviour,* Edinburgh, Scottish Sports Council.

Craig, E. W. S. (1976), *British Electoral Facts 1885-1975*, MacMillanPress Ltd, 3rd edition.

Craig, F. W. S. (1984), *British Parliamentary Election results 1974-1983*, Parliamentary Research Services.

Crampsey, B. (1978), *The Scottish Footballer*, William Blackwood, Edinburgh.

Crick, B. (1991), *National Identities: The Constitution of the United Kingdom:,* Blackwell.

Currie, R. Gilbert, A. Horsley. L. (1977), *Churches And Churchgoers: Patterns of Church Growth in the British Isles Since 1700*, Clarendon Press, Oxford.

Curtice, J. and Gallagher. (1990), in Jowell R, Witherspoon S, Brook L, Edt, *British Social Attitudes; the 7th report,* Social and Community Planning Research, Gower Publishing, pp 183-216.

Curtis, L. (1984), *Ireland The Propaganda War,* Pluto Press.

Curtis, L. (1988), *Nothing But The Same Old Story: The roots of Anti-Irish Racism,* Published by Information on Ireland, 5th edition.

Curtis, L. P. jr. (1968), *Anglo-Saxons And Celts: A study in Anti- Irish Prejudice in Victorian England,* Published by the Conference on British Studies at the University of Bridgeport, Connecticut.

Curtis, L. P. jr. (1971), *Apes And Angels: The Irishman in Victorian Caricature,* Smithsonian Institution Press, City of Washington.

Daniel, W. (1968), *Racial Discrimination In England,* Penguin.

Darby, J. (1976), *Conflict In Northern Ireland: The Development Of A Polarised Community,* Gill and MacMillan Ltd.

Darragh, J. (1978), 'The Catholic Population of Scotland, 1878-1978': in McRoberts D (Eds), *Modern Scottish Catholicism, 1878-1978,* Burns, Glasgow.

Dashefsky, A. (1976), *Ethnic Identity In Society,* Rand McNally/Chicago.

Davey, A. (1983), *Learning To Be Prejudiced: Growing up in Multi- Ethnic Britain:,* Edward Arnold.

Davis, G. (1991), *The Irish In Britain 1815-1914,* Gill and Macmillan.

Dench, G. (1986), *Minorities In The Open Society: Prisoners Of Ambivalence,* Routledge and Kegan Paul.

De, Santis. and Benkin, R. (1980), 'Ethnicity Without Community', in *Ethnicity,* vol 7, no 2, June.

Deutsch, M. (1973), *The Resolution Of Conflict: Constructive And Destructive Proceses,* New Haven and London, Yale University Press.

Devine, T. M. (1983), 'Highland Migration to Lowland Scotland, 1760-1860': in *The Scottish Historical Review,* LX11, 2, No 174, October.

Devine, T. M. Mitchison R (1988), *People and Society in Scotland: Vol 1, 1760-1830,* John Donald, Edinburgh.

Devine, T. M. edt (1991), *Irish Immigrants and Scottish Society in the Nineteenth and Twentieth Centuries,* Proceedings of the Scottish Historical Studies Seminar, University of Strathclyde, 1989/90, John Donald publishers Ltd.

Dickson, T. edt. (1980), *Scottish Capitalism, Class State And Union, From Before The Union To The Present,* Lawrence And Wishart Ltd, London.

Dickson, T. edt. (1982), *Capital And Class In Scotland,* John Donald Publishers.

Docherty, D. (1986), *The Celtic Football Companion,* John Donald Publishers Ltd.

Donaldson, G. (1971), *Scotland:James V-V11,* Oliver and Boyd, Edinburgh.

Donovan, R. K. '(1978), 'Voices of Distrust: The Expression of Anti-Catholic Feeling in Scotland' 1778-1781', in *The Innes Review,* vol xxix, 2, pp111-139.

Douglas, A. M. (1985), *Church And School In Scotland,* The Saint Andrews Press, Edinburgh.

Dowse, R. E. and Hughes, J. A. (1986), *Political Sociology,* John Wiley and Sons.

Dunning, E. G. Murphy, P. Williams, J. (1982), *Working Class Social Bonding and the Sociogenesis of Football Hooliganism,* a report to the Social Science Research Council.

Edelman, M. (1971), *Politics As Symbolic Action:,* Academic Press.

Edwards, J. (1985), *Language, Society And Identity,* Basil Blackwell.

Ehrlich, S. and Wootton, G. (1980), *Three Faces Of Pluralism: Political Ethnic And Religious:* Gower.

Elcock, H. (1976), *Political Behaviour,* Methuen & Co Ltd.

Elliott, R. S. P. and Hickie, J. (1971), *Ulster: A Case Study In Conflict Theory:,* Longman.

Ellis, P. B. (1976, 1989), *The Boyne Water: The Battle of the Boyne 1690:,* Blackstaff Press.

Fairgrieve, J. (1964), *The Rangers; Scotland's Greatest Football Club:,* Robert Hale, London.

Farrell ,E. edt. (1988), *Twenty Years On,* Brandon.

Finn, G. (1994), 'Faith, Hope and Bigotry: Case Studies of Anti-Catholic Prejudice in Scottish Soccer and Society', in G Jarvie and G Walker (edts), *Scottish Sport in the Making of the Nation,* Leicester University Press.

Fishmen, J. (1977), Language And Ethnicity: in H Giles, (ed), 'Language, Ethnicity and intergoup relations', *European Monographs in Social Psychology, no 13,* Academic Press.

Fitzpatrick, T. J. (1986), *Catholic Secondary Education in South-west Scotland before 1972: its Contribution to theChange in Status of the Catholic Community,* Aberdeen University Press.

Forsyth, R. (1990), *The Only Game,* Mainstream.

Foster B D. (1994), Interpreting the Twelfth, *History Ireland,* Vol 2, Number 2, Summer, pp. 37-41

Franklin, M. N. (1985), *The Decline Of Class Voting In Britain,* Clarendon Press.

Fraser, W. H. and Morris, R. J. (1990), *People And Society in Scotland 11 1830-1914,* John Donald.

Free Presbyterian Church of Scotland, *History of the Free Presbyterian Church of Scotland, 1893-1970,* Self publication.

Gallagher, T. (1981), 'Catholics in Scottish Politics', in, *Bulletin of Scottish Politics,* 1, 2.

Gallagher, T. (1985), 'Protestant Extremism in Urban Scotland 1930-9: Its Growth and Contraction', *Scottish Historical Review,* 64, 2.

Gallagher, T. (1987), *Glasgow The Uneasy Peace,* Manchester University Press.

Gallagher, T. (1987), *Edinburgh Divided: John Cormack and No Popery in the 1930s,* Polygon, Edinburgh.

Gallagher, T. (1991), 'The Catholic Irish in Scotland: In Search of Identity': in T M Devine, (edt), *Irish Immigrants and Scottish Society in the Nineteenth and Twentieth Centuries;* John Donald Publishers Limited.

Gilley, S. & Swift, R. (1985), *The Irish in the Victorian City,* Croom Helm, London.

Gourley, T. (1990), 'Catholic Schooling in Scotland since 1918', *The Innes Review,* vol XL1, no1, Spring, pp119-131.

Goward, N. (1981), 'Sport And Politics In Post-Franco Spain: The Barcelona Football Club', *Iberian Studies,* vol x, no 1, Spring.

Gray, T. (1972), *The Orange Order,* The Bodley Head.

Greely, A. M. and McCready, W. C. (1974), 'Does Ethnicity Matter': in, *Ethnicity,* vol 1, no 1, April, pp91-108.

Greeley, A. M. McCready, W. C. McCourt, K. (1976), *Catholic Schools in a Declining Church,* Sheed and Word, Universal Press.

Greenwood, D. (1977), 'Continuity in Change: Spanish Basque Ethnicity as a Historical Process': in, Esman M.J.E, (edt), *Conference on ethnic pluralism and conflict in contemporary western Europe and Canada:* Cornell University Press.

Habgood, J. (1983), *Church And Nation in A Secular Age*: Darton, Longman and Todd Ltd.

Handley, J. E. *The Irish in Scotland:* John S Burns & Sons, Glasgow, (this book incorporates both The Irish in Scotland 1798-1845 and The Irish in Modern Scotland, 1943 & 1947 respectively. Cork University Press)

Handley, J. E. (1960), *The Celtic Story,* Stanley Paul, London.

Hargreaves, J. (1986), *Sport, Power, And Culture*, Polity Press.

Harris, R. (1972), *Prejudice And Tolerance In Ulster*, Manchester University Press.

Harvie, C. (1981), *No Gods and Precious Few Heroes, Scotland 1914-1980,* Edward Arnold.

Hebdige, (1981), 'Skinheads and the search for white working class identity', in *New Socialist,* Sep/Oct , pp39-41.

Heskin, K. (1980), *Northern Ireland: A Psychological Analysis,* Gill and MacMillan.

Hickman, M. (1990), *A study of the incorporation of the Irish in Britain with special reference to Catholic state education: involving a comparison of the attitudes of pupils and teachers in selected Catholic schools in London and Liverpool,* unpublished PhD, University of London.

Hill, D. (1989), *Out Of His Skin: The John Barnes Phenomenon:*, Faber and Faber.

Horne, J. Jary, D. Tomlinson, A. (1987). 'Sport, Leisure and Social Relations', *Sociological Review Monograph* 33, Routledge and Kegan Paul.

Hudson, R. and Williams, A. M. (1989), *Divided Britain,* Belhaven Press.

Inglis, J. (1982), 'The Irish In Britain: A Question Of Identity', in *Irish Studies in Britain* , No 3, Spring/Summer.

Isajiw, W. W. (1974), 'Definitions of Ethnicity', in, *Ethnicity,* vol 1, no 2, July, pp 111-124

Issacs, H. R. (1974), 'Basic Group Identity, The Idols of the Tribe', in, *Ethnicity,* vol 1, no 1, April, pp 15-41

Jarvie G, Walker G (1994), *Scottish Sport in the Making of the Nation; Ninety Minute Patriots,* Leicester University Press.

Jowell, R. Witherspoon, S. Brook L. (1990), *British Social Attitudes; the 7th report,* Social and Community Planning Research, Gower Publishing.

Jowell R, Brook L, Prior G, Taylor B, (1992/93), *British Social Attitudes; the 9th report,* Social and Community Planning Research, Dartmouth Publishing, Company, University Press Cambridge.

Kavanagh, D. (1972), *Political Culture,* MacMillan.

Keating, M. Levy, R. Geekie, J. Brand, J. (1989), 'Labour Elites in Glasgow', in the *Strathclyde Papers on Government and Politics,* No 61.

216

Keating, M. Levy, R. Geekie, J, Brand, J. Evans, R. (1989), 'Glasgow Labour Councillors: An Ideological Profile', in the *Strathclyde Papers on Governemnt and Politics*, No 66.

Kellas, J. G. (1975), *The Scottish Political System,* Cambridge University Press.

Kellas, J. G. (1986), *Modern Scotland, the Nation since 1970,* Pall Mall, London.

Kellas, J. G. (1991), *An Integrated Theory Of The Politics Of Nationalism And Ethnicity,* Paper for the P.S.A Conference, Lancaster University.

Kendrick, S. (1989), Scotland, Social Change and Politics, in, The Making of Scotland: *Nation, Culture and Social Change,* edt by McCrone, D. Kendrick, S. and Straw, P. Edinburgh University Press.

Keyes, C. F. (1976), 'Towards a New Formulation of the Concept of Ethnic Group', in, *Ethnicity,* vol 1, no 3, Sep.

Kircaldy, J. (1981), 'Irish Jokes: No Cause For Laughter', *Irish Studies in Britain,* No 2, Autumn/Winter.

Langton, K. P. (1969), *Political Socialisation:,* Oxford University Press.

LeVine, R. A. Campbell, D. T. (1972), *Ethnocentrism: theories of Conflict, Ethnic attitudes and Group Behaviour,* John Wiley & Sons, Inc.

Linklater, M. Denniston, R. (1992), *Anatomy of Scotland,* Chambers.

Lorimar, D. A. (1978), *Colour, Class And The Victorians,* Leicester University Press.

Machin. (1964), *The Catholic Question in English Politics, 1820-1830,* Clarendon Press.

Maley, Wm. (1939), *The Story of Celtic,* (printed for author at Villafield Press, Bishopbriggs).

Martin, D. Hill, M. (1970). *A Sociological Yearbook Of Religion In Britain* , SCM Press Ltd.

Mason, T. (1988), *Sport in Britain,* Faber and Faber Ltd.

Medhurst, K. (1987), 'The Basques and the Catalans', *The Minority Rights Group Report,* No 9, London.

Medhurst, K. Moyser, G. H. (1989), 'The Church of England and Politics', in, *Parliamentary Affairs, A Journal of Comparative politics,* Vol 42, 2, April.

Medhurst, K. Moyser, G. (1988), *Church And Politics In A Secular Age,* Clarendon Press, Oxford.

Mews, S. (1982), 'Religion And National Identity', *Papers at the 19th and 20th Winter meetings of the Ecclesiastical History Society,* Basil Blackwell.

Miles, R. Phizacklea, A. (1979), *Racism and Political Action in Britain,* Routledge and Kegan Paul, London.

Miles, R. (1982), *Racism And Migrant Labour,* Routledge And Kegan Paul.

Miller, W. L. (1981), *The End Of British Politics :Scottish and English Political Behaviour in the seventies,* Clarendon Press, Oxford.

Mitchell, J. (1990), *Conservatives and the Union: A Study of Conservative Party Attitudes to Scotland*, Edinburgh University Press.

Mitchell, J. (1992), *Religion And Politics In Scotland*, Unpublished paper presented to Seminar on Religion and Scottish Politics, University of Edinburgh.

Moorhouse, H. F. (1984), 'Professional Football and working class culture: English Theories and Scottish evidence' in, the *Sociological Review,* Vol 32, pp 285-315.

Moorhouse, H. F. (1987), 'Scotland versus England: Football and Popular Culture' in, *International Journal of Sport,* Part 4, pp 189-202.

Moorhouse, H. F. (1986), 'Repressed Nationalism And Professional Football: Scotland Versus England', pp 52-59 in Mangan, J. Small, R. (edts) *Sport, Culture, Society,* London E & F N Spon.

Moncrieff, G. S. (1960), *The Mirror and the Cross; Scotland and the Catholic Faith,* Burns and Oates, London.

Montgomery, M. (1989), *Sectarianism and the Labour Movement in Clydeside, with special reference to Govan, 1912-1950,* Strathclyde University, Unpublished undergraduate dissertation.

Muirhead, Rev. I. A. (1973), 'Catholic Emancipation: Scottish Reactions in 1829' *Innes Review,* 24, 1, Spring.

Muirhead, Rev. I. A. '(1973), 'Catholic Emancipation in Scotland: the debate and the aftermath,' *Innes Review,* 24, 2, Autumn.

Mullard, C. (1973), *Black Britain,* Allen and Unwin Ltd.

Murray, B. (1984), *The Old Firm: Sectarianism, Sport and Society in Scotland,* John Donald Publishers Ltd, Edinburgh.

Murray, B. (1988), *Glasgow's Giants, 100 Years of the Old Firm,* Mainstream Publishing.

Murray, D. B. (1969), *The First One Hundred Years,* Published by The Baptist Union of Scotland.

Myers, B. (1992), *Scottish Church and Social Concerns Survey,* Published by Marc Europe, London.

MacDonald, D. J. Middleton, R. Boyd, D. M. (1989), *Free Presbyterians And The Requiem Mass,* published by the Church at Craven Herald Ltd, Skipton, March.

McCaffrey, J. (1983), 'Roman Catholics in Scotland in the nineteenth and twentieth centuries', *Records of the Scottish Church History Society,* 21, 2.

McCaffrey, J. (1979), 'Politics and the Catholic Community Since 1878', pp140-155, in McRoberts, *Modern Scottish Catholicism, 1878-1978.* Burns, Glasgow.

McCall, G. J. S. Simmons, J. L. (1966), *Identities And Interactions,* The Free Press, New York.

McCarra, K. (1984), *Scottish Football: A Pictorial History From 1867 To The Present Day*: Third Eye Centre and Polygon Books.

McCracken, G. A. (1990), *Bygone Days of Yore,* Printed by Orange Heritage for the County Grand Lodge of Glasgow.

McCrone, D. Kendrick, S. Straw, P. (1989), *The Making of Scotland; Nation, Culture and Social Change,* Edinburgh University Press.

McFarland, E. W. (1986), *The Loyal Orange Institution of Scotland 1799 to 1900,* PhD, Glasgow University.

McFarland, E.W. (1990), *Protestants First: Orangeism in 19th century Scotland,* Edinburgh University Press, 1990.

McFarlane, N. (1986), *Sport and Politics*: Willow Books.

McGrain, D. (1978), *Celtic: My Team,* Souvenir Press, London.

McGrain, D/H Keevans. (1987), *In Sunshine or in Shadow*, John Donald.

McGrory, J. (1975), *A Lifetime in Paradise*, McNee, G. (edt), Published by Authors.

McHugh, M. (1982), *Kirk, State And The Catholic Problem In The Western Highlands And Islands Of Scotland 1690-1760*, M.Litt, Strathclyde University.

McIntosh, N. Smith, D. J. (1974), 'The Extent Of Racial Discrimination', *The Social Science Institute*, vol xl, broadsheet no 547, September.

McLelland, V. A. (1967), 'The Irish Clergy and Archbishop Mannings apostolic visitation of the western district of Scotland, 1867', in the *Catholic Historical Review*, L11, 1.

McLeod, H. (1978), *Religion In The City*, Urban History Yearbook.

McNee, G. (1978), *The Story of Celtic, An Official History, 1888-1978*, Stanley Paul, London.

McRae, K. (1986), *Conflict and Compromise in Multilingual Societies*, Wilfrid Lorimer University Press.

McRoberts, D. (1979), *Modern Scottish Catholicism, 1878-1978*, Burns, Glasgow.

O'Conner, K. (1970), *The Irish in Britain*, Torc, Dublin.

O'Dowd, L. (1989), 'Ignoring the communal divide: the implications for social research' in *Northern Ireland, Studies in Social and Economic Life*, Jenkins, R. (edt), Gower.

O Sullivan, P. edt. (1992), *The Irish in the New Communities*, Vol 11 of The Irish World Wide Series, Leicester University Press, London.

O Tuathaigh, M. A. G. (1985), 'The Irish in Nineteenth Century Britain: Problems of Integration', pp 13-36, in Swift and Gilley, *The Irish in a Victorian City*, Croom Helm.

Parry, R. (1988), *Scottish Political Facts*, T & T Clark, Edinburgh.

Patterson, H. (1981), 'Ireland, Unravelling The Knot', *Review In Bulletin Of Scottish Politics*, No 2, Spring.

Payne, S. (1971), 'Catalan and Basque Nationalism', in, *Journal of Contemporary History*, Vol 1, No 1.

Peach, C (1975), *Urban Social Segregation:*, Longman.

Peach, C. Robinson, Smith, (1981), *Ethnic Segregation In Cities*, Croom Helm Ltd.

Platt, J. and Slater, M. (1984), 'Football Hooliganism', in, *Leisure Studies*, 3.

Punnett, R. M. (1980), *British Government And Politics*, 4th edition, London Heinemann.

Rafferty, J. (1973), *One Hundred Years of Scottish Football*, Pan Books, London.

Reformed Presbyterian Church of Scotland. (1932), *Summary of the Testimony of the Reformed Presbyterian Church Of Scotland*, Published by J Hedderwick and Sons Ltd, Glasgow.

Rex, J. 1971), *Race Relations In Sociological Theory*, Weidenfeld and Nicholson.

Rex, J. (1973), *Race, Colonialism and the City*, Routledge and Kegan Paul.

Rex, J. (1981), *Social Conflict: A Conceptual and theoretical analysis*, Longmans.

Rex, J. Tomlinson, S. (1979), *Colonial immigrants in a British city: A class analysis*, Routledge and Kegan Paul, London.

Roberts, D. A. (1971), 'The Orange Order In Ireland; A Religious Institution'? *British Journal Of Sociology,* Vol 22, pp 269-283.

Robertson, D. (1985), *A Dictionary Of Modern Politics,* Europa Publications Ltd, London.

Rokkan, S. Urwin, D. (1983), *Economy, Territory and Identity, Politics of West European Peripheries,* London, Sage.

Ross, A. (1979), 'Development of the Scottish Catholic Community, 1878-1978', pp30-55, in McRoberts, *Modern Scottish Catholicism, 1878-1978,* Burns, Glasgow.

Samuel, R. Jones, G. S. (1982). 'Culture, Ideology And Politics', in, *Essays for Eric Hobsbawm,* Routledge and Kegan Paul.

Schermerhorn, R. A. (1974), 'Ethnicity in the Perspective of the Sociology of Knowledge', in, *Ethnicity,* vol 1, no 2, July, pp 111-124.

Schermerhorn, R. A. (1970), *Comparative Ethnic Relations. A Framework for Theory and Research,* New York, Random House.

Scott, G. (1967), *The RCs,* Hutchinson, London.

Senior, H. (1966), *Orangism In Ireland And Britain, 1795-1836,* Routledge and Keegan Paul, London.

Shaw, D. (1985), 'The Politics of Futbol', in, *History Today,* Vol 35, Aug, pp 38-42

Sibbet, R. M. (1939), *Orangism in Ireland and throughout the Empire.*

Sisson, P. L. (1973), *The Social Significance of Church Membership in the Burgh of Falkirk,* The Church of Scotland, Edinburgh.

Skinneder, M. 'Catholic Elementary Education in Glasgow 1818-1918', in T.R Bone edt, *Studies in the History of Scottish Education 1872-1939,* S.C.R.E, No 54

Smith, C .W. (1962), *The Great Hunger,* New English Library/Times Mirror.

Smith, J. (1984), 'Labour Tradition In Glasgow And Liverpool', pp 32- 56, in, *History Workshop* Issue 17, Spring.

Smout, T. C. (1969), *A History of the Scottish People, 1560-1830,* London.

Soar, P. (1974, 1987), *Encyclopedia Of British Football,* Willow Books, Collins, London.

Stevenson, D. (1973), *The Scottish Revolution, 1637-44.*

Sugden, J. Bairner, A. (1986), (A), 'Northern Ireland: Sport in a Divided Society' in, Allison L, *The Politics Of Sport,* pp 90-117, Manchester University Press.

Sugden, J. Bairner, A. (1986), (B), Observe The Sons Of Ulster; Football And Politics In Northern Ireland, in Tomlinson A, *Off The Ball: The Football World Cup,* pp 146-157, Pluto Press.

Swift, R. and Gilley, S. (e1985), *The Irish in a Victorian City,* Croom Helm.

Tajfel, H. 'The Social Psychology of Minorities', *Minority Rights Group,* London, No 38.

Tajfel, H. (1981), *Human Groups and Social Categories: Studies in social psychology,* Cambridge University Press.

Tajfel, H. (1981), *Social Identity And Intergroup Relations,* Cambridge University Press.

Taylor, D. (1984), 'Ian Paisley and the Ideology of Ulster Protestantism', pp 59-79 in *Culture and Ideology in Ireland,*' edt by C Curtin, M Kelly and L O Dowd, Galway University Press.

Taylor, H. (1961), *We Will Follow Rangers,* Stanley Paul, London.

Tomlinson, G. Whannel. (1986). *Off The Ball: The Football World Cup*, Pluto Press.

Treble, J. H. (1980), 'The Working Of The 1918 Education Act In Glasgow Archdioces', *Innes Review*, 31, 1, pp. 27-50.

Treble, J. H. (1978), 'The Development Of Roman Catholic Education in Scotland, 1878-1978', in, *The Innes Review*, vol xxix, 2, pp.111-139.

Turner, J. C. Giles, H. (1981), *Intergroup Behaviour*, Basil Blackwell, Oxford.

Urwin, D. (1965), 'The Development of the Conservative Party Organisation in Scotland until 1912', *Scottish Historical Review*, 44, 2.

Vinokur, M. B. (1988), *More Than A Game: Sport and Politics*, Greenwood Press, Connecticut USA.

Walker, G. Gallagher, T. (1990), *Sermons and Battle Hymns: Protestant Popular Culture in Modern Scotland*, Edinburgh University Press.

Walker, W. (1972), 'Irish Immigrants in Scotland: their priests politics and parochial life', *Historical Journal*, xv, 4.

Walvin. J. (1978), *Leisure and Society, 1830-1950*, Longman.

Weigert, A. J. Teitge, J. Teitge, D. (1986), *Society and Identity*, Cambridge University Press.

Williams, J. (1986), 'White Riots' in, Whannel, G. and Tomlinson, A. (edt.), *Off The Ball*, Pluto, pp 5-19.

Williams, J. Dunning, E. G. and Murphy, P. (1984), *Hooligans Abroad: The Behaviour and Control of English Fans in Continental Europe*, Routledge and Kegan Paul.

Williams, J. Dunning, E. G. and Murphy, P. (1984), 'Come on You Whites', in, *New Society*, 24th May, pp 310-311.

Williams, J. Dunning, E. G. Murphy, P. (1988), *Hooliganism After Heysel, Crowd Behaviour in England and Europe, 1985-1988*, Sir Norman Chester Centre for Football Research, University of Leicester.

Williams, J. Dunning E. Murphy, P. (1986), 'The Rise Of The English Soccer Hooligan', pp362-380 in *Youth and Society*, vol 17, no 4, June, Sage Publications.

Wilson, B. (1988), *Celtic, A Century with Honour*, Willow Books.

Wood, I. S. (1980), 'John Wheatley, the Irish and the Labour Movement in Scotland', *Innes Review*, 21.

Wood, I. S. (1994). *Scotland and Ulster*, The Mercat Press, Edinburgh.

Wright, F. (1987), *Northern Ireland:A Comparative Analysis*, Gill and MacMillan Ltd, Dublin.